FAITH, HOPE AND POETRY

Faith, Hope and Poetry explores the poetic imagination as a way of knowing; a way of seeing reality more clearly. Presenting a series of critical appreciations of English poetry from Anglo-Saxon times to the present day, Malcolm Guite applies the insights of poetry to contemporary issues and the contribution poetry can make to our religious knowing and the way we "do Theology". This book is not solely concerned with overtly religious poetry and attends to the paradoxical ways in which the poetry of doubt and despair also enriches theology. Developing an original analysis and application of the poetic vision of Coleridge and Seamus Heaney in the final chapters, Guite builds towards a substantial theology of imagination and provides unique insights into truth which complement and enrich more strictly rational ways of knowing. Readers of this book will return to their reading of poetry equipped with new insights and enthusiasm and will be challenged to integrate imaginative ways of knowing into their other academic and intellectual pursuits.

Malcolm Guite, in this wide-ranging and original study, helps us see how poetry is – if we let ourselves be drawn in and shaped by it – a means of making connections with the fundamental way things are, and so too a way of connecting with a God who is himself a pattern of 'connection' as Trinity, open to share the divine reality with created life. Here are materials for a profound theology of the imagination, developed in dialogue with writers both familiar and unfamiliar, beautifully combining close reading with wide horizons.

The Most Revd Dr Rowan Williams

No one with an interest in the history of poetry inspired by the Christian Faith can fail to be impressed with this book. Malcolm Guite has offered us an immensely rich work, ranging from the 8th Century Dream of the Rood, to Seamus Heaney via Shakespeare, John Davies, John Donne and George Herbert, in which the truth-telling available only in poetry is brought into the service of mature theological vision. It is quite simply both astounding and outstanding.

The Rt Revd Professor Stephen Sykes,

Malcolm Guite has the rare gift of being able to open up the depths of poetry and theology together. He is alert to form, content and context, and above all to the nuances of poetic visions of God, the complexities of faith, and spiritual transformations.

David Ford, Regius Professor of Divinity,
University of Cambridge, UK

To enter Malcolm Guite's Faith, Hope & Poetry is to discover a new continent with dazzling possibilities, a landscape where scholarship, vivid faith, word craft, imaginative insight, reflection and careful research are all available at a level that is revelatory to both academics and lay readers alike. Guite, not only an ordained Anglican priest but a poet and scholar of the highest order, invites us to this fresh feast-a summons that will widen our own worlds immeasurably.

Luci Shaw, Author, *Harvesting Fog - New Poems,*
Breath for the Bones: Imagination, Art, & Spirit.

Ashgate Studies in Theology, Imagination and the Arts

Series Editors:

Trevor Hart, St Mary's College, University of St Andrews, Scotland
Jeremy Begbie, Duke University and University of Cambridge, USA
Roger Lundin, Wheaton College, USA

What have imagination and the arts to do with theology? For much of the modern era, the answer has been, 'not much'. It is precisely this deficit that this series seeks to redress. For, whatever role they have or have not been granted in the theological disciplines, imagination and the arts are undeniably bound up with how we as human beings think, learn and communicate, engage with and respond to our physical and social environments and, in particular, our awareness and experience of that which transcends our own creatureliness. The arts are playing an increasingly significant role in the way people come to terms with the world; at the same time, artists of many disciplines are showing a willingness to engage with religious or theological themes. A spate of publications and courses in many educational institutions has already established this field as one of fast growing concern.

This series taps into a burgeoning intellectual concern on both sides of the Atlantic and beyond. The peculiar inter-disciplinarity of theology, and the growing interest in imagination and the arts in many different fields of human concern, afford the opportunity for a series which has its roots sunk in varied and diverse intellectual soils, while focused around a coherent theological question: How are imagination and the arts involved in the shaping and reshaping of our humanity as part of the creative and redemptive purposes of God, and what roles do they perform in the theological enterprise?

Many projects within the series have particular links to the work of the Institute for Theology Imagination and the Arts in the University of St Andrews, and to the Duke Initiatives in Theology and the Arts at Duke University.

Space, Time, and Presence in the Icon
Seeing the World with the Eyes of God
Clemena Antonova, with a preface by Martin Kemp

Theological Aesthetics after von Balthasar
Edited by Oleg V. Bychkov and James Fodor

Faithful Performances
Enacting Christian Tradition
Edited by Trevor A. Hart and Steven R. Guthrie

Faith, Hope and Poetry
Theology and the Poetic Imagination

MALCOLM GUITE
Girton College, Cambridge, UK

ASHGATE

Published by
Ashgate Publishing Limited
Wey Court East
Union Road
Farnham
Surrey, GU9 7PT
England

Ashgate Publishing Company
Suite 420
101 Cherry Street
Burlington
VT 05401-4405
USA

www.ashgate.com

British Library Cataloguing in Publication Data
Guite, Malcolm.
    Faith, Hope and Poetry: Theology and the Poetic Imagination. – (Ashgate Studies in
    Theology, Imagination, and the Arts)
    1. English poetry – History and criticism. 2. Religion and poetry – Great Britain –
    History. 3. Theology in literature. 4. Spirituality in literature. I. Title II. Series
    821'.009382–dc22

Library of Congress Cataloging-in-Publication Data
Guite, Malcolm.
    Faith, Hope and Poetry: Theology and the Poetic Imagination / Malcolm Guite.
        p.   cm. – (Ashgate Studies in Theology, Imagination and the Arts)
    Includes bibliographical references and index.
    1. English poetry – History and criticism – Theory, etc. 2. Knowledge, Theory of, in
    literature. 3. Theology in literature. 4. Christianity and literature – Great Britain –
    History. I. Title.
    PR508.K56G85 2010
    821.009'382–dc22   2010014641

ISBN   9780754669067 (hbk)

Mixed Sources
Product group from well-managed
forests and other controlled sources
www.fsc.org Cert no. SA-COC-1565
© 1996 Forest Stewardship Council

Printed and bound in Great Britain by
MPG Books Group, UK

Contents

Acknowledgements

Many people have helped me in the making of this book not least my students, in both Literature and Theology, whose probing questions and original ideas have all contributed to the formation of my own understanding, and my colleagues at Girton College whose personal warmth and stimulating conversation have sustained me in the long haul. The Cambridge Theology Through the Arts project and the St Andrew's Institute for Theology and the Arts have both been crucial in nurturing my vision and giving me opportunities to teach and publish in this field.

I have also been immensely encouraged by my own teachers and by the pastors and academics who have mentored me over the years. In particular Stephen Sykes, who first suggested I should write this book, and Jeremy Begbie, whose work and teaching in the field of Theology and Arts has been an inspiration to so many and who has personally encouraged me at every stage of my own endeavours in this field.

I also acknowledge gratefully permission from Faber to quote the poetry of Edwin Muir, Phillip Larkin, and Seamus Heaney, from Penguin and Houghton Mifflin Company for permission to quote Geoffrey Hill, from the Gallery Press for permission to quote from Derek Mahon, and from The Lewis Estate for permission to quote C.S. Lewis.

Finally, I am deeply indebted to Niki Lambros, whose insight, critical encouragement, and gifts of time and talent as an amanuensis helped me get the first draft of this work down on paper, and to my wife Maggie, without whose constant encouragement I would never have brought it to completion.

In the course of this work I discuss the 'theology' I find implicit in the works of two great living poets: Geoffrey Hill and Seamus Heaney. When I refer to their 'faith and doubt', or to their imaginative apprehension of transcendent truths as I find it in their writings, I am always speaking of 'the poet in the poem' the imaginative insight is in that arrangement of words, expressed by the poet in the first person. I am not referring to either poet outside their poetry, in their 'ordinary' life. I do not pretend to any knowledge of their own spiritual life, but only wish to observe the ways in which their writings might nurture and illuminate ours.

For Niki and Maggie

Acknowledgements of Copyright

De Magistro

I thank my God I have emerged at last,
Blinking from Hell, to see these quiet stars
Bewildered by the shadows that I cast.

You set me on this stair, in those rich hours
Pacing your study, chanting poetry.
The Word in you revealed His quickening powers,

Removed the daily veil, and let me see,
As sunlight played along your book-lined walls,
That words are windows onto mystery.

From Eden, whence the living fountain falls
In music, from the tower of ivory,
And from the hidden heart, He calls

In the language of Adam, creating memory
Of unfallen speech. He sets creation
Free from the carapace of history.

His image in us is Imagination,
His Spirit is a sacrifice of breath
Upon the letters of His revelation.

In mid-most of the word-wood is a path
That leads back to the springs of truth in speech.
You showed it to me, kneeling on your hearth,

You showed me how my halting words might reach
To the mind's Maker, to the source of Love,
And so you taught me what it means to teach.

Teaching, I have my ardours now to prove
Climbing with joy the steps of Purgatory.
Teacher and pupil, both are on the move,

As fellow pilgrims on a needful journey.

Introduction

Poetry and Transfiguration: Reading for a New Vision

In *The Redress of Poetry*, the collection of his lectures as Oxford Professor of Poetry, Seamus Heaney claims that poetry 'offers a clarification, a fleeting glimpse of a potential order of things "beyond confusion", a glimpse that has to be its own reward'.[1] However qualified by terms like 'fleeting', 'glimpse' and 'potential', this is still a claim that poetry, and more widely the poetic imagination, is truth-bearing; that it offers not just some inner subjective experience but, as Heaney claims, a redress – the redress of an imbalance in our vision of the world and ourselves. Heaney's claim in these lectures, and in his Nobel Prize acceptance speech, that we can 'Credit Poetry', trust its tacit, intuitive and image-laden way of knowledge, is part of a wider debate in modernist and post-modernist times about the relations between imagination and reason as ways of knowing. This debate is leading, in almost every field, to a renewed emphasis on imagination as essential for a fuller knowledge of the world and ourselves, and it has ramifications for every subject. Science in particular has come to acknowledge the vital role imagination plays in shaping and making scientific models and theories as well as the experiments designed to test them.[2] Theology, likewise, has recovered from an atomising, reductive, demythologising period and is beginning to look at the importance of imaginative shaping and symbolic apprehension in the discovery of meaning and theological truth.[3] But, if renewed claims are to be made for the imagination as a truth-bearing faculty, we need both to understand why it came to be marginalised and also to ask in what ways it is consistent with, and complementary to truths arrived at by other means. A great deal has been written about imagination as contrasted with reason in general, but the purpose of this book is to look at poetry as a particular imaginative art-form and ask what kind of 'clarification' it offers, what kind of 'potential order' it reveals. Since the medium of poetry is language, a system of symbols, this involves asking questions about the relations between

---

[1]   Seamus Heaney, *The Redress of Poetry* (London, 1995), p. xv.

[2]   See, for example, Mary Midgely, *Science and Poetry* (London, 2001).

[3]   The emergence of courses like 'Theology through the Arts' in Cambridge and the Institute for Theology Imagination and the Arts at St. Andrew's are a sign of this recovery. So too are the ways in which leading theologians are engaging at depth with the work of contemporary poets, as for example David Ford's engagement with the poetry of Micheal O'Siadhail, in *The Shape of Living* (London, 1997) and *The Musics of Belonging: The Poetry of Micheal O'Siadhail* (Dublin, 2007).

language, symbol and truth, questions which poetry is peculiarly fitted to answer. These questions are particularly pertinent to the study of Christian theology since that theology depends both on written scriptures and also on the radical idea that the Word behind all words and scriptures has been made, not more words, but flesh. Poetry may be especially fitted as a medium for helping us apprehend something of the mystery embodied in that phrase 'the Word was made flesh'.

After a brief summary of the original split between Reason and Imagination as ways of knowing and an account of some of the attempts in our own age to reintegrate them, this book will offer a series of readings of key moments in English poetry (not necessarily explicitly Christian or even 'religious' poetry) which open the reader to an experience of transfiguration or enhanced insight into the world as it is, what Heaney in *The Redress* calls: 'a draught of the clear water of transformed understanding'.[4] We will read these passages not simply for aesthetic pleasure or as material on which to exercise literary critical skills or theories but as clues to the nature of things as they really are. We will ask: Are these poems truth-bearing? Are they offering imaginative insights, which are both internally consistent and consistent with our other ways of knowing? We will explore the power of poetry to renew vision by transfiguring the ordinary, to reveal in 'utter visibility' that things are 'alive with what's invisible'.[5]

If we are to make the case for poetry as a redress or a restoration of lost balance in vision we need to ask what it is that poetry needs to restore and why we lost that balance in the first place. What are the issues at stake if we are to make claims for the poetic imagination as a truth-bearing faculty?

What Must Poetry Restore?

In order to discern why modern Western culture has lost vision, why there is an imbalance that needs to be redressed, we have to look back to the great cultural shift that occurred during the Enlightenment which ushered in a mistrust and marginalisation of imaginative and poetic vision and a particular suspicion of the ambivalent or multivalent language of poetry. Instead of acknowledging, as many thinkers do now, that the *way* we know, *the language through which we know*, may be an essential and helpful part of knowledge itself, some philosophers of the Enlightenment thought that image and imagination simply clouded and obscured the pure dry knowledge which they were after. This attitude is often traced back rhetorically to Francis Bacon, who wrote: 'For all that concerns ornaments of speech, similitudes, treasury of eloquence, and such like emptiness let it be utterly dismissed.'[6] Though Bacon himself cannot say anything without constantly

---

4   Heaney, *The Redress of Poetry*, p. xv.

5   Phrases from Heaney's poem 'Seeing Things'; see below Chapter 8, pp. 232–42.

6   Francis Bacon, *The Philosophical Works of Francis Bacon*, ed. J.M. Robertson (London, 1905), p. 403.

availing himself of metaphor and symbol, nor can there be any scientific discourse without it, as we shall see in the discussion of metaphor, symbol and science in Chapter 3. Others would trace this splitting of knowledge to Descartes's dividing the world between *res extensa* and *res cogitans*, a dualism from which science and philosophy are only just recovering. It is not my purpose to pursue this split to its ultimate philosophical source but rather to observe the ways in which it became current, affected the way people thought, wrote and read, and continues to affect them still. For this purpose it is better to look at more influential texts, which popularised the thought of Bacon and Descartes. The formation of the Royal Society was absolutely central to the development of English life and thought in and through the Enlightenment, and the Royal Society took a clear stand against poetry and the poetic imagination as ways of coming at truth. And here Thomas Sprat's *History of the Royal Society* – really its manifesto – is a seminal text. Sprat urged his readers 'to separate the knowledge of *Nature*, from the colours of *Rhetoric*, the devices of *Fancy* or the delightful deceit of *Fables*'.[7]

This advice, indeed the whole Enlightenment project which it represents, is in very sharp contrast to the wisdom of the previous age which was rooted in the idea that fables, stories and myths were the medium which most completely embodied the deepest truths we need to know. Thus most of the wisdom of the ancient world both Judeo-Christian and Classical was embodied in myth, story and song. The notion of telling a fable in order to get at a truth went very deep indeed, and emerges, for example, even in the light-hearted exchange between Audrey and Touchstone the fool in *As You Like It*, though it should be said that Shakespeare, with a true understanding of the cross, always puts his greatest wisdom in the mouths of his fools:

> *Audrey*:   I do not know what 'poetical' is. Is it honest in deed and word? Is it a true thing?
>
> *Touchstone*:   No, truly; for the truest poetry is the most feigning ...[8]

Sprat's attack was not only on story but also on the poetry of image and metaphor; he goes on to demand:

> a close, naked, natural way of speaking, positive expressions, clear senses, a native easiness, bringing all things as near the mathematical -plainness as they

---

[7]   Thomas Sprat, *A History of the Royal Society of London for the Improving of Natural Knowledge*, first edition 1667. This and subsequent extracts from Sprat's influential work can be found on http://andromeda.rutgers.edu/~jlynch/Texts/sprat.html.

[8]   *As You Like It*, Act III, scene 3, lines 19–20. All references to Shakespeare are to *The Complete Works*, edited, with an introduction and glossary, by P. Alexander (London, 1957).

can, and preferring the language of the artisans, countrymen and merchants before that of wits and scholars[9]

The new Philosophers and Scientists had declared war on the imagination and the consequence of that war was a kind of cultural apartheid: The entire realm of 'objective' truth was to be the exclusive terrain of *Reason* at its narrowest – analytic, reductive, atomising; and the faculties of *Imagination* and *Intuition*, those very faculties which alone were capable of integrating, synthesising and making sense of our atomised factual knowledge, were relegated to a purely private and 'subjective' truth. If it cannot be weighed and measured, these men were saying, it is not really there. How prophetic Blake, the great rebel against this division was, when he wrote:

> What it will be Question'd, 'when the Sun rises, do you not see a round disk of fire somewhat like a Guinea?' O no, no, I see an Innumerable company of the Heavenly host crying, Holy, Holy, Holy is the Lord God Almighty.[10]

The Effect of Enlightenment on Faith

It was not just poetry that was under attack. This new arrangement affected everything, including the Christian faith, which was forced to choose sides in this divide, either to be relegated to something subjective, not there, essentially made up, or to become a pseudo-science, reducing the great mysteries, embedded in the ancient story-telling of scripture, to quantifiable exactitudes, patient only of a literal interpretation. Theology felt itself forced to choose between an increasingly vague and amorphous liberalism, happy to keep reinventing the faith, and an increasingly strident fundamentalism, which tries to treat the vast subtle poem of scripture as a single scientific treatise whose every word is literally and *only literally* true. As Coleridge brilliantly expressed it, writing in the early nineteenth century when this process was already well underway:

> A hunger-bitten and idea-less philosophy naturally produces a starveling and comfortless religion. It is among the miseries of the present age that it recognises no medium, between Literal and Metaphorical. Faith is either to be buried in the dead letter, or its name and honours usurped by a counterfeit product ...[11]

---

9   Sprat, *A History*, p. 113.

10   William Blake, *Descriptive Catalogue*, 1810 (reprinted, Oxford, 1990).

11   S.T. Coleridge, 'The Statesman's Manual', in *Lay Sermons*, ed. R.J. White (Princeton, 1972), p. 30. This is Volume 6 of *The Collected Works of Samuel Taylor Coleridge*, gen ed. K. Colburn (Princeton, 1970–2002), hereafter CC.

This is to put it starkly. In the course of this debate there have been a wide range of intermediate positions and some profound attempts, as we shall see when we look more closely at Coleridge, to reintegrate the deepest insights of post-Cartesian philosophy, especially Kant, with the wisdom, especially the symbolically expressed or encoded wisdom, of the pre-modern age. The first positions were clearly marked in the seminal early modern period but they have seen interesting development, particularly as we enter another cultural shift, contentiously termed 'post-modernism'. Of most concern to us in making the case for poetic imagination as a truth-bearing faculty is the development of thought about the actual and possible range of reference of language itself. I cited the seventeenth-century writing of Thomas Sprat, itself developing Bacon and Descartes, as characteristic of its age but there is a causal link between Sprat's strictures about language, and his attack on imagination itself. His reductive, essentially sceptical approach anticipates similar analytic approaches highly influential in the twentieth century, especially early Wittgenstein, the Wittgenstein of the *Tractatus*. This is well summarised by Paul Avis in his chapter on the fate of the imagination in modernity in *God and the Creative Imagination*. Avis' description of early Wittgenstein almost exactly echoes Sprat's strictures:

> Modern Philosophy in the analytic tradition was obsessed with the search for a precise, disciplined, stripped down language, purged of ambiguity and without fuzzy edges that would correspond as directly as possible to what is actually the case in the real world. Wittgenstein memorably began his Tractatus Logico-Philosophicus of 1922 with the definition 'The World is all that is the case'.[12] His early logical atomism represents, perhaps, the ultimate quest for a pure relation between words and things.[13]

However, there are robust responses to be made to early Wittgenstein and those who developed his line of thinking into logical positivism, and some of these responses were in fact made by Wittgenstein himself in his later writings. Before we turn to those it is interesting to interpose a purely poetic response to the *Tractatus*. It could of course be argued that two other great works published in the same year, namely *The Wasteland* and *Ulysses* are in themselves a more than sufficient demonstration that truth-bearing language does not have to be purged of ambiguity on order to be truthful, but here to focus our thoughts a little further is a poet's response, indeed direct reply, in Derek Mahon's memorable poem 'Tractatus', first published in 1981:

---

[12]   Ludwig Wittgenstein, *Tractatus Logico-Philosophicus*, trans. D.F. Pears and B. McGuinness (London, 2001), p. 5.

[13]   Paul Avis, *God and the Creative Imagination: Metaphor, Symbol and Myth in Religion and Theology* (London, 1999), p. 14.

Tractatus (for Aidan Higgins)[14]

'The world is everything that is the case'
From the fly giving up in the coal-shed
To the Winged Victory of Samothrace.
Give blame, praise, to the fumbling God
Who hides, shame-facedly, His agèd face;
Whose light retires behind its veil of cloud.

The world, though, is also so much more
Everything that is the case imaginatively.
Tacitus believed mariners could hear
The sun sinking into the western sea;
And who would question that titanic roar,
The steam rising wherever the edge may be?'

It is not simply that Wittgenstein excludes the imaginative realm, seen as purely imaginative, as in the second stanza here, but that even in the first stanza we see how his foreclosing on what the world is, leaves no room for what might be discerned 'behind the veil of cloud'. The *Tractatus*, and the school of thought it represents, circumscribes the possibilities of both language and the world in ways that are not adequate to our actual experience of the rich and mysterious ambiguity of both. In order to describe some aspects of our being human an 'inexactitude' may be, paradoxically, more adequate – indeed, more *exact* – than a supposedly exact expression.

And here we need to notice that, over against the reductive position which we have seen running from Bacon and Descartes through Hobbes and Locke to the Wittgenstein of the *Tractatus*, there is a counter-movement, emphasising both knowledge and language as tacit, trustful, ambiguous, imaginatively shaped, and capable of self-transcendence. This is a line that goes back into and behind the beginnings of modernism and runs from Augustine into writers like Donne and Hooker, through into Coleridge and from him to F.D. Maurice, Newman and historians and philosophers of Science like Michael Polanyi, the later Wittgenstein himself and the later writings of George Steiner.

The three leading characteristics of this counter-tradition are that real knowledge requires an element of trust and commitment to counterbalance its element of systematic scepticism, that real knowledge involves an active synthesising and shaping power of the mind, and finally that it will be at home with symbol and metaphor and will see in symbol itself a possibility of transcendence beckoning from within immanence. All three characteristics bring the imagination into play.

So one can go back to Augustine's essential formula: 'Credo ut intellegam', I believe in order to understand, and trace this insight, that reason can only proceed

---

[14]   Derek Mahon, *Selected Poems* (London, 1993), p. 135.

from, test and interpret, a position of faith and trust, including trust in reason itself, which precedes it. It runs through writers like Richard Hooker with his important distinction between the certainty of evidence and the certainty of adherence, to Coleridge's restatement of Augustine in *Aids To Reflection* where he says: 'To believe and to understand are not diverse things but the same thing in different periods of growth'.[15] Reflecting on knowledge as a journey undertaken in faith, he writes in his Notebooks:

> Try it, travel along it, trust in it and … obey in all respects the various guideposts both at its entrance and those which you will find along it – and this is the method, nay this is from the very nature of the thing the only possible method of converting your negative knowledge into direct and positive Insight…'[16]

Avis places Michael Polanyi in this same, as he terms it, 'fiduciary' tradition:

> … Polanyi's account of 'personal knowledge' may be considered as a sustained exposition of the rule that one must trust in order to test. Polanyi insists that 'we know more than we can tell'. This tacit knowledge that cannot be fully specified or articulated is absorbed from the environment that we test for its truth and adequacy by trusting ourselves to it. This environment is constituted by the symbolic.[17]

This reference to the symbolic brings us to the other characteristic of this 'fiduciary tradition'[18] in epistemology; its recognition that there is no language and no knowledge without symbol and metaphor. Two consequences arise from this: one is that we require imagination both to make and to interpret symbols and the other is that symbols themselves beckon us through language to that which is beyond language. In other words, symbols are energised between the two poles (as Coleridge would say) of immanence and transcendence.

These are themes we will explore in more detail through the work of individual poets, but in this introductory account of some of the theoretical underpinning it is worth returning to Wittgenstein and looking at how he revised his own reductive position. In a passage of *Real Presences* critiquing the *Tractatus*, Steiner says that 'The equation of the *Tractatus* between the limits of our language and the limits

---

[15]   S.T. Coleridge, *Aids To Reflection*, ed. John Beer (Princeton 1993), p.194 (Volume 9 of CC).

[16]   S.T. Coleridge, *Notebooks, 1819–1826*, ed. K. Coburn (London, 1990) p. 4,611. This passage is cited in Avis, *God and the Creative Imagination*, p.31, in his helpful summary of what he calls the fiduciary tradition. There will be a much fuller discussion of Coleridge on ways of knowing and imagination in Chapter 6.

[17]   Avis, *Creative Imagination*, p. 31.

[18]   For a fuller account of this tradition, see John Coulson, *Religion and Imagination* (Oxford, 1981).

of our world is almost a banality',[19] but the Wittgenstein of the *Philosophical Investigations*[20] was saying something else. As Avis summarises: 'He ... defends inexactness as more helpful than great exactitude for some tasks, and challenges the common assumption that "inexact" is really a reproach and "exact" is a praise.'[21]

Steiner himself had moved from a reductive or pessimistic view of the possibilities of language to a much more open one, and indeed in his book *Real Presences* most powerfully challenges Derrida's position that language is 'outsideless' that there is nothing beyond the text. *Real Presences* opens with a brilliant summary of the positivist, reductive view, that words that do not have a specific, concrete, unambiguous reference are empty. Steiner cites the word 'god' as the ultimate example, from this perspective, of a non-word a vain and unmeaning sound: 'god ... is a phantom of grammar, a fossil embedded in the childhood of rational speech. So Nietzsche and many after him.'

But Steiner immediately follows his summary of the reductive approach with a direct refutation of that position:

> This essay argues the reverse.
>
> It proposes that any coherent understanding of what language is and how language performs ... is in the final analysis under-written by the assumption of God's presence ... the experience of aesthetic meaning in particular that of literature and the arts ... infers the necessary possibility of this 'real presence' ... this study will contend that the wager on the meaning of meaning ... when we come face to face with the text and work of art or music ... is a wager on transcendence.[22]

The rest of *Real Presences* explores both sides of the phrase 'wager on transcendence' – the tacit, provisional nature of 'wager', and the theological reach of the word transcendence. Indeed Steiner goes on to make explicit his borrowing of another theological word to account for the 'possible impossibility' of meaning in language:

> This wager – it is that of ... every poet ... – predicates the presence of realness, of a 'substantiation' (the theological reach of this word is obvious) within language and form. It supposes a passage, beyond the fictive or the purely pragmatic, from meaning to meaningfulness. The conjecture is that 'God' *is*, not because

---

[19]   George Steiner, *Real Presences* (London, 1989), p. 83.
[20]   Ludwig Wittgenstein, *Philosophical* Investigation,s trans. G.E.M. Anscombe (Oxford ,1968).
[21]   Ibid., p.41, cited in Avis, *Creative Imagination*, p. 42.
[22]   Steiner, *Real Presences*, pp.3–4.

our grammar is outworn; but that grammar lives and generates worlds because there is a wager on God'[23]

One purpose of this book is to explore the 'theological reach' of our encounter with meaning through the poetic imagination

Derrida and Post-Modernism

Since the name of Derrida has been mentioned it is worth briefly reframing this debate about the inheritance from modernism in terms of our entry into a so-called post-modern period. For many the emergence of post-modernism, with its emphasis on reader-response, its acute alertness to symbol at every turn, might have seemed to be a welcome return of imagination over against reductive positivism, but this has not proved to be the case. In some ways post-modernism has turned out be more a form of hyper-modernism. The problem is that when *everything* becomes symbolic, when every decoding is another encoding, there is no transcendent, not so much as a wager on it, and so supposedly meaning-laden language is reduced to ultimate meaninglessness. As Avis remarks, again borrowing his terms from Coleridge:

> In post-modernity everything has the potential to become a symbol but nothing is a symbol of the transcendent. The pan-symbolism is purely immanent. Symbols images and myths interpret one another, interacting immanently, but none of them points beyond the symbolic realm. They do not symbolise a reality in which they participate.[24]

The poets themselves have been alert to the dangers of Derrida's position. Heaney, for example, in a recent interview, discussing his collection *The Haw Lantern*, with its sequence of poems about faith and loss of faith, speaks of his concern for:

> Loss of faith, to a certain extent in language itself, or at least doubts about the 'real presence' behind it, as in 'The Riddle'. I didn't see this clearly at the time, but now I can see also that there's a countervailing impulse at work, a refusal to discredit 'the real thing', however much it may be melting. There's a contest going on between Derry and Derrida.[25]

Theologians are also contesting with Derrida this question of how far every apparently transcendent or in his terms' totalising' sign or symbol can be

---

[23]   Ibid., p.4.

[24]   Avis, *Creative Imagination*, p. 26.

[25]   Dennis O'Drioscoll, *Stepping Stones: Interviews With Seamus Heaney* (London, 2008), p. 287.

deconstructed again into mere immanence. In *After Writing: On the Liturgical Consummation of Philosophy*, Catherine Pickstock makes a long critique of Derrida, locating him as part of modernist dualism rather than its antithesis. Like Avis she advocates a position of 'symbolic realism'. Symbolic realism allows signs, both words and the symbols they describe or evoke, to point not only to other signs and symbols but also to apprehensions of a reality which transcend them: 'These signs are both things (res) and figures or signs – of one another and of that which exceeds appearance.'[26]

I believe Derrida's extreme deconstruction has had its day and, whilst I welcome the return to a more richly layered reading of image symbol and archetype which some aspects of post-modernism have brought to both biblical and literary hermeneutics,[27] I think a full understanding of the mystery of language and the truth-bearing capacity of the poetic imagination requires a critical approach to language which is alert both to the immanent and the transcendent, and indeed to the unique power of imagination to move between the two. This book will explore how this reciprocation between immanence and transcendence is achieved in particular moments of English poetry, and examine the theological implications of such reciprocation.

Reason, Imagination and 'The Fall'

However, before we turn to the poetry itself and the various ways of reading it available to us, we need to look at a second strand of thought which has given rise to our deeply embedded suspicion of imagination as a truth-bearing faculty. This arises not from problems in language or epistemology but from within the theological tradition itself and might be encapsulated in the Biblical phrase 'vain imaginations'. It is the fear and suspicion of images as giving rise to idols, which is imbedded in the Judaeo-Christian, and (even more so) in the Islamic tradition, a fear which was given particular emphasis in the protestant reformation and which in some ways re-enforced the hostility to imagination we have been discussing.

In what sense should we speak of the imagination as fallen? In some quarters, particularly in Classical Calvinism,[28] the imagination is seen as somehow more

---

[26]   Catherine Pickstock, *After Writing: On the Liturgical Consummation of Philosophy* (Oxford, 1998), p. 170. For my own discussion of the relation between signs and things, see my comments on Coleridge's reading of Augustine's *De Magistro* in Chapter 6 below, pp. 170–72.

[27]   For example, in David Brown's *Tradition and Imagination: Revelation and Change* (Oxford, 1999).

[28]   For a perceptive discussion of the way this tension between Calvinism and a more positive 'Coleridgean' understanding of imagination played out in the life of one highly influential writer, see Kerry Dearborn's interesting study *Baptized Imagination: The Theology of George MacDonald* (Aldershot, 2006).

degraded and overthrown than the reason. Theology is therefore pursued and presented in highly syllogistic and logical form, as pared of imagery as possible. The problem with this approach is it privileges one faculty over against another, as though reason were itself somehow less 'fallen' than imagination. This goes together with a misreading of Augustine's doctrine of illumination which assumes that the Logos, as 'Light which lightens everyone who comes into the world', is to be identified with the light of pure reason rather than a direct intellectual apprehension or grasp of truth which involves imagination as well. The consequence of this has been a church culture which starved the imagination, was suspicious of mystery, but was unaware that, in deifying a logical and syllogistic method in theology, it was in fact creating its own idol. This kind of theology refuses the full consequence and meaning of the incarnation, of believing that the word was made flesh. The poet Edwin Muir has described this approach and its consequence, what he calls 'abstract calamity', in his poem 'The Incarnate One':

How could our race betray
The Image, and the Incarnate One unmake
Who chose this form and fashion for our sake?

The Word made flesh here is made word again
A word made word in flourish and arrogant crook
See there King Calvin with his iron pen,
And God three angry letters in a book,
And there the logical hook
On which the Mystery is impaled and bent
Into an ideological argument.[29]

I have given a fuller exposition of the implications of this poem for theology elsewhere,[30] but it is worth observing here that the 'ideological argument' of syllogistic theology is no less 'fallen', provisional, and seen through a glass darkly than any of the resonant and mysterious images available to the imagination. But there is this difference, that abstract language pretends to a precision, a finality which it cannot deliver, and this, ironically, is what makes it potentially more idolatrous than the images of which it is so suspicious.

In fact, the fallenness of our mental capacities may rest precisely in the disordering or imbalance of relations *between* our capacities of Reason and Imagination. The idea that the fall results in a disordering of relations between our own capacities leading to loss of vision and paralysis of will, is a central part of

---

29   Edwin Muir, *Collected Poems* (London,1960), p. 228.
30   Malcolm Guite, 'Through Literature', in Jeremy Begbie (ed,), *Beholding The Glory: Incarnation Through the Arts* (London, 2000), pp. 25–33.

Christian tradition expressed most clearly by St Augustine,[31] rendered famously in English verse by Milton[32] and more succinctly, though less famously, by Sir John Davies in *Nosce Teipsum*:

> Even so by tasting of that Fruit forbid,
> Where they sought *knowledge*, they did *error* find;
> Ill they desir'd to know, and Ill they did;
> And to give *Passion* eyes, made *Reason* blind.
>
> For then their minds did first in Passion see
> Those wretched shapes of *Misery* and *Woe*,
> Of *Nakedness*, of *Shame*, of *Poverty,*
> Which then their own experience made them know.
>
> But then grew *Reason* dark, that *she* no more,
> Could the faire Forms of *Truth* and *Good* discern;
> *Bats* they became, that *Eagles* were before:
> And this they got by their *desire to learn*.[33]

So, whilst we may need to reframe the argument about our fallenness if we are to resist the demonising of imagination itself over against reason, we do not simply wish to turn the tables by exalting imagination at the expense of reason; for as we have seen, and will see in the ensuing chapters, these two ways of knowing are mutually enfolded and depend on one another. The Romantic Movement[34] as a whole, in its reaction to Enlightenment critiques, could be accused of naively 'deifying' the imagination, as if human imagination were not also caught up in the tragedy of our fallenness. Whilst I would argue that our imagination is part of the *Imago Dei* in us, we also need to take cognisance of what might be called false, darkened, or apparently wilful mis-creations in works of 'imagination'. I will be following Coleridge in maintaining that there is a level at which human and divine imagination participate one another such that, even in a fallen world, the imagination, honestly followed, is able be a truth-bearer. The mis-creations arising from our fallenness, our shallow fantasies, work against Imagination in its deepest sense, and this is where Coleridge's distinction between Fancy and Imagination is

---

[31]   Augustine, *The City of God Against the Pagans*, ed. and trans. R.W. Dyson (Cambridge, 1998), Book XIV.15, p. 611.

[32]   John Milton, *Paradise Lost*, Book III. lines 176ff.

[33]   *The Poems of Sir John Davies*, ed. R. Krueger (Oxford, 1975), pp.6–7, For a more detailed discussion of this poem, see Chapter 3 below.

[34]   For an earlier discussion of the relations between the Romantic revival of interest in Imagination and its implications for theology, see Stephen Prickett, *Romanticism and Religion: The Tradition of Coleridge and Wordsworth in the Victorian Church* (Cambridge, 1976).

so helpful. This is also an insight that can be developed from Heaney's profound remark that 'the faking of feelings is a sin against the imagination'.[35]

We have nevertheless still to reckon with the fact that no purely human effort or work, not even the making of great poetry, will in itself deliver us from the Fall and its consequences. So, whilst we might wish to argue that what Coleridge called 'the shaping spirit of imagination'[36] is both part of the *Imago Dei* in us, and is participated by and participates in God's own shaping Spirit of imagination, the imagination is not itself untainted; it is marred but not utterly overthrown. As Tolkien puts it in his poem 'Mythopoeia':

> The heart of man is not compound of lies,
> but draws some wisdom from the only Wise,
> and still recalls him. Though now long estranged,
> man is not wholly lost nor wholly changed.
> Disgraced he may be, yet is not dethroned,
> and keeps the rags of lordship once he owned,
> his world-dominion by creative act:
> not his to worship the great Artefact,
> man, sub-creator, the refracted light
> through whom is splintered from a single White
> to many hues, and endlessly combined
> in living shapes that move from mind to mind.[37]

In offering a theology of imagination, we need to have some criteria for discerning the ways in which imagination might both lapse into idolatry and unhelpful fantasy, and yet also give us our only possible apprehensions of the Kingdom of God.[38]

T.E. Hulme famously called Romanticism 'spilt religion'[39] and both Romantic and some post-modern discourse may seem to offer art and imagination as an alternative to faith, indeed an alternative to Christ. For them, imaginative art

---

[35] Seamus Heaney, *Preoccupations Selected Prose 1968–1978* (London, 1980), p. 34.

[36] 'Dejection: An Ode', line 86, in *Poetical Works I* (part2), ed. J.C.C. Mays (Princeton, 2001), p. 700. (Volume 16 in CC).

[37] J.R.R. Tolkien, *Tree and Leaf* (London, 2001), p. 87. For further discussion of Tolkien's understanding of relations between truth and imagination in the context of his Fellow Inklings Lewis, Barfield and Williams, see R.J. Reilly's excellent book *Romantic Religion: A Study of Owen Barfield, C.S. Lewis, Charles Williams and J.R.R. Tolkien* (Athens, GA, 1971) and Verlyn Flieger's in-depth study *Splintered Light: Logos and Language in Tolkien's World* (Grand Rapids, 1983)

[38] For a contemporary discussion of the tensions and harmonies between imagination and revelation in light of the Fall, see Paul Fiddes, *Freedom and Limit: A Dialogue between Literature and Christian Doctrine* (Basingstoke, 1991).

[39] T.E. Hulme, *Selected Writing*, ed. P. McGuiness (Manchester, 1988), p. 71.

becomes a human exercise in remaking and reintegration which does away with the need for any transcendence or any narrative of salvation as God's sovereign work in Christ. Through a close reading of particular poems I hope to show that, far from becoming a substitute for the salvific action of the Word made flesh, the poetic imagination helps us make sense of that action and is indeed underpinned by it. If part of the *Imago Dei* is itself our creative imagination then we should expect the action of the Word, indwelling and redeeming fallen humanity, to begin in, and work outward through, the human imagination. If this is so then we should be able discern the presence of that Word in the works of art which are the fruit of our imagination.

The Principle of Selection

In the pages that follow I am not offering a summary of the extensive secondary literature of literary and historical criticism with which academic culture has surrounded the poems I wish to cite, interesting as much of that literature is. What I offer instead is a fresh reading of these poems in light of the specific question of how far and in what ways we can trust the poetic imagination as truth-bearing, and how far within the particular discipline of theology we can come through poetry, to what Keats happily called 'the truth of the imagination'.[40]

There is obviously a huge range of poetry pertinent to such an enquiry, but I have borne five broad criteria in mind in making the selection of poetry to examine in this book. The first is historical. There is a continuous poetic tradition which encompasses and transcends the strict periods into which philosophy and history tend to divide the history of ideas; I have chosen poems ranging from the earliest period to the work of contemporary poets so that the reader will have some sense over the course of the book of the development of that tradition. The second principle of selection is thematic. It will be clear from the foregoing discussion that I am particularly interested in poetry as mediating between immanence and transcendence, between the worlds of comprehension and apprehension, and I have chosen poetry which exemplifies this interconnection and for which the notion of 'Heaven in ordinary' (see below p. 24), the invisible in the visible is central, poetry that can be read as a window or gateway between distinct, but not divided realms. Thirdly, I have tried in my selection to cover a variety of poetic genres, to show the myriad possibilities open to poets, so the selection ranges from dream poetry, through drama, epic, metaphysical, conversation poems, ballad, and lyrical sequences. My hope is that a reader unfamiliar with the full corpus of English poetry[41] may nevertheless get a sense both of the chronological development of that

---

[40]   In a letter to Benjamin Bailey dated 22 November 1817; see *The Letters of John Keats*, ed. M.B. Forman, 3rd edn (Oxford, 1947), p. 67 .

[41]   I intend by the term 'English poetry' poetry written in English. Seamus Heaney is emphatically not an English poet, but by writing in English he draws on and develops a

poetry and of its range of style and subject. Fourthly, I wish to address the cultural split between poetry and science, itself a product of the false quarrel between reason and imagination. This issue has been helpfully and profoundly explored by Mary Midgely in her book *Science and Poetry*[42] and I want to support and illustrate her thesis that the poetic imagination is fully engaged in scientific endeavour and also that poetry is capable of refining and expressing the doubt, as well as the faith which is part of the dynamic of both science and theology. These concerns are especially explored in Chapters 3 and 7. Finally, I have included in this book longer and more focused chapters on two poets who have been particularly reflective about their own use of language and about the nature of imagination itself: Coleridge and Seamus Heaney. They are certainly the two poets whose vision most affects the shape and purpose of this volume, and they are quoted, by way of allusion and commentary, in almost every chapter. The chapters on Coleridge and Heaney make explicit a theology of imagination, which has been developed implicitly in the reading of all the other poetry discussed in this book. Through poetry I hope to explore our imagination as an aspect of the *Imago Dei* in humankind, as an active, shaping power of perception exercised both individually and collectively, and as a faculty which is capable of both apprehending and embodying truth. Like reason, its twin faculty, our fallen imagination is shadowed and finite, but like Reason it is also, under God's grace, illuminating and redemptive. Imagination informs reason and is in turn informed by it. My hope is to illustrate the ways in which the poetic imagination can help to redress a lost balance, renew and deepen our vision of the world, and, in so doing, also enrich our understanding of theology.

Poetry and Vision.

After this historical and philosophical excursus, we turn again to the present problem. We have inherited a divided and dualistic culture, how can we set about reading poetry and engaging the poetic imagination in a way that will heal or restore lost vision? Bearing in mind all that may be said about the limits of language, bearing in mind the shadows that fall across every heart (for now we see through a glass darkly), but bearing in mind also that the indwelling Logos is a light who lightens everyone who comes into the world, what can poetry bring to the task of renewing vision, of reintegrating reason and imagination? How do poets change the way we see, and what kind of new vision is it they offer?

Shakespeare set poetry the comparatively modest task of 'holding a mirror up to nature',[43] that is, helping us to see our society and ourselves more clearly, reflecting our known realities back to us. But sometimes (and very often in the works of Shakespeare), the mirror of poetry does more than reflect what we have

wider tradition of English verse.

[42]   Mary Midgely *Science and Poetry* (London, 2001).
[43]   *Hamlet*, Act III, scene ii, line 24.

already seen. Sometimes that mirror becomes a window, a window into the mystery which is both in and beyond nature, a 'casement opening on perilous seas'. From that window sometimes shines a more than earthly light that suddenly transforms, *transfigures* all the earthly things it falls upon. Through that window, when it is opened for us by the poet's art, we catch a glimpse of that 'Beauty always ancient always new', who made and kindled our imagination in the beginning and whose love draws us beyond the world.

It is those moments of *transfiguration*, those moments when the mirror a poem holds up becomes a window into the Divine, which are the subject of this book. My hope is that we will approach poetry, not all by any means avowedly Christian poetry, in such a way that we have this double vision, this experience of transfiguration, of seeing through and beyond, which the poet-priest George Herbert described so simply:

> A man that looks on glass
> on it may stay his eye
> or if he pleases through it pass
> and then the heavens espy.[44]

Two Preliminary Poems

To help us recover this vision I am going to preface the more detailed chapters with a preparatory reading of two poems, which will help us to reflect on the nature of poetry itself, and on how to read it. The poems I have chosen span the gap of which I have spoken. George Herbert's poem 'Prayer' comes from a poet who saw, at the threshold of the modern world, the coming danger of a false and fragmented knowledge (as we shall see when we come later in this book to read his poem 'Vanity') and in his verse he continuously and deliberately wove together the strands of Reason, Faith and Imagination to make a triple cord which not even the coming cultural shift could break. Seamus Heaney, in 'The Rain Stick', from *The Spirit Level*, written in the final decade of the twentieth century, shows us how even in our 'post-modern' world, the old unity of vision, the ancient window on mystery, can be suddenly and beautifully re-opened.

Heaney's 'The Rain Stick'

So let us begin where we are, in our own age and read Heaney's astonishing poem, finding in it an opening, an invitation into the poetry of every age:

---

[44]   'The Elixir', in *George Herbert: The Complete English Works*, ed. A. Pasternak Slater (London, 1995), p. 180.

The Rain Stick[45]

Upend the rain stick and what happens next
Is a music that you never would have known
To listen for. In a cactus stalk

Downpour, sluice-rush, spillage and backwash
Come flowing through. You stand there like a pipe
Being played by water, you shake it again lightly

And diminuendo runs through all its scales
Like a gutter stopping trickling. And now here comes
A sprinkle of drops out of the freshened leaves,

Then subtle little wets off grass and daisies;
Then glitter-drizzle, almost-breaths of air.
Upend the stick again. What happens next

Is undiminished for having happened once,
Twice, ten, a thousand times before.
Who cares if all the music that transpires

Is the fall of grit or dry seeds through a cactus?
You are like a rich man entering heaven
Through the ear of a raindrop. Listen now again.

Water Imagery

The first thing to strike the reader (and I hope the *listener*, for this is a poem which demands to be read aloud) is the sheer particular vividness of the myriad water images which fall like a cataract through the mind and like the sounds of refreshing water upon the ear: 'Downpour, sluice-rush, spillage and backwash' have in their rhythmic and repeated *w* and *sh* the very sound of the water sloshing and washing as it runs down and backs up against itself; and then the new half-line that ends the sentence – 'come flowing through' – itself expresses the sudden clearing of a channel or passage that lets the water flow through smoothly and quietly again. The phrases and images build to a compendium of all that one has ever enjoyed in the many forms of water from the sluice-rush, through trickles and sprinkle, to the beautifully observed detail of 'subtle little wets off grass and daisies'. Such rich imagery demands a slow and succulent reading, a *tasting* of the words as they flow, and this celebration of the very words and sounds as good in themselves, this more engaged way of reading is one of the ways of approaching poetry, which we shall consider later.

---

[45] Seamus Heaney, 'The Rain Stick', in *The Spirit Level* (London, 1996), p.1.

Refreshment from the Dry
After this first sense of the refreshing variety of water the reader then feels all the more powerfully the creative tension between, 'downpour sluice-rush, spillage and backwash' and the phrase which precedes it – 'In a cactus stalk'. Some of this poem's power to move us is generated by the polarity and counterpoint between the world of images that lie behind the little seed-like words – 'grit', 'dry', 'cactus' – and all the lush water sounds, which emerge from this dry cactus. It is this awareness of tension or polarity which moves us towards the heart of the poem, which is the paradox of refreshment from the dry. Not simply of this moment of water music from the cactus, but of every experience in life when there is a sudden blessing from barrenness, a hope from despair, a grace at the zero point. And in that sense this poem is certainly about poetry itself. In *The Redress of Poetry*, Heaney, commenting on a poem of Robert Frost's, says that poetry ' provides a draught of the clear water of transformed understanding and fills the reader with a momentary sense of freedom and wholeness.'[46] Which is certainly what is happening by the time we reach the invitation at the end of this poem to be like one who enters Heaven through the ear of a raindrop.

The Challenge to 'Scientism'
 When once we have been ushered by the poet into this realm of paradox we begin to notice other things through the lens of his poem. We see that it is written as a deliberate challenge, not to Science in its largest and most integrative sense but to 'scientism', the reductive way of seeing things in terms only of what can be weighed and measured; the approach which dissects a living whole into into its measurable constituent parts and then says that the measurable is all that there is. This approach is what Mary Midgely calls 'an unbalanced fascination with the imagery of atomism – a notion that the only way to understand anything is to break it into its ultimate smallest parts and to conceive these as making up something comparable to a machine'.[47] A scientist working in this reductive mode would say *all* you have heard is the fall of dry seeds through a cactus, but the poet replies:

> Who cares if all the music that transpires
>
> Is the fall of grit or dry seeds through a cactus?
> You are like a rich man entering heaven
> Through the ear of a raindrop.

And as we hear the poem's music and through it the music of water springing miraculously from the desiccated, we know that the poem in fact describes what *really* happens, which is more than the bare accuracy of 'fall of grit and dry seeds'.

---

46   Heaney, *The Redress of Poetry*, p. xv.
47   Midgely, *Science and Poetry*, p. 2.

The Theme of Music

This emergence of the music of water from the dry and desiccated prepares us for another great theme of this poem which is music itself; not only heard music but a deeper music 'you never would have known to listen for'. The poem begins and ends with the injunction to *listen*, and once the ear is attuned to this theme it catches the catena of words and images drawn from the world of music: '… listen … pipe being played … diminuendo runs through all its scales … almost-breaths of air … undiminished … entering heaven through the ear …'

The double senses of water and music in many of these phrases is beautifully achieved especially after the phrase 'pipe being played' has delicately suggested to the mind the image perhaps of a flute, then the phrase 'almost-breaths of air', which is first about the fresh air in a garden after rain, at the same time, just as delicately, conjures the wonderful breathy sound the flute can make.

A Shift of Perspective

At the heart of this musical theme comes one of those sudden shifts of perspective whereby the poets shake us to a new understanding. For the first few lines of the poem we are *outside* the instrument, holding and upending the dry stalk, listening for its music, then comes the image of it as a water pipe down which the water is sluicing and rushing, and then suddenly it is we ourselves who *are* the pipe, we are being played:

> You stand there like a pipe
> being played by water.

In this sudden shift you get that entering *into* experience, that coalescing of observer and observed, which was so dreadfully and dryly missing from the Enlightenment perspective.

Repetition

As we re-read it and enjoy it again we discover that 'The Rain Stick' is also a poem about *repetition*, about the relation between the outer repetitions in time and the inner experience in eternity. It is a poem of hope, and realism for it does not suggest as some romantics and false mystics have, that the moment of revelation, when the transfiguring light of heaven falls through the window of an experience, is a one-off, never to be caught again, always to be sought, but never accessible to the ordinary person. Quite the reverse. This poem is about the apprehension of the divine *in* the regular, of 'heaven in ordinary':

> Upend the stick again. What happens next
> Is undiminished for having happened once,
>
> Twice, ten, a thousand times before.

Sacrament

And so this poem is also about sacrament. I read it and it reflects for me my experience as a Christian coming to communion, as a priest celebrating communion. The plain little wafer is as dry as those falling seeds, the daily wine and water are all repeated 'once twice, ten a thousand times', and yet from them also, undiminished, comes the refreshing flow from the source of all things.

And finally, because it is about sacrament, this poem is about entering Heaven. Heaney delicately alludes to one of the hard sayings of Jesus and releases from it somehow an unexpected grace: 'It is easier for a camel to go through the eye of a needle than for a rich man to enter the kingdom of God.'[48] 'The eye of a needle' in Christ's saying becomes in this poem, in a strange and beautiful conflation of images, 'the ear of a raindrop'. In this image we both hear the music of water and see for an instant how the curved reflective surface of the droplet seems to hold the whole world. However, the world it contains is not only a reflection of our own, but also wholly new. The mirror, held up to nature, has become a window; the window has become a gateway through which we may enter – as the last lines invite us again to enter – into the mystery. And we do so by listening to the music of the rain stick *through* the music of the poem:

> You are like a rich man entering heaven
> Through the ear of a raindrop. Listen now again.

Herbert's 'Prayer'

We turn now to a poem of George Herbert's. In a later chapter we will be looking at his poetry in much more detail, but we will anticipate a little as there are themes and motifs in this poem, as in 'The Rain Stick', which will be germane to the reading of other poems and poets in this book. The best way to enter into this particular poem is to let its amazing cascade of images simply to wash over us and refresh our imagination. We should not try to stop and analyse it immediately, just let the images flow on from one another, rather like Heaney's 'downpour sluice-rush spillage and backwash'.

Prayer (1)[49]
Prayer the Churches banquet, Angels age,
  Gods breath in man returning to his birth,
  The Soul in paraphrase, heart in pilgrimage,
The Christian Plummet sounding heav'n and earth;

Engine against th'Almightie, sinners tower
  Reversed Thunder, Christ-side-piercing spear,

---

[48]   Mark 10:25.

[49]   George Herbert, 'Prayer (1)', in *The Complete English Works*, p. 49.

The six-days world-transposing in an hour,
A kind of tune which all things hear and fear;

Softness, and peace, and joy, and love, and bliss,
    Exalted Manna, gladness of the best,
    Heaven in ordinary, man well drest,
The milky way, the bird of Paradise,

Church-bells beyond the stars heard, the soul's blood,
The land of spices; something understood.

A Cascade of Images

Our first impression is of the sheer wealth, almost over-abundance, of beautiful images contained in striking and memorable phrases we are being offered. This is not the honing and concentration on the single vision, but a kind of rainbow refraction of many insights, a scattering of many seeds broadcast. For each of these images is in its own way a little poem, or the seed of a poem, ready to grow and unfold in the readers mind. And the different seeds take root at different times, falling differently in the soil of the mind each time one returns to this poem. I have been reading it for over thirty years now and I still find its images springing up freshly in my mind and showing me new things. For the purpose of this Introduction we will delve in and examine four of these little seeds, these poems in themselves within the images, before we take a wider view and see how they all fit together in the larger poem itself.

'Prayer the churches banquet'   This opening phrase carries, with the choice of the word 'banquet', a picture not of some puritan modicum, some strict or grudging allowance of necessity, but rather of largesse, generosity, and the good measure of a royal occasion. It is a phrase that sets the poem's tone, for of course a *banquet* is exactly what Herbert gives us; course after course, and layer after layer, of nourishing images. In fourteen lines he heaps up twenty-seven different images of the experience of prayer. But the phrase 'churches banquet' alludes to and summons up the rich complex of feast and banquet imagery in Scripture and the Church's life. Behind this passage lie the covenant meal of the Old Testament, the great wedding feast with which Jesus so often compared the kingdom, to which we must bring ourselves 'well drest', and, most importantly, the Last Supper and through it the Holy Communion which is the foretaste of the banquet of heaven (to which, in another of Herbert's poems, Love himself bids us welcome).

'God's breath in man returning to his birth' This line invites us into a very early tradition of prayer and meditation rooted in a reflection on the image of breath and breathing in the Bible. To understand this line we need first to remember that Hebrew, Greek and Latin all use a single word to mean both 'breath' and 'spirit'. 'God's breath in man' evokes that primal image in Genesis of God breathing

the breath of life into humanity, the moment of our wakening as living beings, a moment of tender closeness to our Maker. But after that *inspiration* comes the equally decisive moment of *expiration*. We have to trace our history through fall and alienation, pain and sin and death at last to the foot of the cross where a Second Adam, one in whom also the whole of humanity is bound and involved, stretches out his arms to embrace the pain of the world and breathes back to God that gift of life:

> Then Jesus, crying with a loud voice, said 'Father, into thy hands I commit my spirit!' And having said this he breathed his last.[50]

Then we must look beyond the cross, to the resurrection and the new breath of life that comes with the sending of the Holy Spirit. John's account consciously parallels the first gift of the breath of life in Genesis:

> And when he had said this he breathed on them and said to them, 'Receive the Holy Spirit.'[51]

Contained in the pattern of our breathing is the whole story of our salvation. For a Christian in prayer the very act of breathing can become a return to our birth, a receiving of original life from the breath of God, as we breathe in with Adam in the garden of our beginnings; an offering of all that needs letting go and redeeming, as we breathe out with Christ on the cross; a glad acceptance of new life in the Holy Spirit as we breathe in again, receiving our life and commission afresh from the risen Lord.

'Engine against th'Almighty, sinners tower / Reversed thunder, Christ-side-piercing spear,' This is an extraordinary clutch of related images, all drawing on pictures of warfare and violence *against* God to describe part of our relation with him in prayer. Herbert achieves his effect by a sudden reversal of perspective, much as we saw in the Heaney poem, epitomised here in the phrase 'reversed thunder'. We think of God in Heaven thundering down on us, but in prayer we are at liberty to thunder back at him, as indeed in our desperation we sometimes do – and perhaps those are our best prayers. The 'Engine against the Almighty' is almost certainly intended to conjure the image of a cannon shot at God, since the other 'engine', the siege tower, is already covered in the phrase 'sinners tower'. Herbert uses this image even more explicitly in his poem 'Artillery' where he says:

> then we are shooters both and thou dost deign
> To enter combat with us and contest,

---

[50]   Luke 23:46.
[51]   John 20:22.

With thine own clay.[52]

The image of prayer as a form of weaponry is of course rooted in St Paul's military metaphors,[53] but here Herbert has dared to observe that it is not always the devil, but sometimes God himself, whom we are fighting, as we struggle with our vocation to full humanity. In compressing this idea into the images of his poem Herbert may have been remembering a sermon by his friend John Donne:

> Earnest prayer hath the nature of Importunity; Wee presse, wee importune God … Prayer hath the nature of Impudency; wee threaten God in Prayer … and God suffers this Impudency and more. Prayer hath the nature of Violence; in the publique Prayers of the Congregation we besiege God, saies *Tertullian*, and we take God Prisoner, and bring God to our Conditions; and God is glad to be straightened by us in that siege.[54]

But after the thunders and towers and cannons of the siege imagery, Herbert brings the focus down and sharpens it with that single piercing image: 'Christ-side-piercing spear'. We have become the centurion, making that terrible thrust, but this time it is not cold iron but our own agonies which are piercing the heart of Christ.

'The six-days world-transposing in an hour, / A kind of tune, which all things hear and fear' Transposition is very much what poetry and all literary art is about. To hear snatches from the huge unknowable symphony of experience, to catch them and transpose them to a key that resonates with our understanding, so that at some point they harmonise with that unheard melody from heaven we are always trying to hear, that is the purpose of poetry. 'Transposition' for Herbert in this poem involves taking of the whole story of creation and a reworking of it within our individual life of prayer. Meditating on the six days of creation as a key to understanding one's own place in the order of things was a tradition which had begun for the West with Augustine's beautiful meditation on Genesis at the end of his Confessions. It had been continued in Herbert's age by his older contemporary Lancelot Andrewes whose private devotions were ordered around the governing images derived in each day's creation, and there is a beautiful contemporary example of 'the six days world' transposed literally in 'an hour' in a sermon of John Donne's, 'Remember thy Creator in the days of thy youth',[55] which takes us symbolically through every step in the Genesis creation narrative and was written to be heard in exactly an hour.

---

[52] 'Artillery', lines 25–8, in *The Complete English Works*, p. 136.

[53] For example, Ephesians 6:13 forward.

[54] *The Sermons of John Donne*, ed. G. Potter and E. Simpson, 10 vols (Los Angeles, 1953–62), Vol. V, p. 364.

[55] Ibid., Vol. II, pp. 235–49.

These transpositions lead to the making of 'a kind of tune', and if this is true of prayer it is also true of poetry and of this poem, for here again is Heaney's 'music that you never would have known to listen for'.

One might take each of these twenty-seven images in turn and find as much fruit in them: the window on the mysteries of communion in 'exalted manna', all the sense both of life and sacrifice packed into 'soul's blood', the evocation of the riches of the enchanted and far away in 'land of spices', and perhaps most tellingly the superb compression and paradox in 'Heaven in ordinary', a phrase which in itself sums up the heart of the Gospel in God's incarnation in a stable, but also stands for the heart of the kind of poetry we will explore in this book. It is precisely the restored vision that sees the ordinary afresh, and allows us to see heaven in it, to be with Blake in 'The Auguries of Innocence';

> To see a world in a grain of sand
> And a heaven in a wild flower
> Hold infinity in the palm of your hand
> And eternity in an hour[56]

or, as we did with Heaney, to enter heaven through the ear of a raindrop.

The Integration of the Poem as a Whole
We could meditate further on these individual images but I want to turn now to look at how they are related to each other and to the poem as a whole, for the ability to feel the energy that arises from the forces and tensions within the poem is part of what we need to rediscover in order to enjoy poetry at depth. Looking at the poem as a whole it seems almost modern in the way Herbert allows himself freedom from syntax and logic. The poem is technically a single sentence with only one full stop at the end of it bringing us to a rest after the roller-coaster ride through the images, with the quiescent phrase 'something understood'. But it is a strange sentence. There is no main verb. It makes no statement. Its meaning is not carried on the surface of its grammar. It is a world away from Sprat's 'bringing all things as near the mathematical plainness as we can'.[57] No, the meaning of this poem is carried not by the syntax of the sentence, but by the images themselves, by the way image speaks to image in point and counterpoint. For here there is both a congruence, which gives the poem flow and unity, and also a disparity, which gives it tension and energy. There are lines of congruence between 'banquet', 'softness', 'manna, and gladness, well-drest', 'land of spices', all suggesting sumptuousness and celebration. There is congruence between the music imagery of 'transposing … a kind of tune' and 'church bells beyond the stars heard', but there is a power

---

[56]   'Auguries of Innocence', lines 1–4, in *The Poetical Works of William Blake*, ed. J. Sampson (Oxford, 1952), p. 171.

[57]   See above p. 000.

in the tension of a poem which in lines 4 and 5 has the loud violence of 'engine against th'almighty' and 'reversed thunder' yet has moved in line 9 to 'softness, and peace, and joy, and love, and bliss'. At the end of the poem something is understood precisely because the poem has been able to hold these extremes in tension with each other, which is of course exactly what the life of prayer does for the practising Christian.

Then there is the whole subtle achievement across this poem of transposition and paraphrase, both terms mentioned in the poem itself. The theme of giving back to heaven what heaven first gave – which is what prayer essentially is – is transposed across a series of different keys from 'breath returning to its birth' through 'reversed thunder', to its fullest expression in 'exalted manna', the offering to God of his own gift in the Eucharist. When Herbert speaks of prayer as 'the soul in paraphrase' he is using that term to describe the way in which through prayer we find a new language, a new set of terms in which to express ourselves and, in paraphrasing ourselves to God in our hour of prayer we are, through the terms of our paraphrase, seeing ourselves afresh in his light. And this in turn is what the poem itself does. Each of the twenty-seven images it offers is itself a paraphrase of the experience of prayer. Between them they offer us a series of new understandings of who we are and what we are doing when we engage in prayer. These notions of 'transposition' and 'paraphrase' will be a key to understanding much of the poetry we encounter in this book.

The other thematic key which we have already noted both in this poem and in 'The Rain Stick' is paradox and reversal, the sudden setting of things on their heads, the 'reversed thunder', the 'up-ending' of the rain stick. Through the break in our world made by the shock of paradox there sometimes flows a new light.

It is the combination of all these things, working together within the subtle unity of the poem, which enables us to hear 'a kind of tune', that stirs 'The souls blood', and leads at last to 'something understood'.

Five Ways into Reading Poetry

Having enjoyed these two poems, let us see if we can draw out and recap from the experience of reading them some methods and approaches to reading poetry which we can bring to bear on the other poems we shall examine in this book. For, if we are not simply to 'stay our eye' on the glassy surface of a first and literal meaning, then we have to learn to read in a new and richer way. Though it is not really a new way, but rather a return to that fuller and more holistic way of reading which was taken from us at the Enlightenment. This new or recovered way of reading will include at least some of the following elements:

Tasting the Words

Firstly, we need to recover slowness, and savouring and celebration of the text itself, of the surface and shape and appearance of the words, and most of all a savouring and celebration, a tasting in the mouth of their sounds. Sometimes the very music of the words compels this:

> ... In some melodious plot
> Of beechen green and shadows numberless,
> Singest of summer in full-throated ease[58]

When you read lines like that you simply have to speak them aloud or murmur them at least. Keats was perhaps the greatest master of the music inherent in the English language but all great poetry has it to some degree. And when, in response, we begin to slow down, not to rush the text, then we are beginning to enter into the old way of reading which once went by the name of *Lectio Divina*. The great practitioners and preservers of this art, as of so many other vital arts, were the monks of Europe. They showed it visually in their illuminated manuscripts, and aurally in this practice of *Lectio Divina*, the prayerful form of reading aloud. The Benedictine historian Jean Leclercq describes it in this way:

> To meditate is to attach oneself closely to the sentence being recited and weigh all its words in order to sound the depths of their full meaning. It means assimilating the content of a text by means of a kind of mastication which releases its full flavour. It means, as St Augustine, St Gregory, John of Fecamp and others say in an untranslatable expression, to taste it with the *palatum cordis* or in *ore cordis*. All this activity is necessarily a prayer; the *lectio divina* is a prayerful reading. Thus the Cistercian, Arnoul of Boheriss will give this advice:
>
> > When he reads, let him seek for savour, not science. The Holy Scripture is the well of Jacob from which the waters are drawn which will be poured out later in prayer. Thus there will be no need to go to the oratory to begin to pray; but in reading itself, means will be found for prayer and contemplation.[59]

For the English Church, echoes of this ancient art of reading are preserved in the Prayer Book collect on the scriptures with its petition 'Help us so to hear them, to read, mark, learn, and *inwardly digest* them ...'[60]

---

[58]   'Ode to a Nightingale', lines 6–10, in *The Poetical Works of John Keats*, ed. H.W. Garrod (Oxford, 1939), p. 257.

[59]   Jean LeClercq OSB, *The Love of Learning and the Desire for God* (London, 1978), p. 90.

[60]   *The Book of Common Prayer*, Collect for the Second Sunday in Advent .

We should also come to poetry both for that inner nourishment, and, in that beautiful Cistercian image, for waters drawn up from a well, to be poured out fruitfully later.

Echo and Counterpoint.

The first fruit of this slower savouring of the text will be a new openness to the powers of echo and counterpoint, of the tension between the words themselves, and the way the words of a poem speak to each other across the lines. There are powers of cross-reference and connection inherent in each word and through the words, in the images they evoke. We saw this for example in the way some of the phrases in Herbert's 'Prayer' connect with and re-enforce each other whilst others react against one another modelling the tensions which are actually inherent in a life of prayer. Words are not dry little counters each betokening one meaning. Even the smallest and driest of words is like the small dry seeds that fall through Heaney's 'Rain Stick', suddenly evoking through their music all the refreshing downpour he celebrates. We have to let the words *be* music, and in that music to let them play counter-melodies to one another. This is happening all the time in even the most familiar and apparently simple poetry. Take for example Blake's 'Tiger':[61]

> Tiger! Tiger! Burning bright
> In the forests of the night,
> What immortal hand or eye
> Could frame thy fearful symmetry?

The first invocation of repeated 'Tiger! Tiger!', the uncontrollable power of fire invoked by 'burning bright' picked up from the blazing pattern of the tiger's coat and the uncountable shapes in a shapeless darkness suggested in the phrase 'forests of the night', all these are met by terms of an opposite polarity, almost another realm of discourse, in the words 'frame' and 'symmetry', with their suggestions of limitation, control and power. Part at least of the power of that verse is generated by the counterpoint and tension between the words that are constrained by Blake to share forever the same stanza. It is what makes the symmetry of his poem so fearful.

Images and Allusion:

What is true of the individual words and phrases is even truer of the images they evoke. We must let the images as well as the words have this interplay between one another, and not just within a single poem but across the whole inter-related network of poetry which is our in inheritance:

---

[61]   *The Poetical Works of William Blake*, p. 85.

T.S. Eliot expressed this truth brilliantly in his critical writing and exemplified it in his verse. For Eliot there was a sense in which all poetry is contemporary. What is written now is not only influenced by what has been written in the past but in itself modifies the way we read the poetry of the past. It shines new lights upon it and makes new connections. As he wrote in his seminal essay *Tradition and the Individual Talent*, first published in 1919, we must have:

> a perception, not only of the pastness of the past, but of its presence; the historical sense compels a man to write not merely with his own generation in his bones, but with a feeling that the whole of the literature of Europe from Homer and within it the whole of the literature of his own country has a simultaneous existence and composes a simultaneous order.[62]

At the end of that essay he goes on to say that a good poet lives 'in what is not merely the present, but the present moment of the past, ... he is conscious, not of what is dead, but of what is already living'.[63].

Eliot's poetry is full of this sense of the present moment of the past, of the way an image from another poet changes the way he sees things now, but also the way he sees things now changes the way we read the old poets. For example, there is a powerful moment in *The Waste Land* when Eliot describes London commuters walking mechanically in a great dull crowd all looking down and seeming to breathe in unison and he says: 'So many, I had not thought death had undone so many'.[64] When I first read this poem I felt this line simply as a poetic insight into the 'nightmare life-in-death' that modern living had imposed upon these 'lost' souls, but later I came to read Carey's great nineteenth-century translation of Dante's *Inferno*, and came to his harrowing description of his first sight of the dead, the crowd of souls in Limbo who had just drifted through life neither struggling to the heights of real virtue nor sinking to the depths of real depravity. Looking on them in horror as they trudge in step together endlessly round and round in a circle, Dante exclaims, '... I should n'ere / Have thought that death so many had despoiled'.[65]

What happens at such a moment of echo and allusion, congruence and connection? At one level I am remembering *The Waste Land* and suddenly realising that Eliot had been alluding to Dante and seeing what a brilliant thing it was to compare the rush-hour crowd to the crowds in Limbo. But at another level, at the level of the effect that Dante's poem is having on me now, it is Dante who is alluding to Eliot, Dante who is brilliantly comparing the crowds in Limbo with the London rush hour! There is a profound sense in which, after Eliot, Dante's

---

[62]   T.S. Eliot, *Selected Prose*, ed. F. Kermode (London, 1975), p.38.

[63]   Ibid., p. 44.

[64]   'The Waste Land', lines 62–3, in T.S.Eliot, *Collected Poems 1909–1962* (London, 1974), p. 65.

[65]   *The Vision of Dante*, trans. H.F. Carey (Oxford, 1923), Canto III, lines 53–4, p. 9.

poem is changed forever. Each poem subtly modifies all the poems with which it is connected running backwards and forwards through time across the great web of Poetry itself.

Ambiguity and Ambivalence:

We must be open to, and delighted with, ambiguity. Unlike those original Fellows of the Royal Society we are entering a realm where only multiple meanings will do if we are at last to find 'something understood'. For example, the phrase 'the soul's bloud' in 'Prayer' carries with it both the sense of blood as a sign of woundedness and hurt, of anguish, like Christ's sweating blood in his agony in the garden, and also the sense of blood as the very force and essence of life itself. We must not feel obliged to choose between these senses. Herbert is telling us that prayer is both the blood of our souls in the sense that prayer is what bleeds from us when we are in agony or anguish, and also the blood of our souls in the sense that without prayer our souls are bloodless, anaemic, starved of their real life.

We must also be ready to hear more than one voice, more than one tone in the poetry we read. For poetry as a medium is able to express both faith and doubt in one moment, to express at one and the same moment both the fulfilment and the frustration of our experience. Philip Larkin, whose honesty compelled him to deny himself the comforts of a faith he feared was false, but at the same time to acknowledge its real fruits, was a master of this delicate combination of avowal and denial, as we shall see in more detail in Chapter 7. For now I would like to take notice of the last verse of his famous poem 'An Arundel Tomb', a poem which describes the effigies of an Earl and Countess, who are depicted on their joint monument as holding hands, and whose monument had therefore become something of a romantic icon. Larkin explores the truth or falsity of such ideals of romantic love in the course of the poem, which concludes with the famous last line: '*What will survive of us is love*'.

Taken out of context, as it often is, this line seems quite unambiguous, but in the context of the poem it is not a slogan about love but rather a recognition that something neither the sculptor nor his subjects meant might be *close* to truth. It is not a simple 'I've found something to keep me going in the face of death', but a feeling that what I *almost* want to be true *almost* is, and so the faith hidden in Larkin's honest reticence qualifies his conclusion:

> Time has transfigured them into
> Untruth. The stone fidelity
> They hardly meant has come to be
> Their final Blazon, and to prove
> Our almost-instinct almost true

What will survive of us is Love.[66]

Larkin forces us to keep the ringing finality of his last line in tension with his unsupressed doubts.

Perspective and Paradox

If we want the final and most fruitful shift in our perspective which the moments of transfiguration in poetry, the moments when the mirror becomes a window, will bring, then we must expect, and be trained by, the other shifts in perspective through which a great poet takes us. Like a Zen master with his Koan, like Christ in his parables, the poet sometimes administers a sudden shock of reversal that brings a new level of enlightenment. 'You have not chosen me, I have chosen you',[67] says Christ to the disciples. You think you are reading the poem, but the poem is reading you, or as in the masterstroke we noted in 'The Rain Stick', just as we are the scientific observer looking at the pipe from outside and noting its features, suddenly we *are* what we observe: 'You stand there like a pipe being played by water.'[68]

In many ways this line of Heaney's sums up all I am trying to say about the way we should read poetry. We must allow ourselves to be *played*, to become an instrument, to let the poet's choice and arrangement of words strike chords, find melody, and bring out in us the unexpected music which we had never known was waiting to be played, as Keats says of this experience:

> Heard melodies are sweet, but those unheard,
>   Are sweeter; therefore ye soft pipes, play on;
> Not to the sensual ear, but, more endear'd,
> Pipe to the spirit ditties of no tone[69]

So Heaney says, alluding surely to these lines in Keats, but also giving us a promise of what is to come from great poetry yet to be encountered: 'What happens next is a music that you never would have known / To listen for.'[70]

---

[66]   Phillip Larkin, *Collected Poems*, ed. and with introduction by A. Thwaite (London, 1988), pp. 110–11.

[67]   John 15:16.

[68]   Heaney, *The Spirit Level*, p. 1.

[69]   'Ode on a Grecian Urn', lines 10–14, *The Poetical Works of John Keats*, p. 261.

[70]   Heaney, *The Spirit Level*, p. 1.

Chapter 1

Seeing through Dreams: Image and Truth in
The Dream of the Rood

Truth and Dreaming

One measure of the gulf between our own age and those that preceded it is the complete change in what we believe about dreams. The 'cultural apartheid' outlined in the Introduction, assuming the only 'objective' truths to be those to which strict science gives us access, has changed the way we think about dreams. Dreams, which so resist the weights and measures of modernism, are relegated to the realm of the merely subjective or else treated 'scientifically' as phenomena, to be studied in 'sleep laboratories', whose remembered symbols are to be examined only as yielding clues as to the pathology of the dreamer. Jung might be regarded as an honourable exception to this approach, but he drew many of the ideas that led him to the conclusion that dreams might refer to a more than personal or individual truth, from ancient, certainly from pre-Enlightenment sources.

Now, this narrow focus on the interpretation of dreams as a way of understanding only what is happening in an individual mind has been fruitful in the field of psychotherapy, but it has also limited our expectation of what dreams might teach us. If we are to test the notion that imagination is truth-bearing by entering fully into the early and mediaeval genre of *dream poetry*, then we need to recover the framework of ancient teaching about dreams. The most subtle and influential teaching about the nature of dreams and dreaming came down to mediaeval poets in the form of a (probably) pagan commentary on a (certainly) pagan text. Yet Christian monks treasured this work for its wisdom, preserved, passed on and integrated into that harmonisation of Biblical and Classical texts which formed the intellectual basis of Christendom. The text, the *Somnium Scipionis*,[1] is a fragment of Cicero's philosophical work *De Republica* and thus comes from the high classical period. The commentary is by Macrobius[2] who lived at the end of the fourth and beginning of the fifth century. He was a Neoplatonist living at a time when Christian and pagan could freely mingle and he became the source for much of the later thinking and understanding about dreams. The *Somnium* tells the story of how Scipio Africanus Minor has a dream in which he meets his grandfather, Scipio Africanus Major, who takes him in a dream-journey to look

---

[1]   Cicero, *De Republica, De Legibus*, text and trans. by C.W. Keyes (London, 1928).

[2]   *Macrobius on the Dream of Scipio*, trans. W.H. Stahl (New York, 1952).

down on Carthage 'from an exalted place, bright and shining, filled with stars'.[3] Here Scipio is told by his grandfather about his own future and given the moral encouragement and insight he needs to live well during the rest of his life.

Five Levels of the Somnium

Macrobius in his commentary takes occasion from this episode to make a careful distinction between the various types and levels of dreaming and the various kinds of truth or falsehood we might expect from them. He distinguishes five different levels of dreaming, from three of which we might learn or have revealed to us real truth, from two of which, at more shallow levels we can expect 'no divination' (*nihil divinationis*). He gives his five levels of dreaming as follows:[4]

- *Insomnium*: This is simply the replaying in our mind of things with which we have been pre-occupied, At first Scipio thought this was the kind of dream he was having because he had been talking about his grandfather that evening.
- *Visum*: This occurs when we are not yet fully asleep but we think ourselves awake, we see shapes rushing towards us or flitting hither and thither, nightmares are included in this class.

Then come the higher levels of dreaming from which we can expect a revelation of truth:

- *Somnium*: This shows us truths carried through symbols or veiled under an allegorical form. Pharaoh's dreams in Genesis are of this sort. There is a whole genre of allegorical dream poetry all of which begins with descriptions of a feigned *somnium*. In his exposition of this text in *The Discarded Image*, from which this information is largely drawn, C.S. Lewis points out that 'nearly all dreams are assumed to be *somnia* by modern psychologists'.[5]
- *Visio:* This is a direct unveiled pre-vision of the future, and is quite rare in poetry except as a means of heightening the tension in dramatic narrative.
- *Oraculum*: This is when we encounter someone in a dream – a parent, or 'some other grave and venerable person' – who openly declares the future or gives us advice and guidance.

---

[3]   For a summary of Scipio's dream and Macrobius's commentary, see C.S. Lewis, *The Discarded Image: An Introduction to Mediaeval and Renaissance Literature* (Cambridge, 1964), pp 23–28, and 60–69.

[4]   Ibid., pp.63–64.

[5]   Ibid., p.64.

Most dreams of course and certainly most of the dreams we encounter in early poetry, combine elements of the various levels and move from one level to another. It is important to be aware of this background teaching about dreams both to show that they were regarded as at least potentially serious revelations of truth and because many of the poets who include dreams in their narrative are deliberately alluding to the *Somnium Scipionis* and giving clues as to what level of dream they intend to portray.

The Northern/Celtic Dream-world

Lying behind this tidy classical categorisation of the dream world inherited from the Mediterranean culture which came with Latin, there were other layers of Celtic and Northern (that is to say Norse and Anglo-Saxon) understanding about dreams and the dream-world equally available to native English poets. Alongside the *gravitas* of Scipio's dream, where the dreamer is addressed by a grave and venerable person and given a guided tour of the cosmos with moralising commentary, the English had access to another realm. This was the realm of the marvellous, the coloured lands, the islands of the blest; the realm where 'stones have been known to move and trees to speak',[6] a realm of shape-shifters and sudden transformation, of doors and windows opening into other worlds; a realm where the stories of a pagan past have been woven together with bible stories, where beneath the shimmer of French or Latin courtliness we feel the strength and sinew of heroes from a much more ancient past. This is the world that stretches from the pagan hero Beowulf fighting the monster Grendel, to Arthur and the quest for the Grail. Part of the peculiar power and beauty of English poetry comes from the way it gathers together and makes a new unity of its very diverse roots – the strong sharp rhythm of Saxon epic, the lapidary Latin of the Church, the beautiful gothic interlacing of Anglo-Norman story – and all these shot through with the memories, sometimes preserved only in place and personal names, of the old Celtic past.[7]

The Range of Early Dream Poetry

Now the field of early and mediaeval dream poetry is vast and one could explore the theme of transfigured vision very fully without straying from this period. One could look at the dream poems in Chaucer – *The House of Fame, The Book*

---

6   *Macbeth*, Act III, Scene 4, line 123. This and all subsequent references to Shakespeare are to *The Complete Works*, edited, with introduction and glossary, by P Alexander (London, 1957).

7   For a recent account of this complex multi-layering of old elements in the English sensibility, see Peter Ackroyd *Albion: The Origins of the English Imagination* (London, 2002).

of the Duchesse, The Romance of the Rose.[8] One could, of course, examine the most extraordinary extended *Visio* of all, the great allegorical dream of Dante,[9] which guides us from the classical *Oraculum* in which Virgil speaks to the poet and takes him through all the realms of Hell and Purgatory, into a new Christian *Oraculum* with the restoration of the dreamed and unforgotten Earthly Paradise where the pagan poet steps back and the dream-journey continues into the real heavens guided by a Christian girl until Dante comes at last to the ineffable sight of God. Staying with purely English poetry (though Dante's influence on all English poetry is huge[10]), one could contemplate Langland, the most underrated mediaeval poet, as he recounts, in the alliterative verse of his *Piers Plowman*,[11] the marvellous dream that befell him as he slept on a May morning in the Malvern hills. But perhaps the most telling of all, since we have not time to enter all these dreams, is to go back in time; back before Chaucer, before Langland, before Dante was born, before the battle of Hastings when French with its soft syllables and rhymes began to insinuate into the clashing consonants of Anglo-Saxon, back to the beginning of known English poetry to a dream poem which is both an early Christian achievement and the fulfilment of a still more ancient past.

As we prepare to travel back to the beginnings of English verse it is worth looking at a passage from 'Bone Dreams' a dream poem of Seamus Heaney's in his collection *North*[12] which is an exploration of the Saxon and Norse part of our linguistic inheritance. In these few lines Heaney takes us on a journey back through the different dictions and styles that make up English, back to the kind of language, the kind of poetry, which stands at the threshold of our language:

> I push back
> through dictions,
> Elizabethan canopies.
> Norman devices,
>
> the erotic mayflowers
> of Provence
> and the ivied latins
> of churchmen
>
> to the scop's

---

[8]   In *The Complete Works of Geoffrey Chaucer*, ed. F.N. Robinson (Oxford, 1974).

[9]   A good parallel text, with a brilliant new translation into English verse, is the new version for Penguin Classics by Robin Kirkpatrick: *The Divine Comedy*, 3 vols (London, 2006–8).

[10]   See *Dante in English*, ed. E. Griffiths and M. Reynolds (London, 2005).

[11]   William Langland, *The Vision of Piers Plowman: A Complete Edition of the B-Text*, ed. A.V.C. Schmidt (London, 1978).

[12]   Seamus Heaney, *North* (London, 1975).

twang, the iron
flash of consonants
cleaving the line.[13]

Introducing *The Dream of the Rood*

We are going to look now at a masterpiece of dream poetry which stands at the very beginning of English literature. Nobody knows how old it is, but it must have been composed by the end of the seventh century, or the very beginning of the eighth, for a key passage from it is engraved in the old runic writing on a stone cross in Ruthwell in Scotland, which has been dated to that period. Another small portion of it is engraved on a silver reliquary said to contain a fragment of the 'True Cross' in Brussels, but the full poem is found in its entirety only in one manuscript now in Vercelli in north Italy, once a halting place for English Pilgrims on their way to Rome.[14] The poem may have found its way to an Italian monastery, but the really significant thing about it is that it is not a *Latin* poem. It is aware of the Latin tradition and seems to draw in places on the great Latin hymns which celebrated the cross of Christ and explored the paradox of his victory on the tree of defeat. But the language of this poem and therefore its rhythm, its echoes, and the world it draws with it, is *Old English*, the northern barbarian tongue, the language of the Saxon warriors who had at first come in their long dragon-ships setting flame to the monasteries, celebrating their own heroes in their terse and powerful alliterative verse. At the time *The Dream* was composed the Gospel was still comparatively new to these shores. Not all of the Saxons were converted and the poem arises from the first encounter of Christianity with the ancient pagan culture of the North.

To hear 'the scop's twang, the iron flash of consonants cleaving the line' was to enter the world of those who sprang from *Ask* and *Embla*, ash and elm trees whom in the beginning the gods made human, not from the Semitic world of Adam and Eve, who came to trees as outsiders only to pluck their fruit. The poet certainly knows about Eden and the Tree of Life that grew beside the fatal tree, he knows, as Bede knew, the link embedded deep in the language of symbol, between Adam's

---

[13]   Ibid., p.20.

[14]   For a full discussion of the history and significance of these different textual sources, see Michael Swanton *The Dream of the Rood* (Manchester, 1970), and 'A Vision of a Rood', the opening chapter of J.A.W. Bennett's *Poetry of the Passion: Studies in Twelve Centuries of English Verse* (Oxford, 1982)., which also contains a parallel text giving Bennett's own translation of the first 86 lines. A complete Old English text with parallel verse translation is to be found in Richard Hamer's *A Choice of Anglo-Saxon Verse: Selected with an Introduction and Parallel Verse Translation* (London, 1970), pp.159–71. There is also a fine translation by Helen Gardner in *The Faber Book of Religious Verse* (London, 1979), pp. 25–29.

Tree and Christ's Cross: 'About the same hour in which the first man touched the tree of paradise, the second man ascended the tree of redemption.'[15] But, as we shall see, he also knows about *Yggdrasil*, the world-tree, and how Odin the all-father himself hung there.

Paul had said in the letter to the Romans that even in the pagan places God 'had not left himself without a witness',[16] and in the Acts of the Apostles his famous speech to the pagan Athenians set out the basis on which a fruitful missionary encounter between Christ and pagan culture might take place. He sees the altar to the Unknown God and says 'him whom you worship without knowing, him I preach',[17] going on to develop the idea that even before the coming of the Gospel there are in pagan culture true elements, real revelations from God about who he is, but these elements are mixed with falsehoods and delusions. The coming of the Gospel puts them into their true perspective, fulfilling and completing what was hinted at or half-said in the old myths. Every nation and culture is called 'to seek the lord, if haply they might feel after him and find him, though he is not far from every one of us' and Paul then goes on to quote a pagan poet in support of a truth from the Christian Gospel: 'For in him we live and move and have our being, as certain also of your own poets have said, For we are also His offspring.'[18]

What we witness in this poem is the subtle transformation of a pagan inheritance through the power of the Christian story; but at the same time the Christian story is itself opened up to us in a new way by the emphasis and perspective that comes from the pagan past.

In the Vercelli manuscript this poem has no title and indeed it draws partly on the Saxon tradition of the enigma and the riddle. Although later scholars have always referred to it as 'The Dream of the Rood', we should not let that title influence us or jump to conclusions before the poet brings us to them.[19] Part of the power of this poem comes from the fact that neither the mysterious tree the dreamer sees, nor the young hero whom it bears, are named until well into the poem and at a fitting and climactic moment. The text that follows draws from the original Old English, the late Professor Bennett's translation, which reflects the unrhymed powerful rhythmic alliteration of the original, and Helen Gardner's beautiful alliterative translation.[20] Of course to understand this poem in its depth, and read it in some of the five ways enumerated in the Introduction, we will have to lay the translations aside and savour the untranslatable sounds of the original, as the strong clean, compacted staves of Saxon poetry.

---

[15]   Bede, *De Genesis in litteram*, iii.18, quoted in Bennett, *Poetry of the Passion*, p.15.

[16]   Romans 1:19–21.

[17]   Acts 17:23.

[18]   Acts 17:27–28.

[19]   See Bennett. *Poetry of the Passion* pp. 1ff.

[20]   Bennet, *Poetry of the Passion*, and Gardner, *The Faber Book of Religious Verse*. The name of each translator will be indicated in brackets after the text.

Opening Lines

Let us begin by hearing in its original words the strong opening lines of this masterpiece:

> Hwæt! Ic swefna cyst secgan wylle,
> hwæt me gemætte to midre nihte,
> syðþan reordberend reste wunedon!

> Hearken, the rarest of dreams I purpose to tell
> Which I dreamed one midnight
> When men with their voices were at rest (Bennett lines 1–3)

Hwæt, the opening sound of this poem, is untranslatable. Some modern versions give *Lo!* or *Hearken*! but *Hwæt* is the ritual opening made by the *scop*, the tribal poet, taking his harp in the hall to announce to the company that what follows is epic or high verse, a celebration of the great stories of the gods and ancestors, the stories that tell a people who they are. It is the word that begins the story of Beowulf's struggle with Grendel and with the dragon. Then the poet announces that he will tell the rarest of dreams which he dreamed one midnight 'after the race of men had gone to their rest'. the description of the dream as *rarest* and its placing at midnight give clear signals that what follows is not *Insomnium* or *Visio*, the shallower levels through which the dreaming mind passes first, but is rather a true *somnium,* and more, for it is, as we see, an *Oraculum* the highest form of dream of all.

The reference to the race of men sleeping prepares us subtly for the fact that it is not one of the race of men who speaks in the dream, but it also tells us something about the meaning of humanity for the poet. The Old English word sometimes translated 'race of men' or 'humankind', or as Bennett does 'men with their word', is *reordberend*. This means, literally, *speech-bearers.* To call human beings *speech-bearers* is to distinguish them from the animal kingdom not because they are unique but because they now bear company with the angels who speak God's praises and with the Lord himself who gave men speech, who is himself the Word and as the Word, was made flesh to redeem the word-bearers. The poetic device here is called a *kenning* and is frequent in Saxon and Norse poetry. The northern poets would never call a spade a spade if they could have the pleasure of calling it an earth-biter. A bear is called a bee-wolf (Beowulf) for its love of honey, the sea is the whale-road, a good lord is a ring-giver. Sometimes, especially in Nordic verse, there are kennings within kennings, as the poet's playful riddling helps you to see your world in a new way. So, for example, an amber bracelet round a wrist becomes in a double-kenning *fire of the hawk's high cliff.* The kenning here, *speech-bearer*, has the poetic effect of heightening the drama, for in the dream a speech-bearer is silent whilst a tree acquires powers of speech, powers that inevitably carry echoes of the pagan past in which men could learn wisdom from trees.

What Kind of Tree Is This?

> It seemed to me I saw the strangest of trees,
> lifted aloft in the air with light all around it
> of all beams the brightest. It stood as a beacon
> Drenched in gold; gleaming gems were set
> fair round its foot; five such flamed
> High upon its cross-branch. (Gardner lines 4–9)

It is important that we do not lose the sense that this *sylicre treow* (as it is called in Old English) is a *tree*. We must not immediately impose upon it our later sense of a conventional cross. We must not either literally or symbolically cut it off from its roots, from the sense, to which we have already alluded, of its gathering into those roots the marvellous trees both of Scripture and of the Pagan North. It is first a tree. But this strange tree, lifted aloft and shining in the air, is also a *beacne*, a beacon, that is a sign which has been set up to convey a truth and to shine a light in dark places. I have stood before the Ruthwell cross in Dumfriesshire which bears a part of this poem written in the ancient runic lettering, itself a beacon set up to speak through its signs and symbols to the Celts and Saxons who cast their eyes up to it. J.A.W. Bennett describes it brilliantly in the opening of *Poetry of the Passion*:

> The Passage cited thereon forms part of a complex programme of lettering and sculpture and was evidently chosen because of its peculiar fitness for a rood-like pillar, making it verily a speaking cross. A monument of such dramatic power, carved with such masterly assurance, set up on the very limits of north-west Europe some fifty years after the Synod of Whitby and probably before Charlemagne was born, must still astonish us. It is rightly called a *beacn*, a beacon, a sign. It casts a strong beam of light in what we are pleased to call the Dark Ages. It should be the first object of English pilgrimage.[21]

The tree lifted aloft, the shining beacon wound round with light, becomes a great sign in the sky reaching from earth to heaven, binding together men and angels, and indeed all creation, in a sense of wonder:

> Hosts of angels gazed upon it
> In world-without-end glory. This was no felon's gallows.
> Holy souls in heaven hailed it with wonder
> And mortal men on earth and all the maker wrought. (Gardner lines 9–12)

In these and the foregoing lines we are really being invited to see three things simultaneously, each as it were set through and beyond the other. There is first the beautiful jewelled cross, *begotten mid gold*, gleaming with jewels, like Cuthbert's

---

[21]   Ibid., p.1.

cross in Durham, like the reliquary on which some of these lines were engraved; but then through and behind the gold and jewels are light and the stars themselves. This is a great cross of light in the sky such as Constantine saw and was told *In hoc signo vinces* before his victory at Milvian Bridge in 312. But if we listen to the Old English words a third level becomes apparent; the gems *faegere at foldan sceatum* are rendered in Bennett's more accurate translation not *fair round its foot* but *fair at earth's four corners*, the cross-beam is *thanne eaxlgespanne*, both phrases recalling the axle-tree one of the names of *Yggdrasil* the great ash tree of Norse mythology, whose top was in Asgard or heaven and whose roots were in Hell. This tree spanned and supported the nine worlds of Norse imagination. The name *Ygg Drasil* means literally the steed of *Ygg* or *Odin* for he climbed on it and rode it to the nine worlds. But it was on the tree that Odin underwent the most terrible rite of passage, for like the Christ, the coming one who was to show the true meaning of Odin's story and realise it in history, in the flesh, Odin was wounded to the death with a spear and hung nine days and nine nights upon the sacred tree. It was hanging on the tree that he was able to look down and see where the tree had cut markings into stone with its roots. Over those nine nights Odin deciphered the markings and found in them the secret of the magical alphabet known as runes. When in the refrain of some of the Scottish and border ballads there comes the repeated oath *by him that hung on tree*, scholars are divided as to whether it is a Christian reference, a pagan survival or something of both.

I think the poet here is perfectly clear. I think he is deliberately evoking and gathering the memory and the power of his pagan past, which is carried by the very metre and cadence of his verse, and allowing it to find both its fulfilment and its judgement in the cross of Christ. For though Odin hung on Yggdrasil, though he visited the dead, though he gained the power of resurrection, he was no saviour. He could not meet or deal with human pain and alienation. Through his suffering he acquired personal power and magic knowledge, but he emerges in his resurrection as an incalculable one-eyed god exercising the power he learned from the runic alphabet entirely at and for his own behest, not as a self offering to take away the dreamer's sins and win him heaven. This is why the sculptor of the Ruthwell cross was making such a supremely powerful statement, lighting such a powerful beacon, when he chose the ancient runic alphabet to write the words we are about to read, when the tree itself speaks the real meaning and power of the life and death of the one who hung upon it.

Transfiguration

Having given us this powerful and all-encompassing triple image of such cosmic proportions, the poet, with a master stroke, produces a kind of reverse transfiguration which takes us to the heart of his vision. In the gospel transfiguration, Christ, labouring up Mount Tabor with the disciples in all his obvious humanity, is transfigured at the summit before them so that they glimpse, shining through the weakness of the human body, the eternal glory. But here the poet invites us to look through the light and glory, through the outer decking of gold and jewels, to the pain and agony beneath. And he subtly prepares us for the meaning of the *staining* of the cross with sweat and blood which he is about to describe, of the *wounding* of its wood, by introducing first his own stain and woundedness, and ours: 'Strange was that tree of triumph – and I a transgressor / stained by my sins. I saw the tree of Glory' is how Helen Gardner puts it (lines 13–14), which brings out the juxtaposition of triumph and transgression, glory and stain, though it does no justice to the original's strong *'forwunded mid womum'* which means deeply wounded by defilement.

A weaker poet would have been content simply with this contrast between the glorious golden cross and the poor defiled sinner. But not this poet. He invites us instead to share an extraordinary *double vision* which almost anticipates the effects achieved by some modern photographers and film makers, in which we see alternately and then, as it were, simultaneously in a double-exposure, *both* the gold's glory *and* the sweat and blood upon the wounded wood. Here Helen Gardner's rendering is wonderful:

> Yet beneath the gold I glimpsed the signs
> Of some ancient agony when again as of old
> Its right side sweated blood. Sorrow seized me;
> I was full of fear. I saw the beacon flicker,
> Now dazzling, now darkened; at times drenched and dripping,
> running red with blood, at times a royal treasure (Gardner lines 18–23)

Like the 'souls blood' in Herbert's 'Prayer' which is both the soul's pain and its life, so the vision here does not ask us to choose between a harrowing empathy with Christ in his human weakness or a triumphal affirmation of his glory as God the Son, between a horrified understanding of the cross as a dreadful gibbet, and a devotion to it as a sign of salvation. Instead we are asked to affirm these truths simultaneously and are offered a single image with which to embody them.

If the poem had ended here that would already have been an achievement but it is in the lines that follow that its true dramatic power is realised, for now we move, in the poet's Latin world through *Somnium* and *Visio* to *Oraculum*, and in his pagan world to the memory of the sentient, magical and speaking woods, for now the tree speaks, and here it is worth savouring the sounds of the original Anglo-Saxon.

The Tree Speaks

> þæt wæs geara iu, (ic þæt gyta geman),
> þæt ic wæs aheawen holtes on ende,
> astyred of stefne minum. Genaman me ðær strange feondas,
> geworhton him þær to wæfersyne, heton me heora wergas hebban.

It was long since, yet I well remember
That I was hewn down at wood-edge
Struck off from my stem. Strong foes seized me,
Set me up for a spectacle, bade me raise their felons (lines 27–31, Bennett)

Bennett rightly points out here 'the plain, staccato and intensely human language of the Saxon Rood' with its 'rush of kinetic verbs that pile up as if expressing both the agitation of the speaker and the feverish activity of the men: genamen … geworhton … heton … baeron … asetton … gefaestnodon … This language at once establishes a humility of tone, consonant with the tree's obedience to its Lord.'[22]

The story the tree has to tell starts with disaster for itself:
struck off from my stem. Strong foes seized me
Set me up for a spectacle …
… .foes aplenty fastened me …

So that when it says

… Far off then I saw
The King of all mankind coming in great haste,
With courage keen … (Gardner lines 33–34)

we have a momentary sense that this might be a rescue. In our woundedness, our rootlesness, the captivity and humiliation of our fallen nature, we identify with the tree. As with the tree we see man's lord approaching us *with courage keen*, we have kindled in us a hope that everything will be sorted out forthwith, the enemies simply overthrown, all our cares and suffering dealt with suddenly, dramatically taken away, as it were, in an instant by an intervening hand from on high. So often this is the prayer we make, that is the kind of God we would like. Not a God who enters into and declares himself in the midst of our suffering and alienation, but one who will simply snap his fingers and take these things away. The poet refuses us this fantasy, but having refused the 'vain imagination' he engages a deeper and truer imagination to take us through the images and words of his dream into the real depth of the Christian Gospel which is that our experience of alienation and suffering, our woundedness and coming death are too deep and too real to be magicked away. They must be redeemed, and to redeem them Christ must enter into them, take them into himself, bear them for us. 'He is made to *be* sin who knew no sin',[23] he is made a curse he is obedient even unto death. He cannot ultimately take away our sin unless he takes it on. He must take it on first in the sense of enduring it himself before he can take it on in the second and glorious

---

22   Bennett, *Poetry of the Passion*, p. 5.
23   2 Corinthians 5:21.

sense of doing battle against it and winning victory on our behalf. And this is the meaning of the next half-line and the extraordinary experience the rood goes on to describe. The young hero comes with courage to climb onto him, to embrace him, to identify absolutely with his condition.

Christ the Hero

> The King comes
> With courage keen, eager to climb me
> I did not dare against my Lord's dictate,
> to bow down or break, though I beheld tremble
> The earth's four corners. I could easily
> Have felled his foes; yet fixed and firm I stood.
> Then the young Hero – it was God Almighty –
> Strong and steadfast, stripped himself for battle;
> He climbed up on the high gallows, constant in his purpose,
> Mounted it in the sight of many, mankind to ransom.' (Gardner lines 34–42)

This whole approach is completely different from the purely historical one we might be used to. The poet does not use any of the gospel material about the events leading up to the crucifixion, indeed he has up to this point still not directly named Christ. Instead, building up towards his identity, in the Norse riddling tradition, by a series of titles, 'frean mancynes' ('man's lord'), 'geong helath' ('young hero' or, as Bennett gives it, 'young warrior'), though here, still without naming the name, he draws aside the veil of the young warrior in order to get the full power of the paradox of incarnation between 'young' and 'God Almighty'. So we have in one line: 'The young hero – it was God almighty'.

Where he does reflect the Gospels in this poem, and indeed the rest of the New Testament is not at the level of historical narrative, the telling of the outer events, but at the level of exploring their inner meaning. Running throughout the New Testament is a double strand of understanding about the crucifixion. On the one hand, from a human perspective, we see it as a horrific injustice in which an innocent man is falsely arrested, stripped, beaten and tortured to death, hung upon a felon's gallows. At this level we see Christ in his humanity entering into and enduring the suffering which sinful people inflict on one another. Nailed to the cross, unable to move, he is the picture of total human weakness and vulnerability in the face of evil and death. On the other level, from the perspective of Heaven, from the perspective of God's purpose in Christ from the beginning, Christ is not a passive victim who is done unto, but is in charge of events, embodying the vigorous and active love of God which has come forth from heaven to take on and defeat all that would harm and destroy his beloved creature man. In this sense he really is a mighty warrior coming to our rescue.

Within the Gospels these strands are differently emphasised by their different writers. Mark emphasises the *passio* in passion, after the arrest of Jesus nearly all the verbs about him are passive, he is 'done unto'. John, on the other hand, from the moment of Christ's arrest emphasises the sense in which Christ, not Pilate, is really in control. John uses the title King for Christ more than a dozen times. In John, Christ says at the beginning 'the son of man must be lifted up'[24] and shows the cross as an *exaltation* and a moment of victory, and again John has Christ saying 'no-one takes my life from me it is mine to lay down and mine to take up again'.[25]

The great task for any poet dealing with this matter is to do justice to both sides of this mystery in the combined action and passion of Christ. For at the heart of it is the deeper mystery of what the theologians have called the dual nature of Christ, that he is both fully human and fully divine at one and the same time, the two natures subsisting in one single person. Reason alone, certainly post-Enlightenment reason alone, simply cannot deal with this. It demands a more subtle and complex response. In fact only the imaginative arts – certainly poetry, but also painting and music – have come anywhere close to embracing simultaneously both parts of the paradox and expressing the mystery adequately. The way the poet does it here is so to identify the cross itself, whom the nails also pierce, with the passion of Christ; so that the cross is able to express and symbolise that passion, whilst at the same time witnessing and celebrating the action of Christ the saving hero. We can see in more detail how this happens in the lines we have just examined, and those that follow, hearing them this time in the power of the original language.

Let us consider, for example, 'Ongyrede hine þa geong hæleð, þæt wæs god ælmihtig'. 'Ongyred' is an astonishing word, although Hamer's translation, otherwise good in places, has 'got ready'[26] which is inadequate. In other contexts 'Ongyred' carries that sense of preparing, especially preparing for a contest or a battle, but it actually means 'to strip or divest oneself'. Bennett gives 'stripped himself' and Helen Gardner is even better with 'Stripped himself for battle', but it takes four words strung out in modern English to convey what is in one pithy word of Anglo-Saxon. But what is the thought? What are the allusions lying behind this picture of the young hero stripping himself for battle before he climbs the cross?

At one level there is the image of an athlete stripping himself ready for the race, an image which had already been applied to Christ through the allegorical way the Church read the Bible and through its Latin hymns. The beautiful picture of the sun rising in the Old Testament poem Psalm 19:5 – 'He is as a bridegroom coming out of his chamber and rejoiceth as a strong man to run a race' – had been applied by the Church to that other sun the Son of God, who came from the chamber of the virgin's womb and, as Ambrose's Latin hymn on the verse puts it, eagerly runs his course.[27]

---

24   John 3:14.
25   John 10:18.
26   Hamer, *Coice of Anglo-Saxon Verse*, p. 163.
27   Quoted in Bennett, *Poetry of the Passion,*, pp 18–19.

'Ongyred' here though conveys more then just the preparation of the warrior-athlete, if we take it in its deeper sense of 'stripped'. Firstly, it alludes to, but at the same time reverses the emphasis of the gospel account of the forcible stripping of Christ before the crucifixion. For in a paradox the poet is saying that, although to the outward eye others were stripping Christ for humiliation, in truth, to the inward eye that sees reality, Christ was stripping himself for action. And almost certainly the poet, in choosing this word, has in mind the great passage where Paul speaks of the *kenosis* of God, his self- emptying, his stripping away from himself of the glories of Heaven in order to enter the travail of earth for us:

> [Christ] though he was in the form of God, did not regard equality with God as something to be exploited, but emptied himself, taking the form of a slave, being born in human likeness. And being found in human form, he humbled himself and became obedient to the point of death – even death on a cross.[28]

So stripped and ready, strong and steadfast, the young hero climbed the high gallows. Again it is an active choosing to climb the tree. Behind it probably lies the passage from Bede we alluded to earlier: 'About the time the first man touched the tree of paradise, the second man ascended the tree of redemption.'[29] This climbing of the tree is witnessed by many because it is done for many: 'modig on manigra gesyhðe, þa he wolde mancyn lysan' (line 41)

'Modig' means both bravely and proudly, and is a kind of showing of inner glory in the midst of what is meant to be outward humiliation. And then in the second half of the line the poet reveals what this crucifixion is all for, and returns us as it were to that hope of rescue kindled in the first sight of the young hero: 'þa he wolde mancyn lysan'. Here Gardner has 'mankind to ransom', Hamer 'to redeem mankind'; but both these are too sophisticated, too much after-the event, using theological jargon – something the poet for all his depth and theological subtlety never does. The poet's word 'lysan', gives us modern English 'loosen, loose, untie, set free', which Bennett expands into 'Resolved to loose man's bonds'. With an eye, as always, to the paradox of his mystery, the poet has offered the word for 'loosen' just as Christ is to be 'fastened', 'through-driven with dark nails', as he puts it a few lines later. His fastening is our freedom. 'Mancyn' harks back to the title he gives Christ earlier – 'frean mancynnes'. 'Freah' is the Norse for God or Lord but also puns with 'freog' meaning free. He is 'Freah mancynnes', Mankind's Lord because he will 'loosen' Mankind, set Mankind free. Here, as we have noted, the contrast is implicit with the other Freah, the god Odin, who hung on the tree not openly in the sight of many to set mankind free, but secretly in the occult passage-making of the shaman and in order to acquire the hidden knowledge whereby he would have power, certainly to loose, but also to bind others.

---

28   Phillipians 2:6–8.
29   See above p.000.

The Poem's Polarities

The energy of this poem is generated by the tension between the two sets of polarities from which its power to move us flows: the polarity between Christian and Pagan Faith, and within the Christian gospel, the polarity between the passion of Christ's human suffering and action of his divine battling against, and victory over evil and death. Having evoked the latter with these images of the young warrior, the poet now returns us to the former in the next few lines with his close identification of the tree's experience with that of the suffering Christ:

> Horror seized me when the hero clasped me
> But I dared not bow or bend to the earth
> Nor falter nor fall; firm I needs must stand …
> They drove dark nails through me, the dire wounds still show,
> Cruel gaping gashes, yet I dared not give as good.
> They taunted the two of us; I was wet with teeming blood,
> Streaming from the warrior's side when he sent forth his spirit
> High upon that hill helpless I suffered
> Long hours of torment; … (Gardner lines 42–50)

What is so moving here is the sense of having to restrain all the desire to hurt back, the impulse to vengeance, which was part of the pagan ethic. This desire to give as good as we get is subsumed instead into something, also deep in the pagan ethic, which at last finds its truest expression in this poem, that is the courage of endurance, to be *strang and stidmod*. This is the virtue celebrated so brilliantly in the great last stand against the Vikings in *The Battle of Maldon*, courage which is called upon and inspired just at the point when the beloved leader has died:

> Hige sceal þe heardra, heorte þe cenre,
> mod sceal þe mare, þe ure mægen lytlað.
> Her lið ure ealdor eall forheawen,
> god on greote. A mæg gnornian
> se ðe nu fram þis wigplegan wendan þenceð.
> Ic eom frod feores; fram ic ne wille,
> ac ic me be healfe minum hlaforde,
> be swa leofan men, licgan þence. (lines 312–19)

> Mind must be harder spirit must be bolder
> And heart the greater as our might grows less
> Here lies our leader in the dust …
> … hence I will not
> but I intend to die beside my lord

give up my life beside so dear a chief [30]

The duty to endure all things with the chieftain and die beside him in battle is transformed in the *Dream* into this intense identification with the agony of Christ, this refusal to bend or bow as the dreadful deeds are done simultaneously to Christ and to the cross. The poem then goes on to blend in a brilliant fusion the two pagan forms – on the one hand elegy for the fallen hero, and on the other battle song of his triumph – since uniquely the crucifixion is an instance simultaneously of death and of triumphant victory.

The Climax

Now the poem moves towards its climax when the rood, the mysterious tree, finally names the one who hangs upon it, building towards the naming of that name in perhaps the most concentrated and dramatically placed half-line in all of English verse:

'... I saw the Lord of Hosts
Outstretched in agony; all embracing darkness
covered with thick clouds the corpse of the world's ruler
The bright day was darkened by a deep shadow
all its colours clouded; the whole creation wept
Keened for its King's fall; Christ was on the rood. (Gardner lines 51–56)

Though not even Helen Gardner's brilliant translation can do justice to the terse power of the original text in those last two lines:

wann under wolcnum. Weop eal gesceaft,
cwiðdon cyninges fyll. Crist wæs on rode.

From out of the darkness of *wan under wolcnum* comes the powerful half-line *weop ealgesceaft – all creation wept*. The power these words exercise in gathering in all that has gone before exemplify not only this poet's skill, but also the essence of poetry itself. Firstly, *weop eal gesceaft* picks up and gathers in the earlier phrase *eall peos maera gesceaft – all this wondrous creation*, which he had used in lines 11–12, before the rood began to speak, to show that it was indeed the world-tree that all the levels of being, holy souls, men on the earth and all this wondrous creation, beheld. And now, at the moment of Christ's death, *eall gesceaft* is weeping. The poet's repeated phrase secondly gathers in and echoes a weeping or groaning of all creation which he finds in the New Testament: 'For we know that the whole creation groaneth and travaileth together in pain until now.'[31]

---

[30] Text and translation in Hamer, *Choice of Anglo-Saxon Verse*, pp. 68–69.
[31] Romans 8:22.

But as we have seen, the poetic medium and language in which he has chosen to work is full of echoes from the Norse stories which the poet is also recalling and redeeming. Here *weop eall gesceaft* recalls the story of Balder the beautiful, the shining god of light who was killed by his own blind brother through the machinations of Loki, and who would be restored to life only if *eall gesceaft*, the whole creation, wept for him. The story of Balder's death is perhaps the most moving in the whole Norse cycle. More than simply foreshadowing or reflecting the story of Christ, it actually communicates it to some people, to some imaginations, to some northern souls, in a way that the stories of Latin and Semitic culture simply cannot approach, as we shall see at the end of this chapter when we consider how the issues of this poem resolved themselves in the life of a man of our own time.

Crist wæs on rode is really the climax and the point of the whole poem. The rood's narrative thereafter with its gentle and moving account of the deposition is as much a part of the necessary setting of that line as were all the lines which preceded it.

The Tree Now

In the ensuing lines the cross continues its extraordinary double role as both the witness of the saviour's sufferings and as one who is absolutely identified with the same sufferings, to the extent that the cross, like the saviour, has its own deposition and burial. But the cross continues also as a witness, and by its apparition in the dream, also enters in its own way into a resurrection. The tree has become, through the poem, so completely identified with the Christ who suffered upon it that it is able, as a symbol, to carry to the dreamer all that Christ is:

> Now you have heard beloved hero
> How I endured the evil men did to me,
> Suffered great sorrow. Now the season is come
> When all things honour me, here and everywhere,
> mortal men on earth and all the maker wrought (Gardner lines 78–82)

In the fiction of the poem these words are uttered to the dreamer by the cross about itself; in fact they are the words of the risen Christ about himself. But the tree that bore him speaks with the honour of Christ and invites the dreamer to pray to or rather through him in order himself to participate in Christ's glory as Christ has participated in our suffering. And so there is a resolution of all things when, after the tree has finished speaking, we return to the voice of the narrator whose forebears would once certainly have prayed to a tree and thought of it as one on which Odin had fared forth to other worlds, and who now also prays to a tree, but how transformed a tree, and how transformed his and our vision of the world when he says:

> Then I prayed to that blessed beam, blithe in spirit,

With courage keen; no comrade was by me,
I lay there alone. There was longing in my heart,
I was fain to fare forth ... (Gardner lines122–25)

The Poem in Our Own Age.

Though this poem might be seen as the most remote from us in time, in culture, and from the language of the other poems we shall study, I do not think it is remote at all. It was written in an age of transition, of tension between the old and the new, and we live in just such an age again. Moreover, the mythical northern world of its ancestry was not only alive then, it is still alive now. It still haunts our memories and kindles our imaginations in a way in which even the most ornate Classical myths can never do. It is instructive to look at the influence the world of this poem and the issues it raises exercised on the formation of the mind and faith of someone of our own time. The story of the conversion of C.S. Lewis provides a very interesting sidelight here on what myth, especially great myth of this kind is, and why Orthodox Christianity need not be afraid of it. Lewis, an Ulsterman, fell fully in love with the North, the whole cycle of story and legend which it embodies, as a child. It touched his soul and imagination in ways that Christianity, which he associated with 'ugly architecture, ugly music and bad poetry',[32] had thus far failed to do. This was because the Norse stories addressed themselves directly to his imagination and he did not learn until much later in life that he might encounter the Gospel as much with his imagination as with his post-Enlightenment reason or his sense of duty. He had joy of these great stories, but the cultural apartheid of his day prevented him from feeling he might have truth from them as well, until a great thinker, Owen Barfield (himself drawing on Coleridge), and J.R.R. Tolkien, both personal friends of Lewis's, helped him to break down the barriers and rediscover the unified and transfiguring way of seeing which is really the subject of this book. Here is how it happened. In *Surprised by Joy*, Lewis gives an account of three moments of transfiguration, moments of sudden Joy, experienced in early childhood, which came much later to be part of a thread of experiences that led him to Christ. It is the third 'glimpse', as he calls it, which arose from reading poetry, that concerns us here

> The third glimpse came through poetry. I had become fond of Longfellow's Saga of King Olaf: fond of it in a casual shallow way for its story and its vigorous rhythms. But then, and quite different from such pleasures, and like a voice from far more distant regions, there came a moment when I idly turned the pages of the book and found the unrhymed translation of Tegner's Drapa and read

> *I heard a voice that cried*
> *Balder the beautiful*

---

[32]   In C.S. Lewis *Surprised by Joy* (London, 1987) p 139.

Is dead, is dead

I knew nothing about Balder; but instantly I was uplifted into huge regions of northern sky, I desired with almost sickening intensity something never to be described (except that it is cold, spacious, severe, pale and remote, and then, as in the other examples, found myself at the very same moment already falling out of that desire and wishing I were back in it.[33]

He goes on to describe how this first encounter with Balder developed into a deep engagement with the whole world he inhabited, including of course the stories of Odin and the world-tree which we have looked at. So that when he published *Dymer*, a long poetry cycle, he prefaced it with this line from the Norse Havamal: '*Nine nights I hung upon the tree, wounded with the spear as an offering to Odin, myself sacrificed to myself.*'[34]

Unfortunately, Lewis was fully in the grip of the post-Enlightenment apartheid discussed in the Introduction, in which imagination could have nothing to do with the insights of reason, which was itself thereby weakened and dwindled into mere rationalism. As Lewis himself starkly put it:

Such then was the state of my imaginative life; over against it stood the life of my intellect. The two hemispheres of my mind were in the sharpest contrast. On the one side a many-islanded sea of poetry and myth; on the other a glib and shallow 'rationalism'. Nearly all that I loved I believed to be imaginary; nearly all that I believed to be real I thought grim and meaningless.[35]

The first bridge to be thrown across this great divide was made for Lewis by the thinking and scholarship of his friend Owen Barfield. Barfield was a great student of Coleridge,[36] not only as a poet but as a philosopher, and he was able over the course of many years' friendship and argument to persuade Lewis of the truth which Coleridge, reacting against Enlightenment at its height had hammered out: that Imagination and aesthetic experience have as much right to be considered windows onto real truth as does purely rational argument.[37] Having shown Lewis

---

[33]   Ibid., pp. 19–20.

[34]   [C.S. Lewis], *Dymer* (London, 1926); published under the pseudonym Clive Hamilton.

[35]   Lewis, *Surprised by Joy*, p. 138.

[36]   Barfield's book *What Coleridge Thought* (Oxford, 1972), remains a lucid guide to Coleridge's philosophy and theology of imagination. Another conduit for Coleridge's insights into imagination was George MacDonald. There is a fascinating insight into Macdonald's personal and intellectual links with Coleridge in Kerry Dearborn's *Baptized Imagination: The Theology of George MacDonald* (Aldershot, 2006).

[37]   For a fuller account, see Lionel Adey, *C.S. Lewis' 'Great War' with Owen Barfield* (Wigton, 2002).

that he must take his imagination at least as seriously as he took his capacity for reason, Barfield went on to demonstrate, in a great and much under-valued book *Poetic Diction*[38] (a book he dedicated to Lewis), that Myth, far from being something peripheral or infantile to be left behind as man grows and develops, has in fact a central place in the whole development and meaning of the structures of language and thought by which we know ourselves. Lewis then met and became close friends with Tolkien, a man who deeply shared Lewis's love of all things Northern. As a professor of Old English, Tolkien was thoroughly versed in all the Norse and Anglo-Saxon poetry, but he was also an instructed Catholic Christian, whose faith gave him the basis for a coherent critique of modernism. Tolkien had already achieved the integration of faith, imagination and reason towards which he was now to enable Lewis to struggle. A significant part of that integration especially in the context of this poem and of the conversation which brought insight to Lewis was that Tolkien loved and understood trees, not simply as part of the subject matter of botany but as they actually are, which includes a great deal more than their botany. We take up the account of the impact of Tolkien's ideas as it is told by Humphrey Carpenter in *The Inklings*,[39] drawing largely on the words of Lewis and Tolkien themselves in subsequent letters, for this was a momentous conversation and both of them reflected a great deal on it afterwards. I quote it at length because it revisits almost all the themes we have encountered so far in the consideration of the *Dream* and will continue to explore throughout this book. Indeed, the great passage in which Tolkien considers what a tree really is, relates not only to how we are to read *The Dream of the Rood* but also to the very issue raised by Heaney in 'The Rain Stick': the full reality is always more than 'the fall of grit and dry seeds'. This is Carpenter's account of the conversation that took place almost exactly 66 years ago as Lewis, Tolkien and Hugo Dyson strolled through Magdelen grounds late on a Saturday in September 1931, discussing metaphor and myth:

> Lewis had never underestimated the power of myth. Far from it, for one of his earliest loves had been the Norse Myth of the dying god Balder. Now, Barfield had shown him the crucial role that mythology had played in the history of language and literature.But he still did not *believe* in the myths that delighted him. Beautiful and moving though such stories might be, they were (he said) ultimately untrue. As he expressed it to Tolkien, myths are 'lies and therefore worthless, even though breathed through silver.'
>
> *No*, said Tolkien. *They are not lies*.
>
> Just then (Lewis afterwards recalled) there was 'a rush of wind which came so suddenly on the still, warm evening and sent so many leaves pattering down that we thought it was raining. We held our breath.'

---

[38]   Owen Barfield, *Poetic Diction* (London, 1928).

[39]   Humphrey Carpenter, *The Inklings; C.S. Lewis, J.R.R. Tolkien, Charles Williams, and their Friends* (London, 1978).

When Tolkien resumed, he took his argument from the very thing that they were watching.

You look at trees, he said, and call them 'trees', and probably you do not think twice about the word. You call a star a 'star', and think nothing more of it. But you must remember that these words 'tree', 'star', were in their original forms names given to these objects by people with very different views from yours. To you, a tree is simply a vegetable organism, and a star simply a ball of inanimate matter moving along a mathematical course. But the first men to talk of 'trees' and 'stars' saw things very differently. To them the world was alive with mythological beings. They saw the stars as living silver, bursting into flame in answer to the eternal music. They saw the sky as a jewelled tent, and the earth as the womb whence all living things have come. To them the whole of creation was 'myth-woven and elf-patterned'.

This was not a new notion to Lewis, for Tolkien was, in his own manner, expressing what Barfield had said in *Poetic Diction*. Nor, said Lewis did it effectively answer his point that myths are lies.

But, replied Tolkien, man is not ultimately a liar. He may pervert his thoughts to lies, but he comes from God, and it is from God that he draws his ultimate ideals.. Therefore, Tolkien continued, not merely the abstract thoughts of man *but also his imaginative inventions* must originate with God, and must in consequence reflect something of eternal truth. In making a myth..a person is actually fulfilling God's purpose, and reflecting a splintered fragment of the true light. Pagan myths are therefore never just 'lies': there is always something of the truth in them.

They talked on, until Lewis was convinced by the force of Tolkien's argument. But he had another question to put to his friends, and they decided to go indoors.. There, he recorded, 'we continued on Christianity'.[40]

Given the way all the great themes of this poem were so deeply woven with a life-changing experience for Lewis it is not surprising that he records in *Surprised by Joy* 'I was deeply moved by *The Dream of the Rood*'.[41]

And so, painfully and by great exercise of learning and imagination, Lewis, in the twentieth century, attained to that reintegrated vision, that transfiguration of experience, which was the very atmosphere this anonymous eighth-century poet breathed, and which is implicit in every line he wrote.

---

[40]   Ibid., pp. 42–44. Carpenter writes that 'the account of the conversation between Lewis, Tolkien and Dyson is based on Lewis' letter to Greeves of 22nd September 1931 and on Tolkien's poem "Mythopoeia"' (ibid., p. 268).

[41]   Lewis, *Surprised by Joy*, p. 171.

Chapter 2

Truth and Feigning: Story and Play in
A Midsummer Night's Dream and
The Tempest[1]

The distance in time and culture between the oracular *Dream of the Rood* in eighth-century Northumberland, and the window into the magical world of *A Midsummer Night's Dream* and *The Tempest* which Shakespeare opened in sixteenth-century London, may seem enormous, but for all the differences between the worlds they inhabited the Elizabethan playwright and the Anglo-Saxon poet still have a great deal to connect them. Shakespeare is as aware as the anonymous poet, of the Classical and Patristic tradition that saw dreams as giving potential glimpses of a Heavenly Realm which both transcends and undergirds our own. They both offer us truths which can only be apprehended through story and image. They have also in common the notion that the stories of a pagan past can be transformed into moving figures whose ultimate significance can harmonise with the Christian faith, and Christian faith is of course the other common strand stretching unbroken from the cross at Ruthwell to the Globe in London. Shakespeare enjoyed a cultural freedom to play with language, to play with stories and dreams, to play in the end with even the most sacred things, and yet through that very playfulness to restate the great themes of Transfiguration, Death and Resurrection in a new and wonderfully life-enhancing way.

We noted in the Introduction how much truth there was in the light-hearted remark Shakespeare gave his fool Touchstone – 'The truest poetry is the most feigning';[2] in this chapter we shall explore in more detail the way in which fable and story, far from being the 'delightful deceit'[3] of Sprat's assertion are, in the hands of Shakespeare, a lasting embodiment of truth.

Faced with the works of Shakespeare we obviously have an *embarras de richesse* and everywhere we could find elaborated the theme of this book, the theme of transfiguration, of finding the true through the seeming. What I propose to do therefore in this chapter is to begin with a consideration of the possibilities

---

[1]   A condensed version of this chapter appeared as 'Our Truest Poetry Is Our Most Feigning … Poetry, Playfulness and Truth', in T. Hart and S. Guthrie (eds), *Faithful Performances: Enacting Christian Tradition* (Aldershot, 2007), pp. 199–218.

[2]   *As You Like It*, Act III, Scene 3, line 20 see above Introduction, p.3. All references to works by Shakespeare are to *The Complete Works*, ed. P. Alexander (London, 1957).

[3]   See above Introduction, p.3.

of play and fiction as they are open to the dramatist and how these relate to truth, and then to focus on two specific moments in the works of Shakespeare where we can see some of these themes most clearly. Since we are considering the role of story and the play itself I have chosen two plays in which Shakespeare himself plays with the idea of a play within a play, and specifically those points in those plays where he addresses the idea of imagination and how it relates to truth. We will look at these themes first in the comedy of *A Midsummer Night's Dream*, and then see how, after all the experience of the histories and tragedies, Shakespeare returns to and develops them in the Romance of *The Tempest*, so that we see the ideas transposed between two distinct genres of play.

The Purpose of Play and Fiction

In one sense all poets enjoy the freedom and possibilities of fiction, the stories they tell need not be outwardly true, nor need the voice and tone in which their poem speaks be their own. On the other hand if they are to succeed in moving us, everything in their poetry must be full of truth, it must, as we shall see, 'grow to something of great constancy'.[4] We are so used to the conventions of fiction, so used to engaging in what Coleridge called the willing suspension of disbelief, that we miss the paradox beneath our noses, that truth arises not from the labouring reason of the poet, but from his playfulness, his freedom to invent. The poet of *The Dream of the Rood* achieves his effect by feigning the speech of the cross, by assuming a voice and speaking with an accent not his own, but hereby he not only conveys truth, he conveys it in a way he could not have done had he spoken in with his own voice. A poet who is also a playwright obviously enjoys this freedom to an even greater degree and is perhaps even more conscious both of the deliberate feigning and of the presentation of truth which their art represents.

Playfulness and Truth in *A Midsummer Night's Dream*

We shall begin with the 'playfulness', in every sense, of *A Midsummer Night's Dream* and allow Theseus and Hippolyta's famous dialogue about truth and imagination to set some of our themes. Before we engage with this dialogue it is worth remembering the context in which it takes place. It functions as both an epilogue to the main action of the play, and as a prologue to the play within the play. The four lovers, it will be recalled, leave the day-lit rationalism of the Athenian court to encounter the moonlight transformations of Puck, and find themselves caught up in the elemental quarrel of Oberon and Titania. They leave the court mismatched and miserable, caught in a chain of frustration and betrayal; they return rightly matched and joyful, ready to enter into the fruitfulness of love,

---

[4]   *A Midsummer Night's Dream*, Act V, Scene 1, line 26.

of which the play's closing nuptials are a sign. Puck has so cast a spell on the lovers who are now at last, through the play of magic, rightly linked again to one another, that on waking they imagine that their transformations have only been a dream. They tell their story to Theseus and Hippolyta, not knowing whether they will be believed or whether to believe themselves:

> *Hippolyta*:   'Tis strange my Theseus, that these lovers speak of.
> *Theseus*:   More strange than true: I never may believe
> These antique fables, nor these fairy toys.
> Lovers and madmen have such seething brains,
> Such shaping fantasies, that apprehend
> More than cool reason ever comprehends.
> The lunatic, the lover and the poet
> Are of imagination all compact:
> One sees more devils than vast hell can hold,
> That is, the madman: the lover, all as frantic,
> Sees Helen's beauty in a brow of Egypt:
> The poet's eye, in fine frenzy rolling,
> Doth glance from heaven to earth, from earth to heaven;
> And as imagination bodies forth
> The forms of things unknown, the poet's pen
> Turns them to shapes and gives to airy nothing
> A local habitation and a name.
> Such tricks hath strong imagination,
> That if it would but apprehend some joy,
> It comprehends some bringer of that joy;
> Or in the night, imagining some fear,
> How easy is a bush supposed a bear!
> *Hippolyta*:   But all the story of the night told over,
> And all their minds transfigured so together,
> More witnesseth than fancy's images
> And grows to something of great constancy;
> But, howsoever, strange and admirable.[5]

Like the quarrel between Oberon and Titania, the quarrel between Theseus and Hippolyta is not simply a matter of individuals disagreeing. These characters embody great truths and principles which are in every one of us, quarrelling and also – perhaps through our imaginative participation in this play – on their way to being reconciled. So it is at this moment of the play that, in and through the meeting and the words of Theseus and Hippolyta, we have a meeting in our minds of Reason and Imagination.

---

[5]   Ibid., Act V, Scene 1, lines 1–27.

The Literal Meaning

Let us first look at what Theseus has to say on Reason's behalf against, or apparently against, Imagination. On the surface and most straightforward level he is simply saying: 'I don't believe it! I deny that these events, which the lovers have narrated, actually took place. I think they have been deceived by their overwrought imaginations, and their imaginations were overwrought because they were in love.'

But Theseus goes on to describe the way imagination itself works, and in so doing concedes almost everything his reason hopes to deny. What is more, he generalises from this particular denial to a denial of all 'antique fables' and 'fairy toys', and so, cuts off, in a fine piece of dramatic irony, both the branch on which he is sitting and the stage on which he is standing. For here is Theseus, whose entire existence to us and to our minds and imaginations rests on the fact that he has come down to us from antiquity through the medium of 'antique fables', saying 'well of course you can't believe these antique fables, I don't believe them myself.' Here is Theseus remade in the imagination of Shakespeare, and engendered or embodied in us by the power of Shakespeare's poetry, telling us, in the very medium of that poetry, 'well of course you all know there's nothing in poetry'.

The Dialectic Between Apprehend and Comprehend

Theseus is choosing now to confine reality to that which he can comprehend and to deny reality to that which he can only apprehend, but his distinction, though not his opposition, between these two modes of knowing is potentially helpful and worth examining more closely. In some ways Theseus's speech, with its distrust of antique fable and shaping fantasies, and its emphasis on cool reason and comprehension might be seen as an anticipation of the coming view of the new or modern world exemplified in those passages from the Royal Society in language which is in fact almost exactly anticipated here:

> Lovers and madmen have such seething brains,
> Such shaping fantasies, that apprehend
> More than cool reason ever comprehends.

The errors and omissions of that later rationalism are also anticipated and gently shown up by Shakespeare in Theseus's speech, for the most striking thing about his attack on imagination is not a failure of imagination, which in fact animates the whole speech, but a failure of reason. There is a serious logical flaw in his speech. He begins with a proper and useful distinction between apprehension and comprehension as modes of knowing: we have 'shaping fantasies' which apprehend more than cool reason ever comprehends. But he then goes on to imply, without ever proving, that what we apprehend is not real. And he implies that it is not real first by a sleight of hand and than by a suggestion of motive. The sleight of hand is in the elision from 'things unknown' to 'airy nothing':

> And as imagination bodies forth
> The form of things *unknown,* the poet's pen
> Turns them to shapes and gives to airy *nothing*
> A local habitation and a name.

Just because a thing is 'unknown', or unknown to reason, it does not follow that it is simply 'nothing'. The very fact that imagination is able to discern a form which bodies it forth and find a name for it, may suggest that it not only has its own mode of existence but that its existence is able to impinge on and to have effects on, to operate as a cause within, the realm of things which reason can in fact comprehend. Thus it is that engineers can make use of imaginary numbers to construct real bridges. We require the strong imagination to be active in bodying forth the form of things unknown precisely because, far from being airy nothing, these things, however incomprehensible, may have a huge influence on things we do comprehend. And this is of course exactly the case in the narrative structure of the play. Oberon and Titania are the 'local habitation and a name' given by Shakespeare to realities we could not otherwise picture, but which are nevertheless at play as forces within our own psyche and perhaps within the wider world. One might even say that Oberon and Titania represent two poles of being and meaning, between which are generated the forces upon which other realities in the play depend. When they are in harmony there is felt a measured blessing in the material world, and their discord likewise has a measurable and felt effect on the world, as Titania herself says when she upbraids Oberon, listing the disharmony and unsettledness of the outer world which their quarrel has caused:

> And thorough this distemperature we see
> The seasons alter: hoary-headed frosts
> Fall in the fresh lap of the crimson rose,
> And on old Hiems' thin and icy crown
> An odorous chaplet of sweet summer buds
> Is, as in mockery, set: the spring, the summer,
> The chiding autumn, angry winter, change
> Their wonted liveries, and the mazed world,
> By their increase, now knows not which is which:
> And this same progeny of evils comes
> From our debate, from our dissension;
> We are their parents and original.[6]

---

6   *A Midsummer Night's Dream*, Act II, Scene 1, lines 106–17.

Any narrow form of 'Reason' which refuses to pursue the causes of things into the realm of apprehension, and to enlist the aid of strong imagination in doing so, may well be missing the hidden 'parent and original' of the outer phenomena it seeks to measure. The purpose of imagination, in its playfulness and poetry in particular, is to be a bridge between reason and intuitive apprehension, to find for apprehension just those shapes, those local habitations and names, which make for comprehension. We must not distrust the longings of the imagination. When Theseus says

> Such tricks hath strong imagination,
> That if it would but apprehend some joy
> It comprehends some bringer of that joy

he implies that its comprehension is false; but actually it is only by 'strong imagination' that we ever enjoy the truths we apprehend at all. For every act of communication, including the most rigorously scientific, is built of language – that vast system of metaphors bequeathed us by the possibilities of imagination and by the work of poets. Indeed, you could argue that all great poetry works by holding these two ways of knowing in creative tension. Poetic force is generated between the apprehension of the hitherto unknowable, which gives it its depth, resonance and meaning, and the comprehension of the shapes and images in which it bodies forth its apprehensions which is what allows it to communicate at all. We can see poems failing when they capitulate to either one of these poles: when they are so comprehensible as to lead us nowhere, give us nothing, and remain on a trite surface, or when they are so full of unclothed or un-embodied apprehension that they offer us no common bridge in language or picture to the poet's truth and so remain obscure and opaque. But we can equally see, and indeed we know in all the faculties of our soul, when a poem succeeds, when the knowable form of its comprehended image, the glassy surface of its mirror of imitation, is suddenly a window that lets us pass through into the new world the poet has apprehended.

Seeing and Embodying

Many poets and critics have come to find in Theseus's description of how the poet sets to work, the very best embodiment in words of the relation between imagination, poetry and truth. Let us look again at the process as Theseus describes it:

> The poet's eye, in fine frenzy rolling,
> Doth glance from heaven to earth, from earth to heaven;
> And as imagination bodies forth
> The forms of things unknown, the poet's pen
> Turns them to shapes and gives to airy nothing
> A local habitation and a name.

The work of the poet begins with perception, with the observation of life as he or she sees and feels it. But it is to be a comprehensive observation, nothing is to be omitted or excluded as unreal or unearthly. The poet's eye is to glance from heaven to earth from earth to heaven, not only literally but figuratively as well. The poets observation is to include the things that earth and heaven here symbolise: visibility and invisibility, imperfection and perfection. For the phrase 'from heaven to earth, from earth to heaven' not only expresses the comprehensiveness of all that the poet must take into their observation but also anticipates something of the mystery they will subsequently embody in the shapes and names of their art. For the heart of that art is to express heaven in earthly terms and move us through the comprehension of earth to the apprehension of heaven; so we glimpse 'heaven in ordinary', and are invited through the close, original observation of particular earthly things, to be, in Heaney's phrase, 'like a rich man entering heaven through the ear of a raindrop'.[7] How does the poet achieve this? What role does imagination play in the process?

First there is observation, the poet's eye 'glancing' but then there is a transformation and a bodying forth; the images the poet has seen enter into, and are transformed by, the power of imagination:

> And as imagination bodies forth
> The form of things unknown, the poet's pen
> Turns them to shapes and gives to airy nothing
> A local habitation and a name.

Simple observation is not enough and in fact never takes place, even in science, without some involvement of the shaping spirit of imagination. What imagination does here is to discern that the outer shapes or forms are in fact pregnant with meaning, to realise that things unknown can be made known by being embodied, not in mere copies of nature, but through imitations of nature, so that the things between heaven and earth presented to our senses are so re-presented in the poet's art that they 'body forth' the invisible, that they turn into shape, and so into comprehensibility, truth and experience which would otherwise have been either inaccessible or only accessible once and for a fleeting moment – apprehendable perhaps, but also irretrievable. The poet, however, takes that experience, that apprehension, that potentially fleeting glimpse, and by exercise of the poetic imagination gives to apprehension's 'airy nothingness' a shape, and more than a shape: 'A local habitation and a name'.

This is the heart of the art; to create a shape that can be sounded, a network of vocables, a nameable name, in which to incarnate insight, so that the remote or uncatchable is caught in the net of sound and has a local habitation and a name that can evoke it forever thereafter. Of course this is what language itself does, or rather what language *is*. Every word is made, by the continuous miracle of language,

---

7   Seamus Heaney, 'The Rain Stick', in *The Spirit Level* (London, 1996), p.1.

into a local habitation and a name for something which we would otherwise not experience at all, or not be able to hold, develop and integrate And what is true of language in general is true of an individual poem. So, to return to 'The Rain Stick', the poem we discussed in the Introduction: we can all have the experience of upending a rain stick, we may all have had the separate experiences of rainfall in its myriad forms, but Heaney's poem transforms these experiences. He joins us first in our observation of these things. With ours, his eyes glance from heaven to earth, from earth to heaven, and then he shares with us his own imagination's bodying forth of these things, his pen turns them to shapes, and his poem 'Rain Stick' becomes forever the unique local habitation and name for the experience of refreshment from the desiccate, which it embodies. And because that truth now has a local habitation and a name it becomes available to us not once but many times. Because of its embodiment through the poet's art, the truth of the poem, like the music of the rain stick it celebrates, 'is undiminished for having happened once, / Twice, ten, a thousand times before'.[8]

'Imagination Bodies' and the Incarnation

But can we say more? Does Shakespeare's poetry help us to apprehend something about the Incarnation, the great mystery at the heart of Christian theology? Theologians hoping to reflect on what we might mean by saying 'The Word was made flesh and dwelt among us, full of grace and truth'[9] may find this very passage, for all its imaginary pre-Christian setting full of 'antique Fables and fairy toys', has a direct bearing on the heart of Christian faith. In the Incarnation, the Word which dwells in the beginning richly with God, the Divine Logos which would otherwise be an apprehension or an abstraction in the human mind, is literally 'bodied forth', literally given 'a local habitation and a name', so that in John's Gospel the first question of the disciples to Jesus is 'Master where are you staying?'[10] In Jesus Christ, who 'bodies forth' from the Father truth that would otherwise have remained 'the form of things unknown', we see a continuous movement between 'earth and heaven, heaven and earth'; we see Jesus 'bodying forth' again and again the love which is the essence of heaven and we see the disciples glimpsing in him not only the physical body but also a kind of window or doorway into heaven itself, as at the transfiguration. Indeed in John's Gospel Christ declares himself to be the Door[11] and the Way.[12]

Shakespeare's account of the poetic imagination as the bodying forth in earthly terms of heavenly apprehension provides us with a model for understanding the Incarnation as the supreme act of divine poesis. If this is so then it has rich

---

8   Ibid., p.1.
9   John 1:14.
10   John 1:38.
11   John 10:9.
12   John 14:6.

implications for our understanding of humanity as made in God's image; for it means that we are made as makers ourselves, as imaginative 'embodiers'. If that is the case then we might regard the successful embodiment of truth in Christ, the word made flesh, as the prime imaginative or communicative act which underwrites and makes possible all others.[13] We might see this divine poeisis in Christ as answering exactly to that need of which Steiner spoke in *Real Presences*:

> any coherent understanding of what language is and how language performs …
> is in the final analysis under-written by the assumption of God's presence … the
> experience of aesthetic meaning in particular that of literature and the arts …
> infers the necessary possibility of this 'real presence' … this study will contend
> that the wager on the meaning of meaning … when we come face to face with
> the text and work of art or music … is a wager on transcendence.[14]

Though one might add that this wager on the meaning of meaning is in fact a wager on God's immanence as well as his transcendence. We wager that God has enabled our imagination to create symbols which are energised between the poles of immanence and transcendence; the 'earth' and 'heaven' of Shakespeare's lines. We will see these lines of thought developed more fully when we deal in detail with Coleridge in Chapter 6.

Hippolyta's Reply

Returning to *A Midsummer Night's Dream*, it is extraordinary that a speech which the character intends as a denial of the power and meaning of poetry, should be used by the author as the most perfect embodiment and analysis of that power in the language, though that paradox is itself part of the power and the playful humour of this particular embodied poem. One can imagine that Shakespeare enjoyed giving Theseus, as his own creation, sufficient power in poetry and imagination to deny the power of poetry and imagination that had in fact created him. So Theseus on the literal level denies the lovers' story and makes the case against imagination and for 'cool reason'. How does Hippolyta reply?

> But all the story of the night told over,
> And all their minds transfigured so together,
> More witnesseth than fancy's images
> And grows to something of great constancy …

---

[13] For a systematic attempt to relate God's being as Trinity, and his incarnation, to the human creative process in art, see Dorothy Sayers *The Mind of the Maker*, ed. S. Howatch (1941; London, 1994).

[14] George Steiner, *Real Presences* (London, 1989), pp.3–4.

Just as at a literal level, and in terms of the plot of the play, Theseus' speech attacks the veracity of the lovers' story, so at the same level, Hippolyta defends it. At a literal level she is simply saying: 'When we look at these stories over again, and especially when we put them together, they cohere, they make sense, and all the lovers seem to be referring to the same thing. Their minds are transfigured so together, and their separate stories "grow to something of great constancy", so they can't have been making it up.' But there is more: her defence of 'the story of the night told over' amounts to a defence of imagination and of the poet's art, as well as spelling out the criteria by which its success might be judged. Let us look then in more detail at what Hippolyta says – 'And all their minds transfigured so together'. The achievement of art is the transfiguring of our minds, by means of imagination, so that we see both what the artist sees and what they see through the things they see. In the case of the playwright's art it is the transfiguring of our minds together. There is a corporate transfiguration, a corporate entering into the world of the poet's imagination and a corporate seeing through it, of the truth he intends. This is in fact happening at the very moment that Hippolyta speaks of it and through the very means of her speech. When this speech is spoken by an actress, what is happening is that we the audience have voluntarily succumbed to the enchantment of the playwright, whose art, like Puck's love potion, has so worked on our eyes that our vision is altered. In one sense we know perfectly well that we are sitting in a theatre watching a well-known actress, but at another level we have ourselves been in the fairy wood and lived its moonlit scenes, and we are seeing these two characters who combine in their persons 'antique fable' and 'fairy toy', and who represent in their characters Reason and Imagination, working as forces both within the plot of the play, and in our own lives and minds. Our minds are indeed transfigured, for through the costumes and the lights and the greasepaint, and the outer sounds of the familiar speeches, we are seeing into the heart of language itself, into the very forge and generative place of poetry, as Shakespeare celebrates the mystery of his art.

Inner Coherence and Growth in a Work of Art

Hippolyta goes on to say that there must be some truth in the lovers' tale because when we return to it, when it is 'told oe'r', it 'grows to something of great constancy'. And this is true not just of an episode in this play, but of all great works of art. Once it has been finished, a work of art develops a life of its own which is in some sense independent of its author. A good work of art has an independent inner coherence which does indeed 'grow to something of great constancy' the more often we 'tell it o'er' – that is, enter into its world, and allow it to transfigure our minds. How does this work? How is it that a single play like this one, a finite collection of words composed by a finite mind, can take on such a life of its own, can seem to gather to itself and embody so much, and to do so consistently and with such inner cohesion and integrity? The best hint as to how this happens is to be taken from Shakespeare/Hippolyta's choice of the word 'grows'. The work grows in our minds because its structure and unity are *organic*. The principles of its inner organisation, the way all its parts are related to its whole, is like the organisation and accommodation of a living thing. It has what Coleridge distinguished as an organic unity over against a 'mechanic' one. The sense that a work of imagination might grow and develop according to its own inner laws in just the same way that in the outer world life itself grows and develops is hinted in Shakespeare's choice of the word 'bodies'. Imagination 'bodies forth the form of things unknown'. Coleridge more than any other critic grasped this principle about art in general and Shakespeare's art in particular and developed it very fruitfully,[15] but there is no doubt that the seeds of his critical theory are all here in this exchange between Theseus and Hippolyta. The speech is all the more remarkable when we realise that Shakespeare is giving a sense and power to the word 'imagination' which, since Coleridge's time, is common to us, but in Shakespeare's time was unheard of. In Shakespeare's day the word imagination meant the capacity to hold an interior mental image and no more, as Owen Barfield comments, citing this very passage in his *History in English Words*:

'Phantasia' and 'imaginatio' were in use among the Schoolmen, and fantasy and imagination are both found in Chaucer in the sense of 'a mental image or reflection', or more particularly 'an image of something which either has no existence or does not yet exist'. After the Renaissance Shakespeare suddenly transfigured one of the two words in one of those extraordinary passages which make us feel that genius is indeed more than earthly:

And as imagination bodies forth
The forms of things unknown, the poet's pen
Turns them to shapes and gives to airy nothing
A local habitation and a name.

In such a passage we seem to behold him standing up, a figure of colossal stature, gazing at us over the heads of the intervening generations. He transcends the flight of time and the laborious building up of meanings, and, picking up a part of the outlook of an age which is to succeed his by nearly two hundred years, gives it momentary expression before he lets it drop again. That mystical conception which the word embodies in these lines – a conception which would make imagination the interpreter and part creator of a whole unseen world -is not found again until the Romantic Movement has begun.[16]

---

[15]   For a fuller discussion of Coleridge's Shakespeare criticism, see below Chapter 6 pp. 163–2.

[16]   Owen Barfield, *History in English Words* (Great Barrington, MA, 2002), pp. 213–14.

The Conjunction of Opposites

One way in which the parts and elements of this play are all organically related to the whole can be seen in the way the structure of the plot develops the meaning of the poetry. Theseus and Hippolyta each make a speech defending a particular way of knowing: Reason on the one hand and Imagination on the other. But the context in which they set out their different viewpoints is a preparation for marriage. The entire play is a kind of preface to their marriage and it concludes with a blessing of their marriage bed. Indeed you could argue that the play, which ends with three marriages in the realm of the visible, and a reconciliation of marriage in the invisible realm, is about marriage; about the fruitful conjunction of opposites at every level, the bringing together of contraries that seem to quarrel, but in whose conjunction is not only harmony but a kind of overspill of creative energy into fruitfulness and blessing.

So the marriage of Theseus and Hippolyta represents the necessary and fruitful union of Reason and Imagination. It is saying that the divorce between reason and imagination which Sprat was to propose will only injure us, and prevent us really knowing and being blessed by truth. Rather we must find a way of knowing which involves both the way reason comprehends and the way imagination apprehends. This applies just as much to our understanding of the mysteries of life and growth in the outer world of nature as it does in the inner world of art. Allowing poetry to transfigure our vision heals the false fragmentation our culture has endured since the Enlightenment. To find a way of making a marriage, a fruitful union, of the apparent opposition of Reason and Imagination is perhaps the most urgent task of our own time. In Chapter 1 we saw this struggle played out in the life of C.S. Lewis, and a poem of his called 'Reason' makes an interesting final reflection on the issues raised in this part of the play:

> Set on the soul's acropolis the reason stands
> A virgin arm'd, commercing with celestial light,
> And he who sins against her has defiled his own
> Virginity: no cleansing makes his garment white;
> So clear is reason. But how dark, imagining,
> Warm, dark, obscure and infinite, daughter of Night:
> Dark is her brow, the beauty of her eyes with sleep
> Is loaded, and her pains are long, and her delight.
> Tempt not Athene. Wound not in her fertile pains
> Demeter, nor rebel against her mother-right.
> Oh who will reconcile in me both maid and mother,
> Who make in me a concord of the depth and height?
> Who make imagination's dim exploring touch
> Ever report the same as intellectual sight?
> Then could I truly say and not deceive,

Then wholly say that I BELIEVE.[17]

Reason and Imagination in this poem are distinct but complementary ways of knowing, but figured as Goddesses, as active powers of the soul in a very Coleridgian sense. Lewis recognises that because they deal ultimately with the same reality they must be reconciled, but reconciled in a way that respects their distinct modes of operation; and he sees faith itself as a way of properly integrating reason and imagination.[18]

Performance and 'The Play within the Play'

The exchange between Theseus and Hippolyta forms an interlude between the magical transfigurations of the moonlit wood and the play within the play, the ludicrous enactments of Bottom and his friends, the 'rude mechanicals'. In a way the contrast could not better illustrate the difference between the true work of art, with its imaginative invitation to a 'willing suspension of disbelief', and a mere outward imitation which, failing to engage the imagination, fails equally to please the reason. The success of Shakespeare's play depends on a kind of invited feigning, on a mutual consent that our minds should be transfigured together. In some sense we have to agree to be deceived in order to reach a truth. But the authors and actors of the play within the play cannot grasp this. They are afraid that it would be wrong to deceive the gentry with the appearances of their play in case they frightened them. But all their special efforts not to feign, or rather to 'undeceive', with each of the players solemnly informing their audience, in the middle of the action, as to who they 'really' are, actually prevent them from telling their story at all, and at no point is anybody's mind transfigured. Their very concern with accuracy about the bodily surface of reality prevents them from embodying anything real at all. So, for example, they introduce the moon as a physical character in the play. There is a wonderful irony here, for moonlight is perhaps the central and most beautifully embodied and imagined thing in the whole of Shakespeare's play. *A Midsummer Night's Dream* is flooded with a most unearthly and magical moonlight from its very opening lines, 'but oh methinks how slow this old moon wanes' through to the glimmering light in which Oberon and Titania give the house of Theseus its final blessing. So it is a moment of rich comedy when, into the midst of this imaginatively moon-enchanted play, Shakespeare introduces another play in which a man stands physically in front of people, carrying a lantern they can all see with their outer eyes while announcing solemnly that he is the moon, and thinks that this will be a better embodiment of moonlight than any mere words can provide.

---

[17] *The Collected Poems of C.S. Lewis*, ed. W. Hooper (Fount, 1994), p.65.

[18] For a fuller discussion of this important poem see my chapter 'Poet' in R. MacSwain and M. Wood (eds), *The Cambridge Companion to C.S. Lewis* (Cambridge, forthcoming), chapter 21.

In a way the mechanicals' attempt to keep reminding everybody that they are not really Pyramus or Thisbe or a lion or the moon, but only Snug or Snout or Bottom, and thus destroying their own art, stands as a parable for the whole poverty of our way of knowing the world since the Enlightenment: the poverty of reductionism. We look at the mystery of the world, its moonlight and sunlight, its rains and rivers, and we dissect it all and say it is not 'really' this, not the sublime mystery it seems to be hinting at, it is 'really' only x or y or some other such formula we have devised to describe its constituent parts. It is as though someone at the performance of a great piece of music were to take along an oscilloscope and insist that nothing had happened but the movement of wavy lines on its screen. But the realism of the 'rude mechanicals', the realism of our own age, is not only shallow; it is also false, as this very play shows. The reality is that we live not in a dead world of mere surfaces, but in the midst of a mystery which, if we will let it transfigure our minds, 'grows to something of great constancy; / But, howsoever, strange and admirable'.

Appearance and Reality in *The Tempest*

It is instructive to turn now from the early enchantments of the *Dream*, standing as it does near the threshold of Shakespeare's major work, to *The Tempest*, that other magical play concerned also with the relation of inner and outer, of reality and appearance, which comes at the end of his career and whose epilogue is believed by many to be Shakespeare's own farewell to the stage. Like the *Dream*, *The Tempest* uses magical or imaginary characters to embody aspects of our inner nature and also hidden aspects of the outer nature which surrounds us. Just as Oberon and Titania are in some sense the hidden forms, the 'parents and originals', of much in both the outer and inner worlds of the *Dream*, so Prospero's two servants Ariel and Caliban are the local habitations and names given by Shakespeare to profound aspects of our own human nature, with its greeds and resentments on the one hand, and yearnings for flight and freedom on the other. We are certain to recognise Ariel within ourselves, but equally bound, under the searching light of Shakespeare's poetry, to say of Caliban, as Prospero does, 'This thing of darkness I acknowledge mine'.[19]

Just as we found the themes of truth and imagination, which are woven throughout the *Dream*, focused in the exchange between Hippolyta and Theseus which precedes the play within the play, so we can find many of the themes of *The Tempest* focused in a speech of Prospero's spoken just after the 'play within the play', or more accurately the masque within the play, which occurs at the beginning of Act IV in *The Tempest*. But first *The Tempest* itself, and then Prospero's speech need to be set into context.

---

[19]   *The Tempest*, Act V, scene 1, line 275.

The *Dream* is a comedy and, for all its extraordinary profundity in the matter of imagination and poetry, there is in its lightness of touch, an absence of engagement with the deepest issues of suffering, sin and mortality, especially with the great issues of Judgement and Mercy. Whilst in the late Romances, of which the *Tempest* is the last, Shakespeare can in some sense be seen to return to some of the themes of his earliest plays, it is not a naive return. Between *A Midsummer Night's Dream* and *The Tempest* lie the Histories and Tragedies. By the time he writes *The Tempest* he has faced and outfaced the self-doubts and searching of Hamlet, Othello's terrible twisting of the energy of love, Macbeth's uncanny mapping of the degradation of the soul, and Lear's encounter, in himself and others, with humankind's 'monster's of the deep'. The power of *The Tempest* comes from the fact that it is not a fantasy of escape, but one in which the darkest themes explored in the tragedies can find their resolution. The final affirmations, explicit and implicit, at the end of *The Tempest* have a special value. 'We can say of them what Karl Barth says of the enormous *Yes* at the centre of Mozart's music, that it has weight and significance because it overpowers and contains a *No*.'[20]

Indeed *the Tempest* both begins and builds as though it were a revenge tragedy. It has all the classic elements: Prospero, the wronged Duke, manages by his magic art to summon together all those who have wronged him. Their guilt is proved many times in the course of the play, both by their own confession and by the subsequent scenes Prospero has himself contrived to test their characters. Prospero does not reveal his hand until the very last act, but by the beginning of the Act IV we have a strong sense of the coming denouement. A Jacobean audience might reasonably have expected a Last Judgement-type scene in which Prospero is justly avenged on the guilty, and rewards the faithful. But running throughout the play is a counter-theme of *mercy*, of unexpected graces and salvations, of people being given up for lost only to be saved at the last minute from their own wreckage. This is true of the original story of Prospero and Miranda's survival in the drifting boat; it is true of the opening tempest and the apparent wreck of the ship and loss of its crew, when they are in fact all restored and recovered; and it is true of the love between Ferdinand and Miranda as Prospero's pretended opposition gives way to the reality of his loving purpose and good will to them both. This theme of the sudden revelation of mercy and restoration in the midst of apparent catastrophe is seamlessly woven together with the other two pairs of apparent opposites – Control and Release, and Truth and Illusion – whose tension and interplay does so much to generate the play's energy and meaning.

By the beginning of Act IV, theme and counter-theme are hung finely in the balance; we do not know, and perhaps Prospero himself does not know, whether when he reveals the truth to his brother and the other conspirators he will find it in himself to forgive them or not. When the tension is at its height it is relieved by an

---

[20]   Seamus Heaney alludes to this passage in Barth in praising one of Yeats' last poems in *The Redress of Poetry* (London, 1995), p. 163, but I think his insight applies as much, if not more, to Shakespeare's last plays.

unexpected *jeu d'esprit* on Prospero's part, when he suddenly kindles his own and our imaginations to 'bestow upon the eyes of this young couple, some vanity of my art'.[21] That 'vanity' takes the form of a play or masque in which the goddesses Iris, Ceres and Juno appear to bless the proposed marriage between Ferdinand and Miranda, and fill the stage suddenly with music and images of union and fruitfulness, as though the curtain of the world had for a moment been drawn aside to give us a glimpse of a heaven in which there is at last a resolution of all the tensions with which the play is charged, and we wonder whether it was as much for his own benefit as for Ferdinand and Miranda's that Prospero summoned the vision. But then it vanishes in noise and confusion as suddenly as it had come, and Prospero speaks these words:

> You do look, my son, in a moved sort,
> As if you were dismay'd: be cheerful, sir:
> Our revels now are ended. These our actors,
> As I foretold you, were all spirits and
> Are melted into air, into thin air:
> And, like the baseless fabric of this vision,
> The cloud-capp'd towers, the gorgeous palaces,
> The solemn temples, the great globe itself,
> Yea all which it inherit, shall dissolve
> And, like this insubstantial pageant faded,
> Leave not a rack behind. We are such stuff
> As dreams are made on, and our little life
> Is rounded with a sleep. Sir, I am vex'd;
> Bear with my weakness; my brain is troubled:
> Be not disturb'd with my infirmity:
> If you be pleased, retire into my cell
> And there repose: a turn or two I'll walk,
> To still my beating mind.[22]

Like the exchange between Theseus and Hippolyta in the *Dream*, this speech works simultaneously at a number of different levels, and the 'revels', the 'insubstantial pageant', to which it refers may be understood, in this context, in at least five different ways. Firstly, 'Our revels now are ended' refers to the 'insubstantial pageant' or masque which they (the characters) and we (the audience) have just been watching. These 'actors' were, as Prospero had forewarned, invisible spirits of the air summoned by his art, and they, and the magical glimpses of heaven which were their scenery, have faded back into the air whence they were woven. However, to hear Prospero, at this point in the play, saying that the revels are ended, the dream-playing is over, is bound to carry a reference to the way in

---

21   *The Tempest*, Act IV, Scene 1, line 41.
22   *The Tempest*, Act IV, scene 1, lines 177–94.

which he has in fact been orchestrating the plot of what happens in the play so far. Prospero has been the playwright within the play. He has brought the characters together, he has set the scenes in which they have encountered one another, he has led them through these encounters with each other and with the illusions of his art, till at last they come to a moment of real encounter with him, whom most of them have not yet seen. This encounter is to come in the final act when Prospero lays aside his robes and appears to his brother and the other conspirators plainly as the person he is. The revels are ended, there is a reality of personal encounter, with its perils and its possibilities of redemption for all of them to face. The insubstantial pageant is broken by the arrival of that moment for encounter.

But there is a third level of reference, for here we have an actor in a play, one who has been presenting appearances of reality to us through the medium of his performance, and his words carry beyond the fellow characters to whom they are directed, out to the audience itself, and we cannot help hearing this reference to vanishing actors and beautiful scenery that suddenly fades away, as a reference to the very play that we are watching. For a while Shakespeare has filled our minds with cloud-capped towers, with gorgeous palaces and solemn temples, and now through one of his characters he is reminding us that this beautiful vision will fade from us and return us to those other encounters and confrontations for which the fading vision may perhaps have been preparing us. For the original audience, sensing the widening ripples which the flung stone of this speech cast in their minds, there must have been a particular frisson on the outward movement from 'towers' through 'palaces' to 'temples' and finally 'the globe', which led them to a fourth and particular level of understanding:

> The cloud-capp'd towers, the gorgeous palaces,
> The solemn temples, the great globe itself,
> Yea all which it inherit, shall dissolve
> And, like this insubstantial pageant faded,
> Leave not a rack behind.

If the tradition which maintains that Shakespeare intended this play as his farewell to the theatre, and that he himself played the part of Prospero, is right, then his contemporaries would have felt the reference to the 'great globe itself' - the Globe Theatre, the scene of so many extraordinary visions – and here the artist who had conjured those visions for them, was resigning from his art, dissolving the pageant before their eyes and strangely implying that they themselves will be dissolved with it. And this sense of a wider dissolution brings us to the fifth and deepest reference of these lines, for they refer to the end, or the apparent end, not simply of this episode, this play, or even Shakespeare's art and theatre, but to the end of all things, the end of our lives and the end of the world.

What does Shakespeare intend us to understand by the two key metaphors he uses here for the relation between our present experience and what might lie behind or beyond them; the metaphor of a play and its ending, and of a dream and awakening?

In one sense Prospero is alluding to and developing the idea, used by Shakespeare in many other plays, that 'all the world's a stage', an idea which had been given very forceful expression in Raleigh's brilliant little poem 'What Is Our life?' which gives a good sense of the sort of feel the life/stage metaphor had for Shakespeare's contemporaries, and is worth quoting here in full:

> What is our life? A play of passion.
> And what our mirth but music of division?
> Our mothers' wombs the tiring houses be
> Where we are dressed for this short comedy.
> Heaven the judicious sharp spectator is
> Who sits and marks what here we do amiss.
> The graves that hide us from the searching sun
> Are like drawn curtains when the play is done.
> Thus playing post we to our latest rest,
> And then we die, in earnest, not in jest.[23]

Raleigh here picks up on the brevity and comedy, the illusions and delusions, of our lives, but although the potential bleakness of his juxtaposed womb/tomb imagery has been developed by some moderns, (most notably by Beckett in *Waiting For Godot* where the lines 'they give birth astride of a grave, the light gleams an instant then all is night once more'[24] probably owe something to this poem) Raleigh's poem is not bleak in the modern sense, because, for all its judicious sharpness, 'heaven' is nevertheless the spectator of the play of our lives, and there is at least implicit in the notion of dying 'in earnest' some sense that beyond the illusions and tragicomedies of our lives, we may encounter a heaven so real that in comparison with it all that seemed real before was no more than 'a play of passion'.

The notion of our present life as a play is fundamentally ambiguous: it can be used to suggest falsehood and futility, something that ultimately does not matter; or to suggest that, just as a play is a beautifully wrought work of art which allows us to engage with a feigned truth in such a way as to enable us for a deeper truth (our truest poetry is our most feigning), so the world, and all our experiences in it, may be a great work of art and imagination, beyond which is a reality for which the play of the world has been preparing us. Shakespeare had explored the bleakest side of the metaphor in many of his plays most notably in *Macbeth*, where Macbeth's soul has been so brutalised and alienated by the course of violence on which he set himself that he greets the news of his wife's suicide not with grief,

---

[23]   Collected in *Silver Poets of the Sixteenth Century*, ed. G. Bullet (London, 1960), p. 296.

[24]   Samuel Beckett, *Waiting for Godot* (London, 1956), Act II, p. 89.

but with indifference and futility, as he reaches for this metaphor of life as a play:

> She should have died hereafter;
> There would have been a time for such a word.
> Tomorrow, and tomorrow, and tomorrow,
> Creeps in this petty pace from day to day
> To the last syllable of recorded time,
> And all our yesterdays have lighted fools
> The way to dusty death. Out, out, brief candle!
> Life's but a walking shadow; a poor player
> That struts and frets his hour upon the stage,
> And then is heard no more: it is a tale
> Told by an idiot, full of sound and fury,
> Signifying nothing.[25]

Macbeth's speech here expresses the alienation from life which is the consequence of the dehumanising choices he has made, choices which demand that 'blood will have blood', that from a bloody course once chosen there is no going back – 'I am in blood stepped in so far that, should I wade no more, returning were as tedious as go oer'.[26] By contrast, Prospero is on the threshold of choosing mercy, and for him the ending of our revels and the dissolution of this insubstantial pageant, is itself a prelude to something more, something to which, as the epilogue of *The Tempest* makes clear, mercy is the only key. Whereas for Macbeth the actors in the play of life are 'walking shadows', Prospero's choice of word is spirits – 'These our actors, / As I foretold you, were all spirits'. They are the natural inhabitants of a realm beyond the one in which they have been playing. Although they melt 'into thin air' and, 'like the baseless fabric of this vision', 'leave not a rack behind', there is a strong sense that they, and the 'cloud-capped towers', melt from us into something else, or in their melting reveal something else. This sense is carried by the context of Prospero's speech in the wider plot. These lines occur at the beginning of the *fourth* act not the end of Act V. We witness the dissolution of the pageant but it leaves not a blank stage or a falling curtain, rather a stage set for a moment of encounter, judgement and reconciliation in which Prospero confronts and forgives his brother. But if, on our fifth and final level of reference, the 'insubstantial pageant' is not only the play within the play but the whole world and all of us in it, then the strong implication is that when, at the cosmic level,

> The cloud-capp'd towers, the gorgeous palaces,
> The solemn temples, the great globe itself,
> Yea all which it inherit, shall dissolve

---

[25]   *Macbeth*, Act V, Scene 5, lines 12–28.

[26]   *Macbeth*, Act II, Scene 4, lines 137–38.

And, like this insubstantial pageant faded,
Leave not a rack behind ...

we ourselves will step from the seemings of this world, from the theatre of the
great globe, not into the nothingness of Macbeth's alienation, but into an encounter
as potentially fraught, but also as potentially fruitful, as that which occupies Act V
of *The Tempest*. This motif of the resurfacing of the lost, is there in Shakespeare's
choice of the ambiguous 'rack' in 'leave not a rack behind', for his play opens with
the apparent wreck of a ship and all its crew, who resurface marvellously and for
their own redemption in the rest of the play. Likewise, the device of the play within
the play itself directs the energy of the life/play metaphor Prospero is using. 'The
play is over' he is saying, and yet by virtue of his continued presence on the stage
we know that the play goes on. We might of course object that when the whole
play itself is over then indeed there will be no surviving of the characters beyond
it, then indeed they will 'leave not a rack behind'. But Shakespeare has something
further to add. He ends his last play and his whole work in drama, and his life in
London with what must have been, when it was first performed, a stunning *coup
de théâtre*. All the characters are gathered on stage at the end of Act V, Prospero
gives his peace and blessing to Alonso and his companions for their voyage home,
and, in the beautiful last lines, at last sets Ariel free. The reconciled company
prepare to follow Prospero into his cell to hear his full story before they sail to
Italy, and with Prospero's last words, 'please you draw near', the play is over, the
curtain falls. And then, as the audience are preparing to leave, the curtain moves
and Prospero appears again and speaks this epilogue:

Now my charms are all o'erthrown,
And what strength I have's mine own,
Which is most faint: now, 'tis true,
I must be here confined by you,
Or sent to Naples. Let me not,
Since I have my dukedom got
And pardon'd the deceiver, dwell
In this bare island by your spell;
But release me from my bands
With the help of your good hands:
Gentle breath of yours my sails
Must fill, or else my project fails,
Which was to please. Now I want
Spirits to enforce, art to enchant,
And my ending is despair,
Unless I be relieved by prayer,
Which pierces so that it assaults
Mercy itself and frees all faults.
As you from crimes would pardon'd be,

Let your indulgence set me free.

At one level this is simply the actor/playwright graciously asking for applause, pretending to be confined to the island of the stage unless released by the applause of the audience – 'But release me from my bands / With the help of your good hands'. But, in the context of all that has gone before, it is far more than that. For a second time the revels have ended and still Prospero, who has forgiven and delivered his enemies, survives the dissolution and stands in need of deliverance himself. He steps as it were from the Great Globe, from the whole theatre of life, to find that he is still himself and still has an audience ('Heaven the judicious sharp spectator is', they might remember from Raleigh). And so he appeals to his audience for mercy on the grounds of mercy, both the mercy he has shown and the mercy his auditors might themselves hope for:

> Let me not,
> Since I have …
> … pardoned the deceiver, dwell
> In this bare island by your spell

So he concludes:

> As you from crimes would pardon'd be,
> Let your indulgence set me free.

Something astonishing is happening here. If we accept the sense we have given to the play/life metaphor in Prospero's earlier speech, then by emerging from the curtain after the play is over to sue for prayer and mercy in the epilogue the character Prospero has, as it were, died from the world of the play and emerged into the other transcendent world of the audience, to appeal for mercy and to be released to freedom by them, as surely as he has himself just released Ariel. His dying out of the world of the play into another world must of course set us in mind of the ending of the play of our own life and our own dying out of that to face what? What audience? To ask for what release? The play/life metaphor hovers again between its twin potentials as an alternate expression of despair or of hope and Prospero/Shakespeare, who had after all given those famously despairing lines to Macbeth, picks up the ambiguity in a direct appeal to the audience:

> And my ending is despair,
> Unless I be relieved by prayer,
> Which pierces so that it assaults
> Mercy itself and frees all faults.

If my prayer, says Prospero, pierces and assaults your mercy as I encounter you beyond the world of the play, how much more might all our prayers pierce and assault a Mercy which undergirds and is beyond the play of this world, the baseless fabric of this vision. For as surely as this play has ended and I have had to leave it, so surely shall both you and I find one day this great globe dissolve around us, as we leave it. Then we ourselves will have an encounter! Then we will look for pardon! And he presses his point by playing with the theologically charged word 'indulgence', a word that brings with it forbidden teachings about the power of prayer in the communion of saints and the lost theology of purgatory. Now he brings that home, both our interdependence and the power of prayerful forgiveness, with the flourish of his final couplet before he leaves the stage:

As you from crimes would pardon'd be,

Let your indulgence set me free.

Throughout this play, as throughout all his works, Shakespeare has been playing with ideas about truth and feigning, appearance and reality, the relation between the nature to which his art holds a mirror and that other nature, beyond or behind the nature Reason measures, from which so much light shines through the window of his art. In this final epilogue he throws out a bridge from the reality of the play, through the reality of the actor/playwright, to the reality of the audience's own lives; and the keystone of that whole bridge, binding all these realities together and allowing them to communicate with one another, is the over-arching presence and mercy of One who is present to every level of reality and who is to be apprehended by imagination, and engaged and pierced by prayer.

Chapter 3

Understanding Light: Ways of Knowing in the Poems of Sir John Davies

Sir John Davies is due for a revival. He is an underrated poet not because he is neglected or forgotten, but because he is remembered for the wrong reasons and in the wrong context. He has been pressed into service as a continuous supplier and illustrator of background. He lives in other people's footnotes. From the time he was used to provide a kind of photographer's back-drop to the works of Shakespeare in E.M.W. Tillyard's excellent book *The Elizabethan World Picture*[1], he has been quarried for example and illustration of the cultural background of the Elizabethan age. Relegating Davies to survive as a kind of two-dimensional academic wallpaper, decorating the rooms in which other poets are allowed to live and move and have their being in three dimensions, has done him no service, other than preserving his name and fragments of his verse torn out of context. What I would like to do in this chapter is release him from the background and invite him into the foreground. The background in front of which I would like him to stand, the context in which I think it is now exciting and necessary to read his poetry, is not the cultural riches of his own age but the cultural crisis of our own. Here I am following Coleridge who quotes him in the *Biographia Literaria* not to illustrate a former age but to illuminate a current problem about the relation of reason imagination and knowledge[2].

Davies' two great poems, *Orchestra* and *Nosce Teipsum*[3] are, respectively, a poem about physical nature, the modes of motive and being that animate the physical universe, and a poem about our psychology, the way we know or apprehend things, and ultimately the question of what constitutes the essence of our own inner identity. In technical terms, one concerns ontology and the other epistemology. Now, both these poems were written with an awareness that the way we see ourselves and the world was under challenge and might change, but they were written before that great change which we still call 'the Enlightenment' had actually occurred. To understand the full importance of what Davies poems might be saying to us now we need briefly to review what has happened to our views of the world and ourselves since the Enlightenment.

---

[1]   E.M.W. Tillyard, *The Elizabethan World Picture* (London, 1960).
[2]   See below pp. 160–72.
[3]   Both poems are in The Poems of Sir John Davies, ed. R. Krueger (Oxford, 1975); all subsequent references are to this edition.

As a project, the Enlightenment was essentially about a search for truth, for the real nature and meaning of things as we find them and ourselves in relation to them. It is hugely ironic, then, that the path Western thought and assumptions has taken since then, the path through what was once called positivism, and is now called materialism, has led to an experience of alienation from any notion of truth or meaning at all:

> Amid all the menacing signs that surround us in the middle of this twentieth century, perhaps the one which fills thoughtful people with the greatest sense of forboding is the growing sense of meaninglessness. It is this which underlies most of the other threats. How is it that the more able man becomes to manipulate the world to his advantage, the less he can perceive any meaning in it?[4]

These words written by Owen Barfield in the 1970s seem even truer now. He argues that the problem is rooted in a false division between the subjective and the objective which was part of the Enlightenment quest, part of that dialogue between reason and imagination, between Theseus and Hippolyta with which we were concerned in the last chapter. The 'whole scientific and common-sense concept of objectivity' is flawed, he argues, and these flaws are now surfacing. Barfield is of course not the only one to have observed this and the trickle of unease about the intellectual validity of the Enlightenment project has since become a flood. Reviewing *Where the Wasteland Ends*,[5] Theodore Roszak's important critique of Western cultural and scientific method, and summarising its arguments, Barfield writes:

> The vaunted progress of knowledge, which has been going on since the seventeenth century, has been progress in alienation. The alienation of nature from humanity, which the exclusive pursuit of 'objectivity' in science entails, was the first stage; and was followed, with the acceptance of Man himself as part of a nature so alienated, by the alienation of man from himself. This final and fatal step in reductionism occurred in two stages: first his body and then his mind. Newton's approach to nature was already, by contrast with older scientific traditions, a form of behaviourism; and what has since followed has been its extension from astronomy and physics into physiology and ultimately psychology.[6]

Such is the analysis of our present malaise that Barfield, Roszak and many others share. But Roszak does not leave us in this wasteland – as his title suggests

---

[4]   Owen Barfield, The *Rediscovery of Meaning and Other Essays*, 2nd edn (San Rafael, CA,, 2006), p. 11.

[5]   Theodore Roszak, *Where The Wasteland Ends: Politics and Transcendence in Post Industrial Society* (London, 1973).

[6]   Barfield, *Rediscovery*, p. 216.

he is concerned with where the wasteland *ends* – and he goes on to argue that the bleak reductionism, far from being, as has been generally assumed, a reflection of fact, is an arbitrary mental construct. It is 'a convenient and necessary one for the purpose of manipulation (technology) but in so far as it is assumed to reflect the whole truth, or the most important part of it, it is an illusion.'[7]

Roszak argues that the way out of this illusion will proceed in reverse order from the way in: first with psychology and then with the natural sciences. Completely reductive behaviourism in psychology is no longer seen as comprehensive and satisfying. We challenge it because we know that another person is more than the sum of their observed behaviour, and we know it of others because, by the mystery of our own consciousness, we know it of ourselves. But suppose, Roszak suggests, we extend this counter-mechanistic knowledge beyond the so-called subjective, or the realms of personal psychology:

> Suppose this ability we have to find something of ourselves in people should be expanded, so that the same personal transaction occurred with animal and plant ...
>
> Suppose that ability began to reach out further still, discovering a reality of inventive pattern and communicative vitality even in what we once regarded as the sense dead stuff of the world ...
>
> Suppose the whole of creation began to speak to us in the silent language of a deeply submerged kinship ...
>
> Suppose ... we even felt urged to reply courteously to this address of the environment and to join in open conversation ...[8]

Barfield examines the consequences of these suppositions for science and society in his brilliant and prophetic essay 'The Coming Trauma of Materialism',[9] but in fact the vision, the integration, the possibility of a courteous and open conversation with nature, had already been imagined and realised by the young Sir John Davies almost exactly four hundred years before.

Davies was Shakespeare's slightly younger contemporary and his *Orchestra*, a real *jeu d'esprit*, was published in 1596, at almost exactly the same time as the composition of *A Midsummer Night's Dream*, when Davies was twenty-six and Shakespeare was thirty. It is in many respects a young man's poem, full of a delight in punning, of playfulness with ideas and alternatives, an attractive combination of seriousness and mischief. But it is also a channel for the great ideas and images of Christendom, not simply those of Davies' own day, but the whole integrated body

---

[7]   Ibid., p. 216.

[8]   Quoted in Barfield, *Rediscovery*, pp. 216–17.

[9]   Barfield, *Rediscovery*, pp. 215–30.

of thought and feeling about ourselves and the world, which Lewis so beautifully describes and elegises in *The Discarded Image*.[10]

Orchestra, or A Poem of Dancing, ostensibly tells the story of how Antinous, one of the suitors of Penelope in Ulysses' absence, woos her and asks her to dance. When she refuses he launches into a great paean in praise of dancing which forms the main body of the poem. This 'narrative' is no more than the framework which enables Davies to set out a picture of the universe we inhabit animated by the double emblems of love and dancing. It is a picture in which the traditional hierarchies and interconnections of the great chain of being, which can sometimes seem fixed, frozen and patriarchal in prose accounts, are all set in a swinging motion of delight, a dance which fallen man, if he could only purge himself sufficiently to hear the music, is invited to join.

To give us a taste of this marvellous poem, and relate it to the kind of issues raised by Roszak and Barfield, I shall focus on the description Antinous gives to Penelope of how the very beginning of creation and the cosmos arose from the dance of love, and move on to give extracts of his celebration of love in the four elements and finally his conclusion on the possibilities of music and harmony in human relations.

Penelope refuses to dance on the basis that dancing is 'new-fangled' and that our 'old divine forefathers' would never have engaged in it. On the contrary, says Antinous:

> Dancing, bright lady, then began to be
> When the first seeds whereof the world did spring,
> The fire, air, earth and water did agree,
> By Love's persuasion, nature's mighty king,
> To leave their first disordered combating
> And in a dance such measure to observe
> As all the world their motion should preserve.
>
> Since when they still are carried in a round,
> And changing, one in another's place,
> Yet do they neither mingle nor confound,
> But every one doth keep his bounded space
> Wherein the dance doth bid it turn or trace.
> This wondrous miracle doth Love devise,
> For dancing is Love's proper exercise. (verses 17–18)[11]

Here the very fabric of being in the four primal elements and the very fabric of space itself is imagined, not as a mechanical process, but as an exchange and

---

[10]   C.S. Lewis, *The Discarded Image An Introduction to Mediaeval and Renaissance Literature* (Cambridge, 1964).

[11]   Davies, *Poems*, p. 94; I have modernised the spelling

mutuality, a loving agreement figured as the elements dancing at the persuasion of Love. Love (significantly given a capital) takes the poet beyond the neoclassical God of Love invoked within the fictional framework of the poem, to God the Son, the Word, who was in the beginning through whom everything was made and whose other name, according to St John, is Love.[12]

The next verse gives an account of the creation of the heavens and with them the music of the spheres, that music, lost to man, that moves the rest of the cosmos:

> Like this he framed the gods' eternal bower
> And of a shapeless and confusèd mass,
> By his through-piercing and digesting power
> The turning vault of heaven formèd was,
> Whose starry wheels he hath so made to pass
> As that their movings do a music frame
> And they themselves still dance unto the same. (verse 19)[13]

So he presents the classical picture, Christianised, of a cosmos whose physical being is the outward manifestation of an inner ordering by love and harmony. But this does not mean to say that he is unaware of other possibilities. The materialist positivist reduction of all things and phenomena to the mechanical interaction of atoms (or 'motes' as Davies called them) had of course already been posited by Democritus and was well known to anyone with classical training. Indeed, in the next verse Davies raises that possibility only to dismiss it on the grounds that a world in which both harmony and redemption have meaning cannot be founded on the purely random or meaningless:

> Or if this *all* which round about we see,
> As idle Morpheus some sick brains have taught,
> Of undivided motes compact be,
> How was this goodly architecture wrought?
> Or by what means where they together brought?
> They err that say they did concur by chance;
> Love made them meet in a well-ordered dance. (verse 20)[14]

Here the sense is that, even if we admit – as is generally admitted today – that the basis of solid material reality is the movement of infinitely small particles, we are not committed thereby to saying their movement is random, in the sense of being without meaning. Recent work on the complexity and interrelatedness of subsystems in the cosmos is casting doubt on the theory of concurrence by chance so beloved of nineteenth-century science. It seems that present estimates of the age

---

[12] See 1 John 4:8ff.

[13] Davies, *Poems*, p. 5.

[14] Ibid.

of the cosmos simply do not allow enough time for order to have emerged from the purely random. These developments are well summarised in Roszak's later book *The Voice of the Earth*[15] and, more recently, in the section titled 'Beyond Atomism' in Mary Midgely's introduction to her *Science and Poetry*.[16] As Aristotle might have put it, the Material Science has made discoveries as to the *efficient* cause of the material world, but says nothing one way or the other about its *first, formal* or *final* causes.

Davies goes on in the next verse to develop the idea of music as a model both of creation and redemption:

> As when Amphion with his charming lyre
> Begot so sweet a siren of the air
> That with her rhetoric made the stones conspire
> The ruins of a city to repair,
> A work of wit, and reason's wise affair,
> So Love's smooth tongue the motes such measures taught
> That they joined hands, and so the world was wrought. (verse 21)[17]

Significantly, it is the power of music to redeem that is presented first before it becomes a model for creation. This is the right order both psychologically and theologically. First the ruined city of man's fallen estate must be repaired through the music of redemption; he must be cleansed of his illusion that his world is dead and lifeless, before he can see that the same love which repairs the ruins of his city is the love which is continually inspiring the dance of the 'motes' that make up the world's fabric

Having described the very beginning of creation and the work of redemption in human affairs as the work of the same music and dance of love, Davies goes on to celebrate the four elements. He sees them not as dead matter, nor as some impersonal environment, but as personal, engaged with us, something with which we are in an intimate, mutual and dependent relationship. The air is 'our tender nurse'; the sea at once embraces the earth and dances with the moon; the earth herself is seen as a mother from whose breasts we all draw our sustenance. In this he is both expressing in beautiful language the common understanding of his own age and also prophesying the discoveries of personal interdependence with our planet we have made, almost too late, in our own age.[18] Two of his verses celebrating the air will give something of the flavour of this approach:

---

15   Theodore Roszak, *The Voice of the Earth* (London, 1993), pp. 105ff.

16   Mary Midgely, *Science and Poetry* (London, 2001), pp.7ff

17   Davies, *Poems*, p. 96.

18   See, for example, James Lovelock, *Gaia: Medicine for an Ailing Planet* (London, 2005) and *The Revenge of Gaia* (London, 2007).

And now behold your tender nurse the Air
And common neighbour that ay runs around:
How many pictures and impressions faire
Within her empty regions are there found,
Which to your senses Dancing doe propound!
For what are Breath, Speech, Echoes, Music, Winds,
But Dancing's of the Air in sundry kinds?

For when you breathe, the air in order moves,
Now in, now out, in time and measure true;
And when you speak, so well she dancing loves,
That doubling oft, and oft redoubling new,
With thousand forms she doth her self endue:
For all the words that from our lips repair
Are nought but tricks and turnings of the air. (verses 33–34)[19]

These verses are a celebration of the atmosphere and breathing as at once music's medium and a form of dancing. 'Tender nurse' and 'common neighbour' are more than just poetic metaphors. They express a neighbourliness, a fellow-creatureliness which was once a key part of the Christian world-view but which was tragically lost sight of in the development of a supposedly more scientific and mechanistic view of the creation. Davies' skill in prosody gives him the power in the very medium of his verse to imitate and embody the rhythms and music of breathing which are his subjects:

For when you breathe, the air in order moves,
Now in, now out, in time and measure true; …

The rhythm of these words itself imposes on the reader a kind of calm and ordered meditative breathing, now in, now out, in time and measure true, just as the line 'That doubling oft, and oft redoubling new' exactly imitates in its form what it describes in its meaning.

This reflection on the mysteries and symmetries of speech in time, of a word incarnate as it were in the movement of the air as sound, goes back to Augustine who used it as a way of modelling the mystery of the Incarnation. He compared the pre-existent and eternal Word with the unspoken word in our minds, and the living breathing word made flesh, incarnate in Jesus Christ, with our uttered speech – the word expressed in breath and sound, articulated in time.

Davies goes on to develop the idea of music as a dancing of the air in a beautiful verse given over to a series of linked phrases apostrophising music, which, I think, in terms of form and precedent are the springboard and point of departure for Herbert's poem 'Prayer' which more famously employs the same technique:

---

[19]   Davies, *Poems*, pp.101–2

And thou sweet Music, Dancing's only life,
The ear's sole happiness, the air's best speech,
Loadstone of fellowship, charming-rod of strife,
The soft mind's Paradise, the sick mind's leach,
With thine own tongue, thou trees and stones canst teach,
That when the Air doth dance her finest measure,
Then art thou born, the god's and men's sweet pleasure. (verse 46)[20]

The same sense of kinship and neighbourliness with the rest of creation is evident in his treatment of the other elements as he sees them; his beautiful description of the sea, for instance, as being at once the earth and the moon's dancing partner:

For lo the Sea that fleets about the Land,
And like a girdle clips her solid waist,
Music and measure both doth understand:
For his great crystal eye is always cast
Up to the Moon, and on her fixèd fast:
And as she danceth in her pallid sphere,
So danceth he about his center here.

Sometimes his proud green waves in order set,
One after other flow unto the shore,
Which, when they have with many kisses wet,
They ebbs away in order as before;
And to make known his courtly love the more,
He oft doth lay aside his three-forkt mace,
And with his arms the timorous Earth embrace. (verses 49–50)[21]

Although *Orchestra* is essentially a poem imagining the order of the physical cosmos in terms of musical harmony and the movement of dance, these very metaphors allow Davies to move seamlessly from cosmic to human affairs. He makes the link between these realms, so divorced in our age, under the notions of *concord* and *comeliness*:

The richest jewel in all the heav'nly treasure
That ever yet unto the Earth was shown,
Is perfect Concord, th'onely perfect pleasure
That wretched earth-borne men have ever known,
For many harts it doth compound in one:
That when so one doth will, or speak, or doe,

---

[20]   Ibid., p. 102.
[21]   Ibid., p. 103.

With one consent they all agree thereto. (verse 109)[22]

Having begun with this fairly stock encomium, Davies goes on to develop a notion of Concord understood as mutual agreement, not by domination of the stronger will, nor by compromise, but by a harmonious conjunction of opposites and an ordering of variety into hierarchies. These hierarchies are not fixed and static, but dynamic and energising, which is why its combination of order with the energy of movement makes the art of dance such a useful metaphor for the kind of concord Davies is after:

> Concord's true picture shineth in this art,
> Where divers men and women rankèd be,
> And every one doth dance a several part,
> Yet all as one, in measure doe agree,
> Observing perfect uniformity;
> All turn together, all together trace,
> And all together honour and embrace. (verse 109)[23]

He goes on to use the striking phrase 'do as they dance' to describe ordered and energetic mutuality in a good marriage:

> If they whom sacred Love hath link't in one,
> Doe as they dance, in all their course of life,
> Never shall burning grief nor bitter moan,
> Nor factious difference, nor unkind strife,
> Arise betwixt the husband and the wife:
> For whether forth or back or round he go
> As the man doth, so must the woman doe. (verse 111)[24]

Having developed this image of concord he adds to it the notion of comeliness:

> For Comeliness is a disposing faire
> Of things and actions in fit time and place;
> Which doth in dancing show it self most clear,
> When troops confus'd, which here and there doe trace
> Without distinguishment or bounded space:
> By dancing's rule, into such ranks are brought,
> As glads the eye, as ravisheth the thought. (verse 114)[25]

---

[22]   Ibid., p. 119.
[23]   Ibid., p. 119.
[24]   Ibid., pp.119–20.
[25]   Ibid., p. 120.

This celebration of a 'disposing fair of things and actions in fit time and place' strongly anticipates what is being written now both by cosmologists and by systems theorists.[26]

This awareness of the comeliness and concord of things leads to an apprehension of the life of Reason within the world. This is not an appeal to a crudely mechanistic argument from design, with an image of God as solely a distant and detached clock-maker. Rather it involves a sense of the continuous indwelling of Reason (understood here in a sense that includes what we now call imagination). So although Davies knows and uses the image of the clock-maker, which was to become the sole and mechanistic image of the next three hundred years, he offers it not by itself but as one of a series of other images:

> Then why should Reason judge that reasonless
> Which is wit's offspring, and the work of art,
> Image of concord and of comeliness?
> Who sees a clock moving in every part,
> A sailing pinace, or a wheeling cart,
> But thinks that Reason, ere it came to pass
> The first impulsive cause and mover was?
>
> Who sees an Army all in rank advance,
> But deems a wise Commander is in place,
> Which leadeth on that brave victorious dance?
> Much more in Dancing's Art, in Dancing's grace,
> Blindness it self may Reason's footstep trace:
> For of Love's maze it is the curious plot,
> And of Man's fellowship the true-love knot. (verses 115–16)[27]

The ship in full sail is a beautiful image suggestive of the balance between force and chosen intention, a more fluid and living interrelationship of parts than the clock. This passage leaves us with that beautiful final image of Reason not as dry ratiocination, or the intellectualised and distant designer, but of one who leads us, even when we are blind, through the intricate maze of our life. Love makes the maze which reason dances us through. It was a cultural tragedy for us that in less than fifty years from the time these lines were written Reason had ceased to be the Lord of the Dance and become merely the clock-maker's apprentice.

If *Orchestra* gives us some hints of the relation between reason in us and order in the world, these hints are much more fully and comprehensively developed in *Nosce Teipsum*. A poem of nearly 2,000 lines, published in 1599 just three years after *Orchestra*, *Nosce Teipsum*, which took its title from the famous words of the oracle at Delphi, was subtitled:

---

[26]   See Roszak, *Voice of The Earth*, Chapters 4 and 6.
[27]   Davies, *Poems*, p. 121.

This oracle expounded in two Elegies.

1. Of Humane Knowledge
2. Of the Soul of Man and the immortality thereof.[28]

This poem opens, paradoxically with a great apostrophe against learning.

> Why did my parents send me to the Schools,
> That I with knowledge might enrich my mind?
> Since the desire to know first madé men fools,
> And did corrupt the root of all mankind. (lines 1–4)[29]

In this Davies is following the method of the formal *disputatio*, best exemplified by Thomas Aquinas' *Summa Theologia* which begins by expressing and acknowledging the force of the opposite point of view before enunciating one's own with the phrase *sed contra*.

After giving a pithy account of the Fall, Davies concludes that our fallen condition means that the relation between reason and passion has become disordered. Our failure to see the world as it really is is directly related to our pursuit of an isolated egotism:

> Even so by tasting of that fruit forbid,
> Where they sought knowledge, they did error find;
> Ill they desir'd to know, and ill they did;
> And to giue Passion eyes, made Reason blind.
>
> For then their minds did first in Passion see
> Those wretched shapes of misery and woe,
> Of nakedness, of shame, of poverty,
> Which then their own experience made them know.
>
> But then grew Reason dark, that she no more,
> Could the faire forms of Good and Truth discern;
> Bats they became, that eagles were before:
> And this they got by their desire to learn. (lines 25–36)[30]

However, the answer to this loss of insight is not to abandon reason or to distrust learning per se. It is instead to realise that our knowledge of the world, especially when the appetite for power and exploration drives the search for it, is flawed and dangerous, both for the world and for ourselves. The missing element is self-

---

[28] Ibid., p. 1.

[29] Ibid., p. 6.

[30] Ibid., pp. 6–7.

knowledge, the kind of self-knowledge that would lead us to understand that we are not self-made, we cannot isolate ourselves from the rest of creation and make our own meaning. We cannot account for the world and ourselves unless we look beyond ourselves to a source, a maker both of ourselves and of the world in which we participate. To do this we must begin by acknowledging the mystery of our own minds, we must cast back upon ourselves what Davies calls our understanding light. In so doing, Davies believes, we will encounter another light, an *understanding light* cast upon us from beyond ourselves and our world, a light which is at once the source of our consciousness and the source of the world of which we are conscious. That light is both the light of the world, and the light which lightens everyone who comes into the world, the second person of the holy and undivided Trinity – but this is to anticipate. Before he develops this theme Davies exclaims upon the strange paradox of our sophisticated knowledge of the world set against our wilful self-ignorance and, anticipating both Freud and Jung, suggests that we prefer to hide ourselves rather than know ourselves because we are afraid of what we might find:

> All things without, which round about we see,
> We seek to know, and how therewith to do:
> But that whereby we reason, live and be,
> Within our selves, we strangers are thereto.
>
> We seek to know the moving of each sphere,
> And the strange cause of th'ebs and floods of Nile;
> But of that clock within our breasts we bear,
> The subtle motions we forget the while.
>
> We that acquaint our selves with every Zone
> And pass both Tropics and behold the Poles
> When we come home, are to our selves unknown,
> And unacquainted still with our own souls.
>
> We study Speech but others we persuade;
> We leech-craft learn, but others cure with it;
> We interpret laws, which other men have made,
> But read not those which in our hearts are writ. (lines 89–104)[31]

In the next chapter we shall see how George Herbert develops this line of thought, about the strange ignorance at the heart of so much learning, through his two poems 'Vanity' and 'The Agony', but Davies goes on to ask *why* so much of our learning should be so hollow:

---

[31]   Ibid., p. 9.

Is it because the mind is like the eye,
Through which it gathers knowledge by degrees –
Whose rays reflect not, but spread outwardly:
Not seeing itself when other things it sees?

No, doubtless; for the mind can backward cast
Upon her self her understanding light;
But she is so corrupt, and so defac't,
As her own image doth her self affright. (lines 105–12)[32]

Davies goes on to argue that it is only when we suffer affliction that we are motivated to turn our attention inwards and ask serious questions of ourselves. In the poem affliction appears as a wise woman teaching him what he needs to know, rather as Philosophy appeared to Boethius, and her appearance leads to one of the poem's great set-piece expressions of the ambiguities and paradoxes of being human:

She within lists my ranging mind hath brought,
That now beyond my self I list not go;
My self am centre of my circling thought,
Only my self I study, learn, and know.

I know my body's of so frail a kind,
As force without, fevers within can kill:
I know the heavenly nature of my mind,
But 'tis corrupted both in wit and will:

I know my soul hath power to know all things,
Yet is she blind and ignorant in all;
I know I am one of nature's little kings,
Yet to the least and vilest things am thrall.

I know my life's a pain and but a span,
I know my Sense is mockt with every thing:
And to conclude, I know my self a man,
Which is a proud, and yet a wretched thing. (lines 165–80)[33]

These words conclude the first elegy, 'Of Humane Knowledge'. In the opening of the second elegy, 'Of the Soul of Man and the Immortality thereof', Davies goes on to develop the central idea, to which he alluded at the end of the first elegy, of the soul's 'understanding light', drawing an analogy between outer and inner

---

[32] Ibid.
[33] Ibid., p.11.

light, between the perception by means of sight of what is outward and visible and the self-knowledge that is inward and spiritual. To understand this analogy we have to realise that Davies did not think of sight and perception as passive faculties of the soul but rather as active powers. Perception happens through the meeting and commingling of two kinds of light. The eye takes in the outward light of the world in which it sees objects, but the perceiving soul is not a blank piece of photographic paper on which this light falls so as to record an impression. The perceiving soul goes out towards these objects, envelops them, comprehends their form; there are, as it were, rays from the eye, as well as to the eye which 'spread outwardly':

> Is it because the mind is like the eye,
> Through which it gathers knowledge by degrees –
> Whose rays reflect not, but spread outwardly:
> Not seeing itself when other things it sees? (lines 105–8)[34]

This difference in understanding the faculty of perception is part of a much bigger difference involving his entire understanding of the world. As we have seen from *Orchestra*, the cosmos was, for Davies and his contemporaries, not yet the huge, lifeless, inert thing 'out there'. Human consciousness was not yet seen as an islanded oddity, an accidental by-product of matter peculiar to one organism. Rather, the cosmos was a single thing interrelated in all its parts and the chief of those parts was man; he was the *microcosm* corresponding at every level of his physical and spiritual being with the *macrocosm* which was at once outside him and within him. The world was more like a living body to which we belong than a machine from which we are alienated. The sun and stars were not distant sources of light but eyes that look in on us as surely as our own eyes look out on them. Because Davies understands these lights as being themselves the eyes of this fair world, he also imagines his own eyes as being in some sense the lights of his own world, his microcosm. So he begins the second elegy:

> The lights of heav'n (which are the World's fair eyes)
> Look down into the World, the World to see:
> And as they turn or wander in the skies,
> Survey all things that on this centre bee.
>
> And yet the lights which in my tower do shine,
> Mine eyes which view all objects, nigh and far,
> Look not into this little world of mine,
> Nor see my face, wherein they fixed are. (lines 181–88)[35]

---

34   Ibid., p. 9.
35   Ibid., p.12.

The use of 'lights' to mean eyes survives today only in slang but once it carried with it the whole mysterious sense of our being in our own measure a 'little world' a microcosm. Davies continues:

> Since Nature fails us in no needful thing,
> Why want I means my inward self to see?
> Which sight the knowledge of my self might bring,
> Which to true wisdom is the first degree. (lines 189–92)[36]

He goes on to say that, just as there is an outer visible light to help me perceive the world and this outer and visible light is from beyond me, so likewise there must be a corresponding inner light which enables me to 'see' myself – that is, to be conscious:

> That Power which gave me eyes the World to view,
> To see my self infused an inward light,
> Whereby my soul, as by a mirror true,
> Of her own form may take a perfect sight,
>
> But as the sharpest eye discerneth nought,
> Except the sun-beams in the air doe shine:
> So the best soul with her reflecting thought,
> Sees not her self without some light divine. (lines 193–200)[37]

This is an essential principle of knowledge: each level of truth is only fully understood in terms of a truth beyond it from which it gets its underlying meaning and validation. As Davies says of the soul in a later verse:

> To judge her self she must her self transcend,
> As greater circles comprehend the less;
> But she wants power, her own powers to extend,
> As fettered men can not their strength express. (lines 249–52)[38]

Our current cultural crisis, the death-throes of modernism, has arisen because we have tried to account for the world of perception and consciousness at the reductive level of the material world, not realising that the material world itself can only be accounted for at the level of perception and consciousness. These in their turn are given their being and validation by that which transcends them but which they nevertheless 'participate'. As we are free to direct our attention where we please, there is a real choice to be made between consciously turning

---

[36]   Ibid.

[37]   Ibid.

[38]   Ibid., p. 14.

to and invoking a light which is the source our being, or choosing to ignore our source and constructing instead an imaginary world below or beneath us, of which we can be the abusive masters. This line of thinking was developed in depth by Owen Barfield, particularly in his *Saving the Appearances*.[39] There, he points out that, paradoxically, it is the human construction of a picture of the universe as supposedly dead, inert and merely material which may turn out to be the vain or 'false imagination', the idol from which we need to be liberated in our search for truth.[40]

However, before he can even begin to deal with the question of how our souls are related to our bodies and to the rest of the material world, Davies withdraws his eyes from the outer world of appearances and invokes that other and transcendent light, itself the source of the outward and visible light of our world. And he invokes it not as a desacralised 'energy' or as a *Star Wars*-style 'force', but as a person:

> O Light which mak'st the light, which makes the day!
> Which set'st the eye without, and mind within;
> Lighten my spirit with one clear heavenly ray,
> Which now to view it self doth first begin. (lines 201–4)[41]

'O Light which mak'st the light, which makes the day!' is perhaps one of the most beautiful lines in English verse, but what is it saying? Who is being addressed? Is this just an example of the rhetorical device of personifying abstracts or is there something more? In the context of the whole poem I have no doubt that Davies regards this act of invocation as an essential part of the process of discovering the truth which is the poem's object. All truth comes from and is confirmed by the One who is author both of the knower and the known. 'Lighten my spirit' is not merely an imitation of the classical invocation of the muse, it is a prayer to Christ made by an informed Christian poet. What is of special interest here is that Christ is being invoked not simply as a sign of personal salvation or as the climax of some drama of private piety, but as the *fons et origo* of objective truth about man and the cosmos. One could be forgiven for thinking, on the basis of some evangelistic rhetoric and practice, that *Jesus* was no more than a magic name assuring salvation and a quick fix for emotional crisis. This is because for a long time Christians have ceded the whole world of so-called objective or scientific truth to humanist atheism and contented themselves with a Christ who survives only on the Bantustan of the 'subjective realm' as a 'personal 'Lord and Saviour. To read Davies is to breathe another atmosphere altogether, where we are concerned to discover universal truth not simply to defend a personal life-style option. This 'Light', as Davies understood it, is Christ, from whom, for whom, in whom all things have their

---

[39]   Owen Barfield, *Saving The Appearances: A Study in Idolatry* (London, 1957).

[40]   Ibid., especially Chapter 2 on 'Collective Representations' and Chapter 7 on 'Appearance and Hypothesis'.

[41]   Davies, *Poems*, p. 12.

being. But it may be objected that Davies is here invoking light, or perhaps a kind of meta-light, something which is to light itself, what light is to us. What grounds have we for interpreting this verse as a conscious prayer to Christ for the revelation of truth to the poet? There are two ways of answering this question. The first is that Davies himself makes the identification of this 'Light which makes the light which makes the day' clear some verses later when he addresses Christ more clearly and in terms of incarnation:

> But Thou which didst man's soul of nothing make,
> And when to nothing it was fallen again,
> To make it new the form of man didst take,
> And God with God, becam'st a Man with men.
>
> Thou, that hast fashioned twice this soul of ours,
> So that she is by double title Thine,
> Thou only knowest her nature and her pow'rs,
> Her subtle form Thou only canst define ...
>
> But Thou bright Morning Star, Thou rising Sun,
> Which in these later times hast brought to light
> Those mysteries, that since the world begun,
> Lay hid in darkness and eternal night;
>
> Thou (like the sun) dost with indifferent ray,
> Into the palace and the cottage shine,
> And shew'st the soul both to the clerk and lay,
> By the clear lamp of Thy Oracle divine. (lines 241–48 and 253–60)[42]

But he is deliberate in addressing Christ *first* as light before bringing the rest of his more explicit Christology in. He is trying to appeal to everyone concerned with Reason and Truth, rather than just to those with their own Christian salvation history to tell. Perhaps he senses already that in the new age on whose threshold he stood, Christ was to dwindle into an item in private Christian narratives instead of being honoured as the light that lightens everyone who comes into the world.

The second way of clarifying Davies' intention in this beautiful invocation of Light which precedes his examination of the nature of the soul, is to see how a later poet, possibly taking his point of departure from this passage in Davies, developed this line of thinking. Milton's beautiful invocation of light at the beginning of Book III of *Paradise Lost* precedes his account of the Fall, in much the same way that Davies' invocation precedes his account of the nature of the soul. As we shall

---

[42]   Ibid., p.14.

see, Milton's invocation of light leads him even more deeply than Davies into meditation on the heart of God and his relations with us.[43]

Having invoked Christ as the light of his reason and imagination, Davies proceeds to an examination of the various purely material ways of accounting for the soul – that is, for the mystery of our consciousness. We are accustomed to the modernist myth of 'progress', the idea that a purely material and scientific account of the universe was a discovery made possible by the Enlightenment and, once grasped, became such a simple explanation of the world that God was no longer needed. Reading Davies therefore comes to some moderns as quite a shock. For Davies is perfectly familiar with the sort of reductive mindset we now associate with a writer like Richard Dawkins; ideas which we now express by saying that we are *just* a bundle of neurones, or *just* a set of conditioned responses, *just* the unwinding of a selfish gene. Davies impassively surveys these reductive ideas and sets them alongside some of the more fanciful occult theories of his own day:

> One thinks the soul is air; another, fire;
> Another blood, diffus'd about the heart;
> Another saith, the elements conspire,
> And to her essence each doth give a part.
>
> Musicians think our souls are harmonies,
> Physicians hold that they complexions bee;
> Epicures make them swarms of atomies,
> Which doe by chance into our bodies flee.
>
> Some think one general Soul fills every brain,
> As the bright sun sheds light in every star;
> And others think the name of soul is vain,
> And that we only well-mixt bodies are. (lines 209–20)[44]

Davies then proceeds to deal with the main reductive theories in turn. What he is attacking is what we might call the 'nothing but' or 'only' school of thought, which we called 'Scientism' in the introduction; consciousness is *nothing but* a twist of DNA, human culture is *only* the activity of a selfish gene, and so on. So Davies divides his poem into a series of headings emphasising the phrase 'more than', for example:

> 'That the soul is more then a perfection or reflection of the sense'
> 'That the soul is more than the temperature of the humours of the body'.

---

[43]   See below p.136–43.

[44]   Davies, *Poems*, p. 13.

In his section on the relation of the soul to the operation of the senses, Davies makes some useful distinctions, particularly about the difference between the mere perception, the mechanical registering as it were, of phenomena, and the inner understanding of their form and meaning. This is a distinction that is crucial to our understanding of the difference between art and photography, between reportage and poetry. It allows us to understand the function of art in opening up insight into the inner beauty and meaning of experience, into what Hopkins called *inscape*, rather than just recording the outer experience. So Davies begins by rejecting the (currently fashionable) view that consciousness *emerges* from the mechanical complexity of the human body:

> Are they not senseless then, that think the Soul
> Nought but a fine perfection of the Sense,
> Or of the forms which fancy doth enrol,
> A quick resulting, and a consequence? (lines 209–20)[45]

He goes on to point out that perception involves not simply recording but interpreting, sometimes reinterpreting, what our senses tell us in terms of what our reason has taught us:

> What is it then that doth the Sense accuse,
> Both of false judgements, and fond appetites?
> What makes us do what Sense doth most refuse?
> Which oft in torment of the Sense delights?
>
> Sense thinks the planets, spheres not much asunder:
> What tells us then their distance is so far?
> Sense thinks the lightning borne before the thunder:
> What tells us then they both together are? (lines 393–400)[46]

He also points out that to derive the soul from the operations of the body is to marginalise all those whose bodies are frail or disabled. Instead he shows that it is often from the weak and the frail that we have the truest perceptions and the deepest insights into life:

> If we had nought but Sense, then only they
> Should have sound minds, which have their Senses sound:
> But Wisdom grows, when Senses do decay,
> And Folly most in quickest Sense is found. (lines 421–24)[47]

---

[45] Ibid., p. 18.
[46] Ibid., p. 19.
[47] Ibid., p. 20.

And then he comes to the distinction, so crucial for understanding both of poetry and faith, between the mere recording of experience and the insight which grasps its substance. This distinction is immediately followed by the insight that our perception of the world is not a *passive receptivity* but a conscious extension of the *active power* of the soul (a power which Coleridge came to name and understand as *Primary Imagination*):

> Sense outsides knows; the Soul thro' al things sees:
> Sense, circumstance; she doth the substance view:
> Sense sees the bark, but she, the life of trees:
> Sense hears the sounds, but she, the concords true. (lines 433–36)[48]

Here, Davies is dealing at a philosophical level with the very same issues which Seamus Heaney and George Herbert dealt with emblematically. 'Sense outside knows; the soul through all things sees' is the insight that underlies the verse:

> A man that looks on glass
> On it may stay his eye
> Or if he pleaseth through it pass
> And then the heavens espy.[49]

In just the same way the distinction between merely hearing the sounds on the one hand and hearing the concords true on the other underlies Heaney's discovery in 'the fall of grit or dry seeds' of 'a music you never would have known to listen for'.

Davies is not arguing against the material base of our perceptions; he is including it in his picture. But he is arguing against the positivist reduction of *everything* to the level of the material base. Having made his distinctions, Davies goes on to emphasise that it is not a dualistic division:

> But why do I the Soul and Sense divide?
> When Sense is but a power, which she extends,
> Which being in diverse parts diversified,
> The diverse forms of objects apprehends?
>
> This power spreads outward, but the root doth grow
> In th'inward Soul, which only doth perceiue;
> For th'eyes and ears no more their objects know,
> Then glasses know what faces they receive ...

---

[48]   Ibid.,

[49]   'The Elixir', in George Herbert, *The Complete English Works*, ed. A. Pasternak Slater (London,1995), p. 180.

Then is the Soul a nature, which contains
The power of Sense, within a greater power
Which doth employ and use the Senses pains,
But sits and rules within her private bower. (lines 437–44 and 449–52)[50]

The power of sense lies 'within a greater power'! It would take the passing of another two hundred years for another philosopher poet to develop a fuller understanding of that 'greater power' and to name it as Imagination. Davies was criticising bleak reductionism before it had really got into full swing; Coleridge was fighting for spiritual life and breath when what he called 'the watch-making scheme of things' and the 'despotism of the eye'[51] was at its height. In the *Biographia Literaria* he turned to Davies to try and express the liberating sense of imagination, not as a retreat from reality but as an essential power with which we engage reality. In the wonderful fourteenth chapter of the *Biographia*, 'On the Definitions of a Poem and Poetry', Coleridge says that 'the poet, described in ideal perfection, brings the whole soul of man into activity'.[52] It is perhaps this thinking of the whole soul of man that puts him in mind of Davies, whom he quotes but with the proviso that what Davies imputes to the soul he wants to name as the work of imagination. He cites a passage from this section in which Davies deals with the relations of the soul and the senses. Davies is asking how it is that the materiality of both sense perception and the objects of sense perception can be, as it were, transmuted or sublimated into spiritual perceptions. For Coleridge, the active power of imagination is the key:

'Doubtless,' as Sir John Davies observes of the soul (and his words may with slight alteration be applied, and even more appropriately, to the poetic IMAGINATION.)

Doubtless this could not be, but that she turns
Bodies to spirit by sublimation strange,
As fire converts to fire the things it burns,
As we our food into our nature change.

From their gross matter she abstracts their forms,
And draws a kind of quintessence from things;
Which to her proper nature she transforms
To bear them light on her celestial wings.

Thus does she when from individual states

---

[50]   Davies, *Poems*, p. 20.

[51]   See, for example, *Samuel Taylor Coleridge, Biographia Literaria*, ed. J. Engell and W.J. Bate (Princeton, 1983), I, p.107, and II, p. 75n (Volume 7 in CC).

[52]   Ibid., II, pp. 15–16.

She doth abstract the universal kinds;
Which then re-clothed in divers names and fates
Steal access through our senses to our minds.[53]

Coleridge was not quoting directly from a copy of Davies' works but from an entry in his notebooks made in 1811. Typically, both memory and imagination were at work as Coleridge responded to Davies, and in fact the third stanza quoted here he had substantially re-written, improving on Davies' verse. 'Steal access through our senses to our mind', for instance, is pure Coleridge and a real improvement on Davies' original line 548: 'and can be lodged but only in our minds'.[54]

Having wrestled with the relation between sense impression and spiritual insight, Davies goes on to deal with the more general question of how the soul is united to the body, that is to say what is the relation in us between the spiritual and the physical. If we agree that it is absurd to locate the soul in a physical organ such as the heart or the brain, but agree equally that our intrinsic person-hood is nevertheless linked at every turn with our bodies, how are we to picture this union of our natures? In a beautiful passage addressing this question, Davies throws off a whole series of possibilities, each of which has merit and represents a well-established position in this ancient debate, only to reject them all in favour of his original and beloved image of light:

In what manner the Soul is united to the Body.

But how shall we this union well express?
Nought ties the soul; her subtlety is such
She moves the body, which she doth possess,
Yet no part toucheth, but by virtue's touch.

Then dwells she not therein as in a tent,
Nor as a pilot in his ship doth sit;
Nor as the spider in his web is pent;
Nor as the wax retains the print in it;

Nor as a vessel water doth contain;
Nor as one liquor in another shed;
Nor as the heat doth in the fire remain;
Nor as a voice throughout the air is spread:

But as the faire and cheerful Morning light,
Doth here and there her silver beams impart,
And in an instant doth her self unite

---

[53]   Ibid., II, p. 17.
[54]   Davies, *Poems*, p.23.

To the transparent air, in all, and part:

Still resting whole, when blows the air divide;
Abiding pure, when th'air is most corrupted;
Throughout the air, her beams dispersing wide,
And when the air is tossed, not interrupted:

So doth the piercing Soul the body fill,
Being all in all, and all in part diffus'd,
Indivisible, incorruptible still,
Not forc't, encountered, troubled or confused.

And as the sun above, the light doth bring,
Though we behold it in the air below;
So from th'Eternal Light the Soul doth spring,
Though in the body she her powers do show. (lines 897–924)[55]

There is a great deal of food for meditation in this suggestion that the soul is to the body what light is to the air. The sense of its being diffused in every part, rather then reserved in some special place, does justice to our incarnate physicality, our sense of identity with every part of our bodies. At the same time the independence of light from air, its pure continuance as light even when the air, which is its medium, is troubled divided or clouded, speaks of the proper independence of our spiritual nature from being fundamentally impaired by the vicissitudes of our bodily life. This understanding, which led Davies to praise the insights of the weak and frail, has a special relevance to our approach to people with Alzheimer's disease, and other conditions which manifest in apparent disturbance of the essential person but whose root is in a disturbance of their bodies. Is a person brain-damaged in an accident essentially wounded in their innermost being, or only in its medium of expression? Because that person's soul has always shone to us through the whole body and can hardly speak through the broken one we are tempted to feel that the person we love is lost or changed. This beautiful stanza of Davies' challenges that attitude:

Still resting whole, when blows the air divide;
Abiding pure, when th'air is most corrupted;
Throughout the air, her beams dispersing wide,
And when the air is tossed, not interrupted …

How well the language of 'blows', 'corruption' and 'dispersal' answers to our experience of bodily life, our own physical fragility and the vulnerability of those we love, and how much therefore we also need to hear the counterweighted words,

---

[55]   Ibid., p. 35.

which Davies sets down for the soul on the other side of the scales: 'still resting whole, abiding pure, not interrupted'.

And so, at the end of this section, Davies returns to the insight in his first invocation of light, that even the soul's 'understanding light', cast backward in meditation upon herself, has a source beyond herself in that eternal Light who is not simply a substance but a person, whose being is in the communion of Love:

> And as the sun above, the light doth bring,
> Though we behold it in the air below;
> So from th'Eternal Light the Soul doth spring,
> Though in the body she her powers do show.

The rest of the poem involves a great deal of technical discussion about the way the soul operates within and through the body, but Davies ends by returning to the question of the soul's immortality. He supplements the old Platonic image of death as jail-delivery with the more Christian and incarnate image of death as a new birth. He begins by imagining birth from the point of view of the babe in the womb who knows only the world he is leaving and not the unknown world into which he is being born:

> The first life, in the mother's womb is spent,
> Where she her nursing power doth only use;
> Where, when she finds defect of nourishment,
> She expels her body, and this world she views.
>
> This we call Birth; but if the child could speak,
> He Death would call it; and of Nature plain,
> That she would thrust him out naked and weak,
> And in his passage pinch him with such pain. (lines 1865–72)[56]

He goes on to describe our growth in the new life to which we are born and the awakening of Reason, which, as we have seen, includes for Davies the awakening of the spiritual and imaginative life:

> Yet, out he comes, and in this world is placed
> Where all his Senses in perfection bee:
> Where he finds flowers to smell, and fruits to taste;
> And sounds to hear, and sundry forms to see.
>
> When he hath past some time upon this stage,
> His Reason then a little seems to wake;
> Which, though the spring, when sense doth fade with age,

---

[56]   Ibid., p. 65.

Yet can she here no perfect practise make. (lines 1873–80)[57]

This awakening of reason can itself be a preparation for the next departure and discovery which is death, reimagined by Davies as a new birth:

> Then doth th'aspiring Soul the body leave,
> Which we call Death; but were it known to all,
> What life our souls do by this death receive,
> Men would it birth or gaol delivery call.
>
> In this third life, Reason will be so bright,
> As that her spark will like the sun-beams shine,
> And shall of God enioy the real sight.
> Being still increased by influence divine. (lines 1881–88)[58]

The whole poem ends with an acclamation appealing to us not to despise, marginalise or ignore the hidden spiritual dimension of our life, this light that pervades the atmosphere of our bodies. It is as though Davies could foresee the coming disaster of reductionism, could foresee the modern consumerist world into which most of us were born: a world in which no one is credited with a soul, everyone is analysed as complexes and chemicals and valued only as a potential consumer; a world where no meaning or value is given us or lasts for ever, where we choose, not between eternal destinies but between life-style options; a world where we compensate for our meaninglessness and poor self-esteem with sex and shopping, but still despair when death comes. Davies stands at the threshold of that modern world, but still carrying in every fibre of his being the spiritual insights of the ancient world, its symbols and its courtesies. Looking out from that perspective at the generations to come, those who would be born robbed of their spiritual inheritance, he says in the closing stanzas of his poem:

> O ignorant poor man! what dost thou bear
> Locked up within the casket of thy breast?
> What jewels, and what riches hast thou there!
> What heavenly treasure in so weak a chest!
>
> Look in thy soul, and thou shalt beauties find,
> Like those which drowned Narcissus in the flood:
> Honour and Pleasure both are in thy mind,
> And all that in the world is counted Good. (lines 1889–96)[59]

---

57 Ibid., p. 65.
58 Ibid., pp. 65–66.
59 Ibid., p. 66.

And having affirmed that inner treasure our age has hastened to write off, he goes
on to encourage us in the face of death:

> And when thou think'st of her eternity,
> Think not that Death against her nature is;
> Think it a birth: and when thou goest to die,
> Sing like a swan, as if thou went'st to bliss.
>
> And if thou, like a child, didst fear before,
> Being in the dark, where thou didst nothing see;
> Now I have brought thee torch-light, fear no more;
> Now when thou diest, thou canst not hoodwinked be. (lines 1905–12)[60]

Finally, in a characteristic touch of humility, he makes a fitting end to a poem
about self-knowledge by returning to a sense of his own self-ignorance as well as
self-knowledge. At the end of his own effort as a maker, a poet he loses himself in
praise of his own Maker:

> And thou my Soul, which turn'st thy curious eye,
> To view the beams of thine own form divine,
> Know, that thou canst know nothing perfectly,
> While thou art clouded with this flesh of mine.
>
> Take heed of over-weening, and compare
> Thy peacock's feet with thy gay peacock's train:
> Study the best and highest things that are,
> But of thy self an humble thought retain.
>
> Cast down thy self, and only strive to raise
> The glory of thy Maker's sacred Name:
> Use all thy powers, that Blessed Power to praise,
> Which gives thee power to be, and use the same. (lines1913–24)[61]

Davies stood at the threshold of modernism and tried to foresee and forestall
some of its worst excesses. We stand at the end of the modernist period, on the
threshold of post-modernism, when the consensus of the Enlightenment project is
breaking up on every side. We need to return to the teaching of poets like Davies
who mediate to us the insights of the pre-modern age, which speak directly to the
heart of a post-modern cultural crisis. The Enlightenment apartheid of which we
spoke in the Introduction, beginning in Davies' own day, became more and more
pervasive as the years passed. But Davies was not a lone voice and the poets

---

[60]   Ibid.
[61]   Ibid., p. 67.

and artists kept a counter-vision alive, ready for the time when, in our own age, not only other artists but philosophers and scientists would be ready to share and explore their vision. Mary Midgely makes a strong case that the time for such a reintegration of our vision has arrived, particularly in her discussion of 'The Cognitive Role of Poetry' in the chapter on 'Rationality and Rainbows' in *Science and Poetry*.[62] In the next chapter we shall look at some of the seventeenth-century poets who, against the more hostile spirit of their age, continued and developed some of the ancient insights which Davies had preserved, before examining how Coleridge has laid the philosophical foundations for the reintegration of ours ways of knowing which we so desperately need.

---

[62]   Midgely, *Science and Poetry*, pp. 38ff

Chapter 4

A Second Glance: Transfigured Vision in the Poems of John Donne and George Herbert

Introduction

> ... our concern was speech, and speech impelled us,
> To purify the dialect of the tribe
> And urge the mind to aftersight and foresight ...[1]

These words (spoken by the familiar compound ghost, who is part-Dante part-Yeats part-Milton, to Eliot in the last of the *Four Quartets*) embody the changeless task of poetry in every generation, which is to give us more than merely outward or momentary sight of our lives. Here Eliot emphasises the 'double vision' of aftersight and foresight; and indeed the simultaneous vision of past and present, the full realisation, in a moment of intense awareness, of what he called 'the present moment of the past',[2] is both a feature of Eliot's own poetry and a characteristic he noticed and emphasised in the poetry of others. The role of poet as guardian and purifier of speech, as the one who would enable language to open up new vistas rather than close them down, would become more and more important as the tenor and spirit of the age moved from late mediaevalism towards modernism.

Davies had made the distinction between vision of the surface and vision of the depth:

> Sense outsides knows; the Soule thro' al things sees:
> Sense, circumstance; she, doth the substance view:
> Sense sees the barke, but she, the life of trees:
> Sense heares the sounds, but she, the concords true.[3]

The poet's task is to allow the vision of the soul to underlie the vision of the senses so that for a moment we see both the outside and the essence.

The old culture had inherited the notion that the two great books we are given to read are the Word and the Works of God. Both these books were revered and read as mysteries, as poetry. Every story in scripture was seen to contain multiple

---

[1] T.S. Eliot, 'Little Gidding', lines 126–29, in *The Four Quartets* (London, 1944).

[2] T.S. Eliot, *Selected Prose*, ed. F. Kermode (London, 1975), p. 44.

[3] *Nosce Teipsum*, lines 433–36, in *The Poems of Sir John Davies*, ed. R. Krueger (Oxford, 1975), p. 20.

layers of meaning in allegory, symbol and typology. Understanding the first and literal meaning was just the first step in penetrating the mysteries of God's word. Likewise, God's works, the book of nature, were read in an equally polysemous and symbolic way. Natural philosophers were concerned both to discover the literal content of God's works, the physical properties of nature, and also to read the symbolism of nature, to understand the truths and meanings being conveyed to humanity from God through the language of his works. As our culture approached modernity, however, it became more one-levelled and literal in its interpretation of the world of exterior phenomena. The phenomenal world around us was to be understood only at the level of what could be measured and observed; the sun and stars to be understood only as a physical objects blindly obeying the laws of motion, rather than as the eyes of heaven, the living symbols and celebrants of a light greater than their own. This new naively literal reading of a once polysemous nature was the foundation of the new science. A parallel loss of subtlety, a parallel reduction of the multiplicity of symbol and suggestion into a single and literal denotation was taking place in the reading of the other book, the book of the scriptures. Just as the world was being reduced from Davies' Love-led dance to Newton's piece of clockwork, so in the same spirit the scriptures were being read less as inspired poetry and more as the clock-maker's manual. It fell to the poets, caught between these two blinkered rationalisms, to preserve and develop the power inherent in language to mean more than one thing. Davies' 'double vision', the experience of seeing at once a surface and a depth, of 'staying our eye' on glass at one moment, and passing through it the next, is mirrored in the action of metaphor in language. When language is used metaphorically we see at one and the same time the literal image and, through it, another reality or experience, which the image symbolises. By making metaphors with words that had been relegated to the merely literal, poets could restore to the imagination the possibility of transcendence. They could suggest by the very form of their art that, just as words are signs of something beyond themselves, so the things to which words point might also be the signs and symbols of a language, and not simply the parts of a clock.

In the course of this chapter we shall look at the work of two of the so-called Metaphysical Poets, John Donne and George Herbert, considering this vocation of poetry to enable us to see with a 'double vision'. In Donne, we will see how playfulness with language, delight in sudden reversals of perspective and the discovery in the everyday of metaphors which transform our understanding leads to the deepest perspective shift of all, the movement from our own vision and gazing to the transfiguring gaze that God casts on us. In Herbert, we shall see how the poet's power to turn the glassy surface of outer knowledge into a window on the heavens leads us to the possibility of a knowledge transformed by the One who is both the light of heaven and the light of the world

Mapping New Worlds, John Donne and the Power of Metaphor

Donne's intellect and imagination delighted in double visions and multiple meanings. He was fascinated by the representation of one thing within and through another, by the correspondences between inner and outer worlds, by the shifts in perspective and dimension which could be produced by moving suddenly, by means of metaphor, between the many worlds of his intellect and imagination. It is not surprising to discover that he was fascinated by the reflections of the great cosmos in the tiny world of an eye or a teardrop, by the mapping of the *microcosmos* of man onto the huge *cosmos* of the world and the heavens, and fascinated therefore by maps and mapping of all kinds. He saw especially in the new science of projection, particularly Mercator's projection whereby the round, three-dimensional world could nevertheless be represented in two dimensions on paper, a real model for the way in which his art could re-present our this-worldly experience to include or suggest its hidden other-worldly dimension. This playful but concentrated fascination with representation and mapping extends through both his love poetry and his devotional poetry. Emotional, imaginative, sexual and spiritual insights are all integrated and interlinked in Donne in a way that is perhaps unequalled in any other writer.

Pursuing his inter-connected person/world/map metaphors first through two 'secular' and then through two 'sacred' poems can open up these powers and possibilities in Donne's poetry. We will begin with 'The Good Morrow':[4]

> I wonder by my troth, what thou, and I
> Did, till we lov'd? were we not wean'd till then?
> But suck'd on country pleasures, childishly?
> Or snorted we in the seven sleepers den?
> T'was so; But this, all pleasures fancies bee.
> If ever any beauty I did see,
> Which I desir'd, and got, t'was but a dream of thee.
>
> And now good morrow to our waking souls,
> Which watch not one another out of fear;
> For love, all love of other sights controls,
> And makes one little room, an every where.
> Let sea-discoverers to new worlds have gone,
> Let Maps to other, worlds on worlds have shown,
> Let us possess one world, each hath one, and is one.
>
> My face in thine eye, thine in mine appears,
> And true plain hearts doe in the faces rest,

---

4   In *The Poems of John Donne*, ed. H. Grierson (Oxford, 1949), p. 7; I have modernised the spelling.

> Where can we find two better hemispheres
> Without sharp North, without declining West?
> What ever dyes, was not mixt equally;
> If our two loves be one, or, thou and I
> Love so alike, that none doe slacken, none can die.

The poem opens in a natural and conversational way, with direct language and the rhythms of natural speech (something which was to be lost from English poetry for most of the next century until Wordsworth and Coleridge recovered it in *Lyrical Ballads*). We are disarmed by the frankness of his opening exclamation and are expecting something very straightforward and literal, when at the close of the first stanza Donne introduces the first of his metaphors of a multi-levelled reality, of 'worlds on worlds' nested within one another:

> If ever any beauty I did see,
> Which I desir'd, and got, t'was but a dream of thee.

At their first and simplest level these lines are simply a combination of amorous boasting and apology. *If* ever any beauty I did see which I desired, might leave the emphasis on the *if,* and let the person to whom this poem is addressed guess she is the first, but the barely concealed pride in Donne's little rider 'and got' leaves us in no doubt that at the very moment he appears to be apologising for his sexual experience he is actually making a boast of it. *If,* indeed. Then comes the brilliant turn whereby he offers his past conquests up to his present love – ''twas but a dream of thee'.

Suddenly, in the midst of this back-handed compliment we have one of Donne's vertiginous shifts of perspective: what was the real world just half a line ago turns out to have been only a dream from which he wakes to and with his present lover, and all the former beauties of his life were like the shadows in Plato's cave, images which beckon us beyond themselves to another and greater beauty from which they drew their grace. Our imagination is prepared in these lines for the worlds on worlds to be encountered by our 'waking souls' in the next stanza:

> For love, all love of other sights controls,
> And makes one little room, an every where.

The power of making one little room an everywhere ascribed here to love is of course also the power of imagination working in and through both reader and poet. The whole world can be re-presented recapitulated in a room and its furnishings (an idea Donne develops in 'The Sun Rising') or in the bodies of two lovers each representing and recapitulating the great world they inhabit as surely as a map. Donne summons the exuberance and adventure of his age of discovery and makes it also mean the adventure and discovery of his loving:

Let sea-discoverers to new worlds have gone,
Let Maps to other, worlds on worlds have shown,
Let us possess one world, each hath one, and is one.

The bodies of the lovers become the maps of worlds yet to be discovered, a conceit he developed in more detail in poems like 'Love's Progress'[5] and 'On Going to Bed'.[6] With a play on 'discover' - 'O my America, my new-found land … how blest am I in this discovering thee' (lines 27–30)[7] – we move then (naturally) from discovery to possession. A lesser poet would have left it here, probably with something very obvious about planting the flag, but Donne in another perspective-shift moves us first from one possessing another to both possessing a mutual world, through to being worlds themselves: 'Let us possess one world, each hath one, and is one' (a variant reading has 'let us possess *our* world'. It is not simply that their love makes a new world, which they share, but that each of them as a microcosm of the great world is a world for the other to know and explore.) Further, just as the great world of the macrocosm is recapitulated afresh in the little worlds of Donne and his lover, so they are each in turn recapitulated in each other, each carrying the other's heart – an idea expressed under the image of their mutual reflections in each other's eyes:

My face is thine eye, thine in mine appears,
And true plain hearts doe in the faces rest …

This wonderfully detailed observation, like Heaney's 'ear of a raindrop', is the outward image and expression of true lovers' inward desire to be in some otherwise inexpressible way within one another. The curvature of the surface of the eye suggests the curvature of the hemispheres of the great world and we return for a second to that macro-level. But this time it is the inner-world of Donne's imaginative fantasy that becomes greater than, and forms a critique of, the outward and visible hemispheres we inhabit:

Where can we find two better hemispheres
Without sharp North, without declining West?

The outer hemispheres of the visible world are subject to change and decay, the 'sharp north' representing the cold that might freeze the warmth of love, the declining west representing sunset; the end of love's day, and ultimately, as we shall see in the other poems, Death itself. Donne holds out to us, as to himself and his lover, the tantalising possibility that this world of change and decay might be only the copy, shadow or dream of the real world of their love that transcends

---

5   Donne, *The Poems*, pp. 103–6.
6   Ibid., pp. 106–8.
7   Ibid., p.107.

it. The imperfect mixture of the elements, in the macrocosm, the humours in the microcosm which make for change and decay, are perhaps reordered and perfectly mixed in the new and transcendent world Love makes; but of course in a last tease Donne makes it all hang on an 'if' – a pretty big if, perhaps the same if with which he closed the first stanza:

> If our two loves be one, or, thou and I
> Love so alike, that none do slacken, none can die.

The notion that love can make this little room an everywhere is developed at large in 'The Sunne Rising'[8] another love poem, like 'The Good Morrow', in the tradition of the aubade:

The Sun Rising

> Busie old fool, unruly Sun,
>   Why dost thou thus
> Through windows, and through curtains call on us?
> Must to thy motions lovers' seasons run?
>   Saucy pedantic wretch, go chide
>   Late school boys, and sour prentices,
>   Go tell Court-huntsmen, that the King will ride,
>   Call country ants to harvest offices;
> Love, all alike, no season knowes, nor clyme,
> Nor houres, dayes, moneths, which are the rags of time.
>
>   Thy beams, so reverend, and strong
>   Why shouldst thou think?
> I could eclipse and cloud them-with a wink,
> But that I would not lose her sight so long:
>   If her eyes have not blinded thine,
>   Look, and to morrow late, tell me,
>   Whether both the'India's of spice and Mine
>   Be where thou leftst them, or lie here with me.
> Ask for those Kings whom thou saw'st yesterday,
> And thou shalt hear, All here in one bed lay.
>   She is all States, and all Princes, I,
>   Nothing else is.
> Princes doe but play us; compar'd to this,
> All honour's mimic; All wealth alchemy.
>   Thou sun art half as happy as we,
>   In that the world's contracted thus;
>   Thine age asks ease, and since thy duties bee
>   To warm the world, that's done in warming us.

---

8   Ibid., pp. 10–11.

Shine here to us, and thou art every where;
This bed thy center is, these walls, thy sphere.

Coleridge said of this poem that it showed a 'Fine vigorous exaltation, both soul and body in full puissance'[9] and certainly one feels the bliss of love fulfilled filling the language with a kind of careless glory, a happy splendour before which even the sun in his glory is only a busy old fool. Love fulfilled has filled the present moment with an experience of such intensity that the passage of time outside that love seems poor and ragged:

Love, all alike, no season knows, nor clime,
Nor hours, days, months, which are the rags of time.

Donne is here celebrating secular, erotic love, but he was well aware that such ecstasy, in which time itself and the world are for a moment transcended, was a type of that greater awareness of the eternal which arises when the soul is wooed by God. Indeed he was not afraid, in a later sermon when he was Dean of Saint Paul's, to take up again his great phrase about the rags of time in relation to God's mercy:

We begin with that which is elder than our beginning, and shall overlive our end,
the mercy of God ... The names of first and last derogate from it, for first and
last are but rags of time, and his mercy hath no relation to time, no limitation in
time, it is not first nor last, but eternal, everlasting.[10]

In his second verse Donne plays with the analogy between the sun and the eye which we saw was so strong in Davies, introducing a characteristically playful reversal of perspective whereby the sight of the sun, the great eye of nature, depends on our eyes and not the other way round. In the poem Donne and his lover are the centre, the *fons et origo* of a new world, and every outer reality depends on them. He has only to blink and the corresponding eye of the sun is closed:

Thy beams, so reverend, and strong
Why shouldst thou think?
I could eclipse and cloud them-with a wink,
But that I would not lose her sight so long: ...

---

[9]   Samuel Taylor Coleridge, *Marginalia*, vol. II, ed. G. Whalley (Princeton, 1984), p. 219 (Volume 12 in CC).

[10]   Preached Christmas 1624. Collected in *The Sermons of John Donne*, ed. G.R. Potter and E.M. Simpson, 10 vols (Los Angeles, 1953–62; re-issued 1984), vol. VI, p. 170.

In the normal world the light of the sun might blind our eyes, but in the poem the eyes of Donne's lover shine so brightly that she might blind the sun; Donne then shifts perspective and, from being luminaries themselves, he makes the lovers and their bed into an entire world, reversing the usual microcosm/macrocosm analogy. We are the macrocosm, the great world, Donne is saying, it is the so-called real outer world that is the tiny and pale imitation:

> If her eyes have not blinded thine,
>   Look, and to morrow late, tell me,
> Whether both the'India's of spice and Mine
>   Be where thou leftst them, or lie here with me.
> Ask for those Kings whom thou saw'st yesterday,
> And thou shalt hear, All here in one bed lay.

Donne maps the great world onto his lover's body; in bed with her he has explored the two Indias of spice and mine. (The detail of this nice analogy is made more explicit in Loves Progress,[11] a journey across the body; here it is just a hint). One little room has indeed become an 'everywhere', and he can boast that 'Nothing else is'. He delights in the power of imagination to incarnate the vast into the tiny, a kind of shadow of the incarnation, the worlds 'contracted thus'. Of course he is playing, impishly and in a kind of glad wantonness, with powerful ideas whose truer meaning and proper application he also knew and revered, the answering poem to this conceit of the world contracted to a lovers' bed is in the beautiful line on the incarnation in his sonnet to Mary: 'Immensity cloistered in thy dear womb'.[12]

That lovely line from 'Nativity' in *Holy Sonnets* brings us to consideration of two sacred poems in which Donne continues to explore the possibilities in the triple vision which overlays world/body/map. We will look first at his 'Hymn to God my God, in my Sickness':[13]

> Since I am coming to that holy room,
>   Where, with thy choir of saints for evermore,
> I shall be made thy music; as I come
>   I tune the instrument here at the door,
>   And what I must do then, think here before.
>
> Whilst my physicians by their love are grown
>   Cosmographers, and I their map, who lie
> Flat on this bed, that by them may be shown
>   That this is my south-west discovery,

---

[11]   Donne, *The Poems*, pp. 103–6.

[12]   Ibid., p. 290.

[13]   Ibid., pp. 336–37.

Per fretum febris, by these straits to die,

I joy, that in these straits I see my west;
 For, though their currents yield return to none,
What shall my west hurt me? As west and east
 In all flat maps (and I am one) are one,
 So death doth touch the resurrection.

Is the Pacific Sea my home? Or are
 The eastern riches? Is Jerusalem?
Anyan, and Magellan, and Gibraltar,
 All straits, and none but straits, are ways to them,
 Whether where Japhet dwelt, or Cham, or Shem.

We think that Paradise and Calvary,
 Christ's cross, and Adam's tree, stood in one place;
Look, Lord, and find both Adams met in me;
 As the first Adam's sweat surrounds my face,
 May the last Adam's blood my soul embrace.

So, in his purple wrapp'd, receive me, Lord;
 By these his thorns, give me his other crown;
And as to others' souls I preach'd thy word,
 Be this my text, my sermon to mine own:
 'Therefore that he may raise, the Lord throws down.'

This poem opens with a metaphor drawn from music making; life is a tuning of the instrument before we enter the holy room of heaven:

Since I am coming to that holy room,
 Where, with thy choir of saints for evermore,
I shall be made thy music; as I come
 I tune the instrument here at the door,
 And what I must do then, think here before.

This verse almost stands alone like an opening chord in a composition as for the rest of the poem Donne turns not to music but to map-making and cosmography for a key to transfiguring his experience. For transfiguration is what this poem is all about; glimpsing the possibility of renewal in the midst of sickness and death, catching a phrase of the music 'you would never have known to listen for' in the 'fall of grit and dry seeds' which is Donne's approaching physical death. After the first stanza's glimpse of heaven by way of prelude, the poem returns to the grim insistence of Donne's present experience as a fevered patient, flattened and sweating on his bed, being pored over and prodded by his doctors as though he had already ceased to be human and had become a mere object, hearing their diagnosis of steady decline and death by fever. Can poetry and the transfiguring power of imagination release any hope from that?

> Whilst my physicians by their love are grown
>   Cosmographers, and I their map, who lie
> Flat on this bed, that by them may be shown
>   That this is my south-west discovery,
>   Per fretum febris, by these straits to die,

Once more the body is a map of the world, pored over and read, this time not in the joy of love-making but in the anxiety of diagnosis. The cosmographer/physicians make a 'South-west discovery'. In the common symbolism in which this poem participates south stands for heat, the heat of Donne's fever, and west, the quarter into which the setting sun descends, stands for decline and death. The cosmographers and explorers, Donne's contemporaries in the outer-world, had been searching for a south-west passage, some narrow strait through which they could sail west into the Pacific. The cosmographers of Donne's body have found that south-west passage, those narrow straits of fever through which he will pass into death 'per fretum febris', by the straits of fever.

But having by this metaphor expressed the worst, Donne, by the same metaphor, begins to redeem the worst. For the outer cosmographers, what lies beyond the straits of their 'south-west discovery' is not annihilation but the new and unimagined world of the Pacific Ocean, and in a round world the mariner who sails west into night and declination far enough finds he has arrived in the east, the east of morning and resurrection. So Donne, having closed his second stanza with those two hard words 'to die', goes on:

> I joy, that in these straits I see my west;
>   For, though their currents yield return to none,
> What shall my west hurt me? As west and east
>   In all flat maps (and I am one) are one,
>   So death doth touch the resurrection.

For Shakespeare, death was 'that undiscovered country from whose bourn no traveller returns', Donne had read in mariners' tales of narrow straits whose currents were so swift that any vessel caught and borne by them could never hope to win a way back against them. So in his metaphor the strait of death is par excellence the strait 'whose current yields return to none'. But Donne knows from those same tales that eastern riches and Pacific promise were never reached except through narrow straits, as he says in a later verse:

> Is the Pacific Sea my home? Or are
>   The eastern riches? Is Jerusalem?

Anyan, and Magellan, and Gibraltar,
    All straits, and none but straits, are ways to them ...'

And so he says of the narrow straits of death, 'I joy, that in these straits I see my west.' For in this brilliant metaphor he sees how, in the flat Mercator projection, the extreme points of east and west appear to be separated at opposite edges of the map but the line of extreme west and the line of extreme east represent the same line and the same space in the real three-dimensional world of which the map is a two-dimensional image. So equally death seems the extreme edge of the map in the two-dimensional world of our physical experience, but in the three-dimensional world of God's reality the 'west' of death curves round to touch the 'east' of resurrection. Our bodies are only the deceptive flat maps of our true selves and when we stand in the true dimensions of heaven then we will know how 'death doth touch the resurrection'.

This fruitful paradox leads Donne beyond the map-making metaphor to develop in the rest of the poem a whole range of paradoxes on the identity of death and resurrection, paradise and Calvary, Christ's cross and Adam's tree, until he reaches this complex poem's simple and powerful conclusion: 'Therefore that he may raise, the Lord throws down.'

If the 'Hymne' mirrors and answers the map metaphors of 'The Good Morrow', transposing them from a secular to a sacred key, then it is equally true that the play with worlds and spheres and time which makes up 'The Sun Rising' is revisited and transformed by Donne in this next poem:

Good Friday, 1613. Riding Westward[14]

LET mans Soul be a Sphere, and then, in this,
The intelligence that moves, devotion is,
And as the other Spheres, by being grown
Subject to foreign motions, lose their own,
And being, by others hurried every day,
Scarce in a year their natural form obey:
Pleasure or businesses so, our Souls admit
For their first mover, and are whirled by it.
Hence is't, that I am carried towards the West
This day, when my Soul's form bends toward the East.
There I should see a Sun, by rising set,
And by that setting endlesse day beget;
But that Christ on this Crosse, did rise and fall,
Sin had eternally benighted all.
Yet dare I almost be glad, I do not see
That spectacle of too much weight for me.

---

[14]   Donne, *The Poems*, pp. 306–8.

Who sees God's face, that is self life, must die;
What a death were it then to see God die?
It made his own Lieutenant Nature shrink,
It made his footstools crack, and the Sun wink.
Could I behold those hands which span the Poles,
And tune all spheres at once, pierced with those holes?
Could I behold that endlesse height which is
Zenith to us, and our Antipodes,
Humbled below us? or that blood which is
The seat of all our Souls, if not of his,
Made dirt of dust, or that flesh which was worn
By God, for his apparel, rag'd, and torn?
If on these things I durst not look, durst I
Upon his miserable mother cast mine eye,
Who was Gods partner here, and furnished thus
Half of that Sacrifice, which ransomed us?
Though these things, as I ride, be from mine eye,
They're present yet unto my memory,
For that looks towards them; and thou look'st towards me,
O Saviour, as thou hang'st upon the tree;
I turn my back to thee, but to receive
Corrections, till thy mercies bid thee leave.
O think me worth thine anger, punish me,
Burn off my rusts, and my deformity,
Restore thine Image, so much, by thy grace,
That thou may'st know me, and I'll turn my face.

Although this is one of Donne's most subtle and complex poems, packed densely with allusions to the science and theology of his day, its basic scenario is clear: Donne travels west on business in the outer world, whilst his soul turns eastward in devotion; and out of the particular moment of journeying which is the poem's occasion Donne brings out and develops dilemmas and paradoxes of universal significance. As with all Donne's poems we are invited to see with a double vision both an outward and visible journey over the earth's surface and an inward and spiritual journey, a journey of humanity towards God and God towards humanity. In the outward and visible world Donne, constrained by business, is riding westward, a direction which symbolises the journey of all our bodies towards sunset, decline and death, westering away from the eastward moment of our morning and birth. The business that forces Donne's body to journey west also stands for the mortality which forces all our bodies along the long day's journey into night. But Donne is constrained, he does not actually want to journey west, any more then any of us want to journey away from our morning into death. Whilst Donne feels outwardly constrained to journey west, in heart and soul he wants to turn east, to turn and face towards the place, outside Jerusalem, where the great drama of all our deaths and resurrections takes place. Just as the heavenly bodies are deflected by 'foreign motions' from their true course, so likewise the business of this world diverts us from our true priorities and sets up a conflict between what carries us outwardly and where we are inwardly yearning to be:

> And as the other Spheres, by being grown
> Subject to foreign motions, lose their own,
> And being, by others hurried every day,
> Scarce in a year their natural form obey:
> Pleasure or businesses so, our Souls admit
> For their first mover, and are whirled by it.
> Hence is't, that I am carried towards the West
> This day, when my Soul's form bends toward the East.

We may have changed the specifics of our astronomy but we can still relate to Donne's account of how our souls allow pleasure or business to become so much our first mover that our whole life gets out of kilter, as we are carried out of our true course. Donne's personal dilemma riding westward while his soul's true form bends towards the east, is a good picture of our whole culture. We are 'hurried every day' away from our true course, away from the deep springs of truth, away from vision and purpose and love, hurried into triviality until we are, as Eliot would later put it, 'distracted from distraction by distraction'.[15] But in the midst of his hurried westering the poet's soul yearns towards the east, and there his imagination embraces a series of paradoxes which prepare us for the great paradox of God's death which forms the poem's climax:

> There I should see a Sun, by rising set,
> And by that setting endlesse day beget;
> But that Christ on this Crosse, did rise and fall,
> Sin had eternally benighted all.

Then comes the admission that, although he longs to turn back from his 'business' and seek God's face, he is in fact afraid to do so. It may be that his 'business' is, like our everyday hurriedness, something deliberately chosen as a way of hiding from God. From here the rest of the poem turns on images of seeing and being seen:

> Yet dare I almost be glad, I do not see
> That spectacle of too much weight for me.
> Who sees Gods face, that is self life, must die;
> What a death were it then to see God die?
> It made his own Lieutenant Nature shrink,
> It made his footstools crack, and the Sun wink.

---

[15] T.S. Eliot, 'Burnt Norton', section III, line 101, in *The Four Quartets*.

Here the conceit, in 'The Sun Rising' of eclipsing the sun with a wink is revisited as the sun darkens and the earth gapes at God's death on the cross. Donne's imagination of a body which could be all kingdoms, of one person's passion affecting the whole cosmos, whose body is mapped out against the stars and yet crushed to the ground by human malice, is here made real by the creator's endurance of a passion within his own creation:

> Could I behold those hands which span the Poles,
> And tune all spheres at once, pierced with those holes?
> Could I behold that endlesse height which is
> Zenith to us, and our Antipodes,
> Humbled below us? or that blood which is
> The seat of all our Souls, if not of his,
> Made dirt of dust, or that flesh which was worn
> By God, for his apparel, rag'd, and torn?

Then, after his reflection on the terrible figure of Mary standing by the cross, comes the paradox of present absence and piercing vision which is at the very heart of the poem and forms the transition from the speculation with which it begins to the impassioned prayer that ends it:

> Though these things, as I ride, be from mine eye,
> They're present yet unto my memory,
> For that looks towards them; and thou look'st towards me,
> O Saviour, as thou hang'st upon the tree; …

The line 'For that looks towards them; and thou look'st towards me' is the hinge upon which the whole poem turns. Up to this point the poem has been about Donne's looking, or failing to look, towards the east where the crucifixion takes place, but suddenly the tables are turned. Just as Donne thinks he is contemplating an image of something distant and in the past in his own memory, he finds the image he contemplates is neither distant nor in the past, but close and present. He finds that it is not he who looks, or fails to look, upon Christ but Christ who looks upon him. In this, as in other poems, Donne shows how a human gaze, looking intently on an outward scene, could pierce through its veils and in that piercing glance transfigure it. So he discovers at this crux of the poem that the gaze of his saviour looking back at him from his imagined image of the cross is ready to pierce and transform him. Suddenly he realises that, for all his protestations, he still has his back to God. Here is a profound revision and reversal of the Old Testament archetype of man's encounter with God. There Moses climbs the mountain searching for God and finds that he can only glimpse a God whose back is turned to him so great is the barrier of human sin. But with the coming of God into human flesh in Christ the world is indeed turned upside down. God descends from the mountain to seek for humanity and this time it is humanity whose back is turned. Just as Moses was afraid to see the face of God, now Donne is afraid to turn and let God see his face and so he prays instead that, even with his back turned, the piercing gaze of the crucified will begin to transform and purge him to make him able even to begin to turn and show his face. His fear is that he has lost himself so utterly in the rust and deformity of sin, that he will no longer be recognisable to the God whose image he is to bear. Yet he longs to be known and so he begins with the fearful image of punishment and correction, the back turned to receive blows, but even as he writes the word 'corrections' he discovers in those corrections God's hidden mercy and prays for a burning-off of rust and deformity so that the lost image can be restored. When the last line of the poem comes the word 'turn' has acquired the fullest sense of metanoia, repentance understood as a complete turning around of oneself and so also of one's perspective:

> I turn my back to thee, but to receive
> Corrections, till thy mercies bid thee leave.
> O think me worth thine anger, punish me,
> Burn off my rusts, and my deformity,
> Restore thine Image, so much, by thy grace,
> That thou may'st know me, and I'll turn my face.

Many-storied Windows: Double Vision in Herbert

If Donne gives us those giddying shifts of perspective where the gazer is suddenly the gazed-upon (rather as Heaney did in 'The Rain Stick' where at one moment we are playing the pipe and at the next we stand there like a pipe being played), Herbert, is concerned with the intentness of a gaze which transfigures vision. In the Introduction we remembered Herbert's moment of insight in which we can choose to look beyond the glassy surface of what apparently meets the eye and glimpse the heaven behind it:

> A man that looks on glass
> On it may stay his eye
> Or if he pleaseth through it pass
> And then the heavens espy.[16]

Sometimes it is not simply that we look through the mirror, now become a window, to catch a glimpse of heaven, but that the very light of heaven shines back through that window to transfigure the supposedly ordinary world of our everyday lives. Herbert was especially interested in the way that transfiguring light can shine through other people who become, in spite of and perhaps even through the stain

---

[16]   George Herbert, 'The Elixir', in *The Complete English Works*, ed. A. Pasternak Slater (London, 1995), p. 180.

of sin with which they struggle, windows on to Christ for us. He explores this idea in the beautiful poem 'The Windows',[17] one of a series in which he reads the everyday features of a parish church – the porch, the steps, the windows, the altar – as all carrying a more than literal meaning:

> Lord, how can man preach thy eternal word?
>   He is a brittle crazy glass:
> Yet in thy temple thou dost him afford
>   This glorious and transcendent place,
>   To be a window, through thy grace.
>
> But when thou dost anneal in glass thy story,
>   Making thy life to shine within
> The holy Preacher's; then the light and glory
>   More rev'rend grows, & more doth win:
>   Which else shows watrish, bleak, & thin.
>
> Doctrine and life, colours and light, in one
>   When they combine and mingle, bring
> A strong regard and awe: but speech alone
>   Doth vanish like a flaring thing,
>   And in the ear, not conscience ring.

The question, with which this poem opens, is the essential problem of the meeting of the eternal with time, of the holy with the sinful, of the Word with the flesh. At first, he seems to imply that such a meeting is impossible: 'Lord, how can *man* preach thy *eternal* word? / He is a brittle crazy glass: ...' The contrast is made between man the time-bound creature and the unattainable eternity of the Word. 'Man' is figured as a piece of 'brittle crazy glass'. In the process of glass-making in the seventeenth century it was almost impossible to produce the clear flawless sheets to which we are accustomed and there was a trade-off in the process between clarity and brittleness. The crazed or uneven surfaces sometimes made for stronger glass, but as often as not glass was both crazed, in the sense that it distorted what you saw through it, and brittle. And yet, as Herbert casts his eyes towards the stained-glass windows of his parish church, this image of man as the brittle crazy glass suddenly gives him, in the light that shines through church windows, the key to his opening problem of how the eternal Word can shine through man; and in the rest of the poem he meditates richly on what it might mean to be 'a window through thy grace'.

In the opening of the next stanza – 'But when thou dost anneal in glass thy story' – he draws once more on the science of glass-making. Colour is annealed into stained glass not painted on to it. The glass has to be reheated, almost melted,

---

17   Ibid., pp. 64–65.

in a sense brought back to its birth and beginning, before the colour can be added, so that before the glass cools the colours have run into the glass itself, not over it, and have become part of its very substance. This is a rich way of thinking about the life of Christ in the lives of those who are members of his body – 'thou dost anneal in glass thy story'. To become a Christian is to realise that Christ's story, which is also history, is our story too. His birth, his baptism, his walk in the wilderness, his temptation, his sorrow, his crucifixion and his resurrection, are not just outside us, running over our glassy surface, but in us as we are in them. And just as the 'brittle crazy glass', with its frozen surface, has to be reheated, melted and brought back to its birth in order to be annealed with the colour, so we have to pass through the heating and melting of our proud surfaces and to be born again and re-formed, this time with the colour of Christ's passion within. The point at which the saving presence and power of the risen Christ, the light that lightens everyone who comes into the world, becomes real is precisely the point where his hurt touches ours, where our wounds are healed by his stripes. Herbert seems to be saying in these two verses, that it is just at the point when the otherwise well-known and abstract story of Christ touches base and is made particular in the everydayness and individual colouring of real Christian lives that it suddenly shines out with the colours God intends it to have. Christ meets us through other people. He makes his life 'to shine within the Holy Preachers'. We should not divide the truths we abstractly know and the lives we concretely live, but rather bring them dramatically together and let each transform the other:

> Doctrine and life, colours and light, in one
>   When they combine and mingle, bring
> A strong regard and awe: ...

When we reflect on how even the darker colours of our sins and failings, if given to God, annealed and remade by him, can still transmit his light, it is interesting to reflect that 'stained glass' is the one context in all its use in which the word 'stained' is redeemed of all its dark connotations to mean something unambiguously beautiful.

Herbert continues to explore the problem of replacing a false, shallow or wordy knowledge with a true knowledge which involves the heart as well as the mind, and changes lives as well as opinions, in 'Vanity (1)' and 'The Agony'. Like Davies in *Nosce Teipsum*, Herbert wants to move us away from a too-facile knowledge of the outer world, a knowledge which deadens and de-natures that world because it ignores the other inner world of the human heart and the vital relationship there should always be between the inner and the outer. In a sense we will never have a true knowledge of the outer world, which science attempts to describe, until that outer knowledge is harmonised with a concomitant inner knowledge of the two primal realities of sin and love which are the subject of Herbert's poem 'The Agony'. In some ways one might say that his poem 'Vanity' sets out the problem of human knowledge acquired only with a single vision while 'The Agony' offers a solution in a double vision which sees both the outer and the inner.

Vanity(1)[18]

The fleet astronomer can bore
And thread the spheres with his quick-piercing mind;
He views their stations, walks from door to door,
    Surveys as if he had design'd
To make a purchase there; he sees their dances
        And knoweth long before
Both their full-ey'd aspects and secret glances.

The nimble diver with his side
Cuts through the working waves, that he may fetch
His dearly-earned pearl; which God did hide
    On purpose from the venturous wretch,
That He might save his life, and also hers
        Who with excessive pride
Her own destruction and his danger wears.

The subtle Chymick can divest
And strip the creature naked, till he finds
The callow principles within their nest;
    There he imparts to them his mind,
Admitted to their bed-chamber before
        They appear trim and drest
To ordinary suitors at the door.

What hath not man sought out and found,
Bur his dear God? Who yet his glorious law
Embosomes in us, mellowing the ground
    With showers and frosts, with love and awe,
So that we need not say, Where's this command?
        Poor man, thou searchest round
To find out death, but missest life at hand!

The word 'Vanity' which is the title of this poem, referred in Herbert's day not just to the small emptiness of human vanity in the modern sense of self-preening, but to the bigger and more complete emptiness which lies behind it, to all things done in vain and uselessly. It was a bold stroke for Herbert writing in the midst of all the excitement and self-congratulation of an 'age of discovery' and scientific

---

[18]   Ibid., p. 83.

advance to survey the whole scene with its supposed discoveries and achievements and call it 'Vanity' – emptiness. It was prophetic too. His survey of the science of his day anticipates the science of our own, anticipates the achievements but also the underlying arrogance and the obvious exploitation. His image of the astronomer who, far from being disinterested, not so much studies as surveys with an eye to possession.

'Surveys as if he had design'd / To make a purchase there' anticipates the commercial interest that goes hand in hand with modern science: the staking of claims on the moon, the filing of patents on the human genome. The second image, of the pearl diver risking his life for the greedy jewel merchant, who in turn feeds and serves the dangerous vanity of the rich, also links the glamour of exploration with the sordid reality of exploitation; a link with which we are only too familiar. The strange image, drawn from alchemy, of the 'subtle Chymick' in the third verse, who can 'divest / And strip the creature naked, till he finds / The callow principles within their nest' in order that he can redesign things to serve his own need, 'impart to them his mind', only too clearly anticipates the stripping down and rebuilding of our given nature which we propose to ourselves in genetic engineering and its prospect of designer babies. Then, just as he brings this survey of man's scientific achievements to a climax, Herbert asks the great unanswered question, the question which is still taboo in many scientific communities today: 'What hath not man sought out and found, / But his dear God?' Without this other knowledge our science may bring us nothing but cheated promises, emptiness and corruption. And how are we to have this 'other knowledge' of God? Like Davies, Herbert says 'look within'. Echoing Paul, he reminds us that this God whom we have chosen to ignore is not a distant deity, he is not far from each one of us. Indeed his closeness as both the Law-giver and the gardener of our souls is brought home in Herbert's beautiful new verb 'embosoms':

> What hath not man sought out and found,
>   Bur his dear God? Who yet his glorious law
>   Embosomes in us, mellowing the ground
>   With showers and frosts, with love and awe, ...

The final image of the poem is the almost comic picture of the busy man searching everywhere for what he thinks is life, but finding only death, whilst all the time life is standing beside him with hands open ready to save: 'Poor man, thou searchest round / To find out death, but missest life at hand!' Herbert's readers would not have needed to be reminded of the text which identifies the life at hand that the poor man missed: 'In him was life and the life was the light of man, the light shines in the darkness and the darkness comprehended it not.'[19]

In 'The Agony', Herbert helps us to imagine what it might be like not to miss that life at hand. What it might be like to turn from our empty knowledge of the

---

[19]   John 1:4–5.

outer to find a truer knowledge of those two vast and spacious things which are a
key to understanding everything else:

The Agony[20]

  Philosophers have measur'd mountains,
Fathom'd the depths of seas, of states and kings;
Walk'd with a staff to heav'n and traced fountains:
  But there are two vast, spacious things,
The which to measure it doth more behove;
Yet few there are that sound them, – Sin and Love.

  Who would know Sin, let him repair
Unto Mount Olivet; there shall he see
A Man so wrung with pains, that all His hair,
  His skin, His garments bloody be.
Sin is that press and vice, which forceth pain
To hunt his cruel food through ev'ry vein.

  Who knows not Love, let him assay
And taste that juice which, on the cross, a pike
Did set again abroach; then let him say
  If ever he did taste the like,
Love is that liquor sweet and most divine,
Which my God feels as blood, but I as wine.

The first three lines of this poem sum up the apparently impressive but actually
empty way of knowing dealt with in 'Vanity'. From there Herbert turns to deal
with what is missing from the empty heart of such merely outer knowledge: 'The
which to measure it doth more behove; Yet few there are that sound them, – Sin
and Love.'

'Sin and Love'. How are we to know these things? Our own age would make
the knowledge purely personal and self-contained – a little dip into what we think
we know about our private psychology. Herbert has a quite different approach. Our
only hope of really knowing ourselves is to look for a light beyond ourselves and
come to know God, for he himself knows us better than we can know ourselves, so
that one day we can 'know even as we have been fully known'.[21] For Herbert, the
only way we know God, the only possible place and person in which we can meet
Him, is Christ. In Christ, God meets us in our humanity. Herbert's epistemology is
Christocentric. It is from the passion of Christ that we learn both who God is and
who we are. In the second stanza of this poem, with its vivid images of Christ's

---

[20] Herbert, *Complete English Works*, p. 34.

[21] 1 Corinthians 13:12.

agony in the garden, Herbert is saying that the image of Christ's agony is also an image of our inner condition – an image both of what sin does to a person and also of God's loving response which bears and transforms the sheer weight of sin. For Herbert, the very fact that Jesus had to endure such agony in order to deliver us from that press and vice, reveals how serious a thing sin is. The image of Christ crushed in the press and vice is profound because it expresses not only the pain and pressure of Gethsemane, squeezing the very blood to the surface of Christ's body, but also because it alludes to the rich biblical symbolism of the winepress, a symbol both of wrath and of generosity. There is the wine press of wrath from the Old Testament: 'I have trodden the wine-press alone ... for I will tread them in mine anger, and trample them in my fury and their blood shall be sprinkled upon my garments and I will stain all my raiment.'[22] But this image, of a wrathful God coming covered in the blood of those upon whom he has taken just vengeance, was daringly and paradoxically applied to Christ by the Church Fathers, both to suggest that, in making atonement, it is his own blood which Christ spills instead of ours, and to make a symbolically profound reversal of the Old Testament metaphor. In Isaiah, the wine crushed from the grapes symbolises blood; in the radical Christian reading of that passage, the garments dipped in blood presage Christ's gift of his own blood as wine. And all this symbolic background is focused and *expressed* (in every sense of that term) in the concentrated imagery of the poem: the sign of wrath becomes the sign of redemption as 'Sin' is transmuted by 'Love' and from this 'press' flows the wine which will be the life of the communicant church. So, in his third and final stanza, Herbert moves from the contemplation in Christ of 'sin' to contemplation in Christ of that 'love' which redeems sin. He who trod the winepress alone becomes the cask of wine to be pierced, 'set abroach,' opened, to refresh his people. It is an astonishing and daring metaphor to make the moment the soldier's pike pierces Christ's heart on the cross a vision of the 'setting abroach' of a wine cask:

> Who knows not Love, let him assay
> And taste that juice which, on the cross, a pike
> Did set again abroach; ...

In this final verse Herbert offers a transformation in the kind of our knowledge, in our way of knowing, not by choosing between ways of knowing, but by integrating two ways of knowing, offering us 'both and', rather than 'either or'. This inclusiveness is embodied in the phrase 'Let him assay *and* taste'. The 'assaying' is that outer and speculative knowledge, the measuring, the reasoning, the head-knowledge. Tasting is the inner and realised knowledge, the knowledge given not to the sceptical head but only to the committed heart. He calls on the 'poor man' of his poem 'Vanity', on the 'philosophers' of his opening stanza, lost as they are in a wilderness of 'assaying', to 'assay *and* taste'. This invitation to

---

22   Isaiah 63:3.

'assay and taste' the wine of love flowing from this tree of life is a divine and redemptive recapitulation of the Devil's invitation to assay and taste wickedly and on our own terms in another garden which constituted our fall. The poem finishes with an expression of the mystery of incarnation and sacrament which is God's divine exchange and intercommunion offered to man on the cross:

> Love is that liquor sweet and most divine,
> Which my God feels as blood, but I as wine.

Conclusion

All these poems bear witness that the task of knowing either ourselves or our world fully cannot be a self-contained human work. It requires light and validation from beyond itself. Davies' two poems on knowledge of the world and of ourselves both acknowledge this. The knowledge in *Orchestra* depends on the knowledge of Love figured as the one whose music both creates and redeems the world. The self-knowledge pursued in *Nosce Teipsum* turns out to depend not on the light of our own reason but on another light which floods the soul, the 'light which made the light which makes the day'. Donne and Herbert explicitly name that Love and know that light as Christ, and their engagement with the God who meets them in Christ is not simply a matter of private devotion but becomes the essential key to their perception of themselves and the world. In the next chapter we will see how Vaughan, supremely the poet of redemptive light, and seer of the unseen, and Milton, whose blindness caused him to reimagine his entire understanding of the relations between the visible and the invisible, both elaborated and mediated their transfigured vision by means of the poetic imagination.

Chapter 5

Holy Light and Human Blindness: Visions of the Invisible in the Poetry of Henry Vaughan and Milton

Yearning and Illumination in the Poetry of Vaughan

If George Herbert was calling us away from the emptiness, the 'Vanity', of ways of knowing and seeing that dealt only with the outwardly visible, calling us to a renewed vision of the inner, the invisible, the realities of light and love, then his disciple Henry Vaughan certainly answered that call. Vaughan is a poet whose palpable experience of the darkness and ambiguities of life in this world, particularly his experience of civil war, never eclipsed his equally strong sense of the light of heaven, both shining beyond us and, as it were, buried within us. As E.C. Pettet put it in his 1960 study *Of Paradise and Light*, Vaughan's poem 'Friends Departed' 'expresses … Vaughan's "intense and continuous yearning for the illumination of heaven and the end of this mist-obscured mortal life" and it is the most concentrated impression he has left us of his light-obsessed imagination'.[1]

I would like to look briefly at this poem 'Friends Departed' and at 'The World'; both as a continuation of the desire for a transcendent light in which to see and understand both the light of day and the light of reason which we saw in John Davies, and as a preface to the direct invocation of Christ as light which we will find in Milton.

Vaughan's poem 'The World'[2] begins with a moment of direct vision without any intermediary and announces that vision with a conversational directness he borrowed from Donne and a clarity of mystical experience which is all his own:

> I saw Eternity the other night
> Like a great Ring of pure and endless light,
>   All calm, as it was bright;
> And round beneath it, Time, in hours, days, years,
>   Driven by the spheres
> Like a vast shadow moved, in which the world

---

[1]   E.C. Pettet, *Of Paradise and Light: A Study of Vaughan's Silex Scintillans* (Cambridge, 1960)., pp. 156–57

[2]   'The World', in *Poetry and Selected Prose of Henry Vaughan*, ed. L.C. Martin (Oxford, 1963), pp. 299–301.

And all her train were hurled.
The doting Lover in his quaintest strain
    Did there complain;
Near him, his lute, his fancy, and his flights,
    Wit's sour delights;
With gloves and knots, the silly snares of pleasure;
    Yet his dear treasure
All scattered lay, while he his eyes did pour
    Upon a flower.

The darksome Statesman hung with weights and woe,
Like a thick midnight fog, moved there so slow
    He did nor stay nor go;
Condemning thoughts, like sad eclipses, scowl
    Upon his soul,
And clouds of crying witnesses without
    Pursued him with one shout.
Yet digged the mole, and, lest his ways be found,
    Worked underground,
Where he did clutch his prey; bur One did see
    That policy,
Churches and altars fed him, perjuries
    Were gnats and flies;
It rained about him blood and tears, but he
    Drank them as free.

The fearful Miser on a heap of rust
Sat pining all his life there, did scarce trust
    His own hands with the dust;
Yet would not place one piece above, but lives
    In fear of thieves.
Thousands there were as frantic as himself,
    And hugged each one his pelf.
The downright Epicure placed heaven in sense
    And scorned pretence;
While other, slipped into a wide excess,
    Said little less;
The weaker sort, slight, trivial wares enslave,
    Who think them brave;
And poor despised Truth sat counting by
    Their victory.

Yet some, who all this while did weep and sing,
And sing and weep, soared up into the Ring;

> But most would use no wing,
> O fools [said I], thus to prefer dark night
>   Before true light,
> To live in grots and caves, and hate the day
>   Because it shows the way,
> The way which from this dead and dark abode
>   Leads up to God,
> A way where you might tread the sun, and be
>   More bright than he.
> But as I did their madness to discuss,
>   One whispered thus,
> *This Ring the Bridegroom did for none provide*
>   *But for his Bride.*

This poem's opening paradox in which the vision of 'eternity' is located at a particular moment in time, 'the other night', brings to Vaughan a new perspective about time itself. Vaughan sees time not as an absolute, but as a kind of shadowy pendant to the bright ring of eternity:

> I saw Eternity the other night
> Like a great *Ring* of pure and endless light,
>   All calm, as it was bright;
> And round beneath it, Time, in hours, days, years,
>   Driven by the spheres
> Like a vast shadow moved, …

With the phrase 'Time, in hours, days, years' Vaughan may well have been consciously echoing Donne in his listing of the passing 'rags of time' as 'hours, days, months'.[3] For the rest of the poem, the world and everything in it is seen from the perspective of Heaven and its light, which is why Vaughan speaks of the world as being like a vast shadow. Vaughan begins with the light and shows the shadows, whereas Shakespeare speaks of the shadows so as to infer the light. Vaughan's picture of the world goes beyond the mere 'vanity of human knowledge' to look at the deliberate perversity through which we do not simply miss the light but positively shun it. And here he brings an enlightened imagination to bear on the very problem of what is fallen and darkened in both Reason and Imagination. For example, 'the darksome statesman' moving slowly through the 'thick midnight fog' of his own false imaginings, condemned by his own thoughts which 'like sad eclipses scowl upon his soul'. Vaughan depicts him as surrounded all this time by clouds of witness and yet running from them rather than seeking in them a liberating vision. Likewise the 'miser', who might seem to be in a palace of riches

---

3   'The Sun Rising', in *The Poems of John Donne*, ed. H. Grierson (Oxford, 1949), p. 11.

but, from the perspective of eternity, pines on a heap of rust. It is a brilliant poetic effect that in his rhyme scheme Vaughan imprisons the word 'trust' between the words 'rust' and 'dust' as a mimesis of the miser's actual situation.

> The fearful Miser on a heap of rust
> Sat pining all his life there, did scarce trust
>   His own hands with the dust; …

In the final verse though, Vaughan pays tribute to those who, whilst weeping with all of us in the darkness, nevertheless can sing and in that singing find themselves caught up beyond the 'rags of time' into the 'ring of light'.

> Yet some, who all this while did weep and sing,
> And sing and weep, soared up into the Ring; …

This couplet is probably a tribute to Herbert himself whose 'singing', his poetry, dared to include his experience *both* of sorrow *and* of love and praise. When he wrote of some who 'weep and sing, and sing and weep', Vaughan may have been thinking of Herbert's little poem 'Bittersweet':

> Ah, my dear angry Lord
> Since Thou dost love, yet strike,
> Cast down, yet help afford;
> Sure I will do the like.
>
> I will complain, yet praise,
> I will bewail, approve;
> And all my sour-sweet days
> Will lament and love.[4]

Vaughan was explicit about his spiritual and literary debt to Herbert 'whose holy life and verse gained many pious converts (of whom I am the least)'.[5] Certainly Vaughan had learned from his master Herbert that the key is to move from a shallow discursive knowledge, the knowledge of 'assaying', to a redeeming relational knowledge, the knowledge of 'tasting' in the movement at the very end of the poem – from 'I did their madness so discuss', to the rediscovery of the true meaning of the *ring* of light. For at the end of this poem the 'great ring of pure and endless light' suddenly becomes the intimate ring of a shared relationship, the ring which the bridegroom offers to his bride:

---

[4]   George Herbert, *The Complete English Works*, ed. A. Pasternak Slater (London, 1995), p.167.

[5]   Cited by L.C. Martin in the Introduction to *Poetry and Selected Prose of Henry Vaughan*, p. xvii.

But as I did their madness so discuss,
   One whispered thus,
This Ring the Bridegroom did for none provide
   But for his Bride.

In 'The World', Vaughan seems to be saying that most men 'prefer dark night / Before true light', but he nevertheless makes it clear that there is, should we choose it, a 'Way which from this dead and dark abode / Leads up to God', and that light, even in the small glimpses of it we experience here, is the beginning of that way; a way which leads eventually to a true light, not only outside us, but shining from within us: 'A way where you might tread the sun, and be / More bright than he'.

In 'Friends Departed' Vaughan return to this theme of the contrast between the light of heaven and the darkness of a shadowy world, but this time he pursues the idea that even in the midst of this world we have moments of transfigured vision that 'some strange thoughts transcend our wonted themes / And into glory peep'. Indeed he goes further – the dominant image of the poem is of a buried star, of a light which is not simply beyond us but also hidden within us:

'Friends Departed'[6]

They are all gone into the world of light!
   And I alone sit ling'ring here;
Their very memory is fair and bright,
   And my sad thoughts doth clear.

It glows and glitters in my cloudy breast,
   Like stars upon some gloomy grove,
Or those faint beams in which this hill is drest,
   After the sun's remove.

I see them walking in an air of glory,
   Whose light doth trample on my days:
My days, which are at best but dull and hoary,
   Mere glimmering and decays.

O holy Hope! and high Humility,
   High as the heavens above!
These are your walks, and you have show'd them me
   To kindle my cold love.

Dear, beauteous Death! The jewel of the just,
   Shining nowhere, but in the dark;

---

[6]   Ibid., pp. 318–19.

What mysteries do lie beyond thy dust
 Could man outlook that mark!

He that hath found some fledg'd bird's nest, may know
 At first sight, if the bird be flown;
But what fair well or grove he sings in now,
 That is to him unknown.

And yet as angels in some brighter dreams
 Call to the soul, when man doth sleep:
So some strange thoughts transcend our wonted themes
 And into glory peep.

If a star were confin'd into a tomb,
 Her captive flames must needs burn there;
But when the hand that lock'd her up, gives room,
 She'll shine through all the sphere.

O Father of eternal life, and all
 Created glories under thee!
Resume thy spirit from this world of thrall
 Into true liberty.

Either disperse these mists, which blot and fill
 My perspective still as they pass,
Or else remove me hence unto that hill,
 Where I shall need no glass.

At first Vaughan interprets this light simply as memory, the memory of the light of heaven as it shone through other people, very much as in the way described by Herbert in 'Windows':

They are all gone into the world of light!
 And I alone sit ling'ring here;
Their very memory is fair and bright,
 And my sad thoughts doth clear.

It glows and glitters in my cloudy breast,
 Like stars upon some gloomy grove,
Or those faint beams in which this hill is drest,
 After the sun's remove.

But this is only memory. The friends whose departure he mourns have their true being in the light of heaven and the contrast seems only to emphasise the shadowed and trampled world in which Vaughan still finds himself:

> I see them walking in an air of glory,
>   Whose light doth trample on my days:
> My days, which are at best but dull and hoary,
>   Mere glimmering and decays.

Then, in the fifth stanza, comes the beginning of a genuinely transfigured vision. At first sight death must surely seem the darkest cave in this 'dead and dark abode'. But the remembered vision of light as it once shone in his departed friends transfigures Vaughan's vision of death and returns him again to the image not of light on high but of buried light:

> Dear, beauteous Death! The jewel of the just,
>   Shining nowhere, but in the dark;
> What mysteries do lie beyond thy dust
>   Could man outlook that mark!

The whole effort of Vaughan's poetry becomes a matter not simply of looking but of *outlooking*. The first part of the poem has looked at the mark of death, not just in the metaphor of the archer taking aim to look at the 'mark', but also in the deeper sense of the 'mark' of death the way we are all marked by grief for friends departed and fear of our own death. But now Vaughan's art summons us to *outlook*, to look through and so beyond, the mark of death. Death has become a mark in another sense; a sign. Those black marks on the paper which make the poem are themselves signs for words, and the words themselves the signs of vision; and we 'outlook the mark' to find the word, 'outlook' the word to see the vision. So now in the poem Vaughan is inviting us to make of death not a full stop, but a word in God's poem, through which, out beyond which, we look at the mysteries which 'do lie beyond that dust'.

He begins to give us this double vision, this sense of the possibility of a presence, even in the midst of an observed absence with the image of an empty nest:

> He that hath found some fledg'd bird's nest, may know
>   At first sight, if the bird be flown;
> But what fair well or grove he sings in now,
>   That is to him unknown.

The key phrase in this stanza is 'at first sight'. By reminding us of what is knowable to first sight he prepares us by implication for the second sight which is at the heart of this poem. And begins to give us at least the imagined possibility of the unknown but actual well or grove in which the fledgling sings. Vaughan is fully conscious of the image of the bird as an archetype not only of the poet, but also of the soul. This verse looks back to John Davies' image of death as birth in Nosce Te Ipseum and forward to Keats' 'Ode to a Nightingale' with its yearning to fly to where the bird has flown. And now Vaughan moves from the analogy of the fledged bird's nest to a direct address to the soul, and an appeal beyond a rational knowledge of the outer, to an intuitive knowledge of the inner, suggesting that the inner yearnings are not echoes in the cave of our lostness, but rather callings from heaven itself:

> And yet as angels in some brighter dreams
>   Call to the soul, when man doth sleep:
> So some strange thoughts transcend our wonted themes
>   And into glory peep.

Then, after all these hints and foreshadowing, comes the key image. The image which had been hinted at in the idea of something fair and bright glittering 'in my cloudy breast', and again in the idea of the jewel 'shining nowhere but in the dark'; it is the image of the buried star:

> If a star were confin'd into a tomb,
>   Her captive flames must needs burn there;
> But when the hand that lock'd her up, gives room,
>   She'll shine through all the sphere.

Vaughan has come a long way from the simple and desolate contrast between light above and darkness below with which the poem opened. In the very act of grieving he has discovered afresh the captive flames of his own immortal soul. And now the death, which at the beginning of the poem had robbed him of his friends, has become instead the hand that will give him liberty. He is ready at last to speak directly to his Father, able to rejoice in eternal life without despising the glories of time. True, he prays for liberation from this world, but it is a prayer which acknowledges that God's light can shine in the creation as well as beyond it, and that sometimes that light will disperse the mists which blot and fill the glass through which we darkly see the world. Indeed, Vaughan's poetry has exactly that effect on our 'perspective', in both its old and modern sense. Vaughan closes his poem with a prayer to the 'Father of eternal life' that, if he cannot now find himself in heaven, he may have the 'mists dispersed' so that he may 'peep' into glory. In some ways the answer to that prayer is the poem itself – the power of the poetic imagination to disperse mists and give us at least a 'peep' into realms of glory:

> O Father of eternal life, and all
>   Created glories under thee!
> Resume thy spirit from this world of thrall

Into true liberty.

Either disperse these mists, which blot and fill
    My perspective still as they pass,
Or else remove me hence unto that hill,
    Where I shall need no glass.

Milton and the Theology of Vision

We turn now to the work of a poet who found himself on the opposite side of the
Civil War from Vaughan, and yet wrestling with and resolving some of the same
issues in both poetry and spirituality. As a young poet of wide culture and deep
reading, seeking an imaginative synthesis of faith and vision in a rapidly changing
world, Milton, even in earlier works like *Comus* and *Lycidas*, had begun to explore
the themes of transfigured vision, the seeking of light in darkness and the 'bodying
forth' through the poet's imagination of the 'form of things unknown' which he had
found in Shakespeare, in Davies, in Donne and in Herbert. But this common poetic
quest 'to see and tell of things invisible to mortal sight', this yearning towards a
'light which makes the light, which makes the day', was given a new urgency,
a new depth and, ultimately, a new authority in Milton's work because he was
confronted with the personal tragedy of physical blindness. His was not the 'thick
midnight fog' of Vaughan's poetic rhetoric but a real 'irrecoverable darkness',
'total eclipse / Without all hope of day'. And yet it was in the very act of wrestling
with his God in this darkness that Milton was able to celebrate and articulate that
light which is the life of humanity.

I propose in the rest of this chapter, to look first at three very different passages
of poetry in which Milton deals directly with his own experience of blindness and
then to show the way in which, in *Paradise Lost*, he was able to address the task
that he had set himself to 'see and tell / Of things invisible to mortal sight'.[7] In
many ways Milton is not only the stateliest but also the most impersonal of all
the English poets. His sense of poetic decorum leads to an almost complete self-
effacement when he is addressing himself to the task of his great epic. Only where
some aspect of his experience is genuinely pertinent to the task in hand does he
give it voice. He is utterly removed from the later Romantic and modern vogue for
self-expression. The sonnet 'XVI On his Blindness'[8] is therefore a rare exception
in which he opens his soul and exposes his doubts and anguish; and even this
poem, although it begins with a private and particular experience, ends with a

---

[7]   John Milton, *Paradise Lost*, ed. A. Fowler (London, 1971), Book III, lines 54–55,
p. 146.

[8]   In John Milton, *The Complete Shorter Poems*, ed. J. Carey (London, 1968), p.
328.

public commentary on Christ's Parable of the Talents[9] and an objective vision not of private pain but of the eternal community of Heaven. The sonnet begins with a frank admission of his sense of helplessness, uselessness and frustration, struck blind less than half-way through his life and before he had written the great work for which he believed God was fitting him:

> When I consider how my light is spent,
>   Ere half my days, in this dark world and wide,
>   And that one talent which is death to hide,
>   Lodged with me useless, though my soul more bent
> To serve therewith my maker, and present
>   My true account, lest he returning chide, …

Here Milton makes a bitter and almost hidden allusion to the story of Christ's Parable of the Talents in which the man who was given only 'one talent' buried it in the ground because he feared that his master would chide him for having risked it, only to be chidden for having buried it. But who buried Milton's 'one talent' in the earth of blindness? Does he not at least imply that it was the very God whose chiding he fears? There is a terrible urgency, contrasted with the sensation of uselessness, in Milton's lines 'my soul more bent/ To serve therewith my maker, and present / My true account, lest he returning chide …'[10] In this cataclysmic period in English history, Milton and many others did in fact expect the bodily return of Christ in their own lifetime. The question 'Doth God exact day-labour light denied?' was an agonisingly real and practical one. And yet in the turn of the sonnet (on line 8), Milton, having expressed his frustration and implicit accusations of God, confesses just as freely his foolishness in those three simple words 'I fondly ask'. ('Fondly' in Milton's day still carried its fuller and older sense of 'foolishly or without foundation'.) Milton's 'fond' question rouses 'Patience' to make a reply. This reply sends Milton back to the heart of his gospel, a gospel of grace not of works. He realises the implicit arrogance of working his salvation by his own achievements, of trying to put God in his debt, which had animated the first part of his poem. As Patience replies he finds the very image of waiting which had seemed so unbearable to him, is redeemed, and reoriented to Heaven. Milton, waiting on God, trapped in a 'dark world and wide', frustrated by his disability, finds himself suddenly in the company of angels and of all the redeemed in heaven who are also waiting before the throne and crying out 'How long?' He has discovered that God can be glorified as much in his passion as in his action

> God doth not need
> Either man's work or his own gifts, who best

---

9   See Matthew 25:14–30.

10   See also *Samson Agonistes*, lines 81–82, see note 12 below.

> Bear his mild yoke, they serve him best, his state
> Is kingly. Thousands at his bidding speed
> And post o'er land and ocean without rest:
> They also serve who only stand and wait.

This famous last line is often quoted out of context, as though it implied a mere passive resignation and were not, as it is in the context of the poem, a ringing declaration of active victory over the temptations of frustration and despair. For Milton, the word 'stand' carries as much weight as the word 'wait'. It carries the sense it has when it is used twice in Ephesians 6: 13 and 14:

> Wherefore take unto you the whole armour of God that ye may be able to stand
> in the evil day and having done all, to stand. Stand therefore, having your loins
> girt about with truth, and having on the breastplate of righteousness.

Milton stood and withstood the crisis marked by this poem and began to discover how his blindness, far from burying 'that one talent', might actually be refining it.

We will look now at two ways in which he made the experience of his blindness an essential part of his poetry. In *Samson Agonistes*, a reworking of the Old Testament story through the structure and method of Greek tragedy, Milton had the opportunity to make a living connection between the most painful and apparently unredeemed part of his personal experience of blindness and the story of Samson. Through the mouth of Samson, Milton can pour out the darkest and most bitter of his complaints and 'yet praise' because, by voicing his agony through Samson whose death was part of God's providence, Milton is placing his own pain in the arena of salvation. Milton's picture of what it is to be blind, to be vulnerable, and to be open in a cruel society 'to daily fraud, contempt, abuse and wrong' is unsurpassed in English literature:

> O loss of sight, of thee I most complain!
> Blind among enemies, O worse than chains,
> Dungeon, or beggary, or decrepit age!
> Light, the prime work of God, to me is extinct,
> And all her various objects of delight
> Annulled, which might in part my grief have eased,
> Inferior to the vilest now become
> Of man or worm; the vilest here excel me,
> They creep, yet see, I dark in light exposed
> To daily fraud, contempt, abuse and wrong,
> Within doors, or without, still as a fool,
> In power of others, never in my own;

Scarce half I seem to live, dead more than half. (Lines 67–79)[11]

Then comes his unforgettable contrast between his own experience of darkness and the guessed-at light around him:

> O dark, dark, dark, amid the blaze of noon,
> Irrecoverably dark, total eclipse
> Without all hope of day! (Lines 80–82)

But here, at this point of total bleakness, there is the possibility of prayer, even if it is the prayer of anguish and anger. The bare word 'day' is enough to carry his mind to that light which is more than the light of day, the primal light of Genesis. And it is to that light and that light alone he must carry his question, from that light and that light alone he can hope for any answer.

> O first-created beam, and thou great word,
> Let there be light and light was over all;
> Why am I thus bereaved thy prime decree? (lines 83–85)

Samson's pleas to the 'first-created beam' and its link with the 'great word' echoes the deepest resolution of these issues of darkness, light and vision which Milton had found in the writing of *Paradise Lost*. Setting about the task of his epic as a blind man had forced Milton to search for that more-than-visible light which Davies had invoked in Nosce Te Ipsum. At the beginning of Book III in *Paradise Lost* Milton must lift his vision, and that of his readers, from the horrors of hell which had occupied the first two books, to the reality of heaven. Any poet would of course feel inadequate to this task. Any poet would invoke divine aid and remember that they were now being asked to describe what 'eye has not seen nor ear heard'. But what might have been a merely conventional admission of weakness, a conventional plea for divine illumination, has a special force in *Paradise Lost* because it is the only point in the poem where Milton introduces himself and refers to his own blindness. It is also the point in English literature where all the invocations of light made by previous poets find their fullest expression and are placed in the context of a deeply realised theology of God as Holy Trinity.

One of the most interesting aspects of Milton's great invocation of light is its openness and plurality. He does not offer us sharply drawn lines or the dogmatic foreclosing of possibilities, but rather a sense of openness, of alternative images of different paths to the brink of the mystery. The key conjunction, in his wonderful long sentences is not a monolinear 'and' but a playful, speculative 'or':

> Hail, holy Light, offspring of heaven first-born,
> Or of the eternal co-eternal beam

---

[11]   Milton, *Complete Shorter Poems*, pp. 346–47.

May I express thee unblamed? (III, lines 1–3)[12]

Milton is aware that in the Genesis narrative there was a light before ever there was a sun, he is aware that in the preface to John's Gospel Christ is seen as a light which can lighten everyone who comes into the world and that in the letter of James God is seen as light. He also knows that he encounters God, and God encounters him, as Father, Son and Holy Spirit. He knows that our different experiences of light can express our experiences: of God as Father, dwelling in unapproachable light; of God as Son and Logos, the light which lightens all who come into the world; and of God as Holy Spirit, the hidden fountain of light. In his invocation of light Milton hesitates before the mystery of these things. Almost, he plays with the possibilities; he wonders whether in speaking directly *to* light he is speaking to God or whether he is asking the God who says 'Let there be light' to infuse into his mind a light which is neither the created visible light, nor yet the inexpressible essence of God Himself. At one level, this surface hesitation between alternative theological ideas about the relation of created and uncreated light to the Holy Trinity is less important than the powerful movement in the poetry of images, and in the verbs, which are all expressive of power and creative energy:

> Hail, holy Light, offspring of heaven first-born,
> O of the external co-eternal beam
> May I express thee unblamed? Since God is light,
> And never but in unapproached light
> Dwelt from eternity, dwelt then in thee,
> Bright effluence of bright essence increate.
> Or hear'st thou rather pure ethereal stream,
> Whose fountain who shall tell? (III, lines 1–8)

Milton takes us back to the primal image of creation, to the image of a light which was before the sun:

> Before the sun,
> Before the heavens thou wert, and at the voice
> Of God, as with a mantle didst invest
> The rising world of waters dark and deep.
> Won from the void and formless infinite. (III, lines 8–12)

But even as he invokes this primal light, with its power to bring order to the 'void and formless infinite', he makes it a sign of the power and purpose of his own poetry. Milton remembers again how vainly he turns to find the outer and visible light of the sun:

---

[12]   Milton *Paradise Lost*, p. 141.

> thee I revisit safe,
> And feel thy sovereign vital lamp; but thou
> Revisit'st not these eyes, that roll in vain
> To find thy piercing ray, and find no dawn (III, lines 21–24)

However, this reminder of his outer blindness only leads Milton to a renewal of inner vision, and he continues with a ringing 'yet' – like the 'yet' or the 'nevertheless' which is so often the fulcrum and turning point in which a dark psalm is transfigured suddenly into praise:

> Yet not the more
> Cease I to wander where the Muses haunt
> Clear spring, or shady grove, or sunny hill.
> Smit with the love of sacred song; ... (III, lines 26–29)

We are given here a glimpse into the inner space of Milton's imaginative life and we find that this blind old man, living in obscurity, had within him whole kingdoms, mountains, valleys and rivers which he roamed at will, and that in that inner realm he could walk in the sunlight. One is reminded of the vivid imagery of a vast inner space within the mind so much greater than the body or the world the body inhabits, which St Augustine gives us in the Confessions when he speaks of walking through the vast fields of his memory: 'See how much I have travelled about in the spaciousness of my memory while looking for thee, O Lord.'[13] So, imprisoned by blindness in London, Milton still wanders 'where the Muses haunt' and sunlight strikes Parnassus. On the wings of thought he can travel from the haunts of classical poetry with which his mind was so richly furnished, to Zion and to the source or fountain of Judaeo-Christian inspiration. As Milton gives an account of his nightly visits to 'Sion', to the streams that make glad the city of God, we sense the connection between that eternal and 'ethereal stream whose fountain who shall tell', which is the source of all things, and the sacred spring in Milton's imagined Sion which is the source of his poetry:

> but chief
> Thee Sion and the flowery brooks beneath
> That wash thy hallowed feet, and warbling flow,
> Nightly I visit: ... (III, lines 29–32)

After remembering the examples of other blind poets and prophets, whose lack of outer sight had been compensated with a gift of inner vision, Milton introduces the image of the 'wakeful bird' singing through the dark and coins the beautiful word 'darkling' which was to echo through English poetry thereafter, and always with the suggestion of hidden hope and power:

---

[13]   St Augustine, *Confessions*, trans. R.S. Pine-Coffin (London, 1961), p. 230.

> Then feed on thoughts, that voluntary move
> Harmonious number; as the wakeful bird
> Sings darkling, and in shadiest covert hid
> Tunes her nocturnal note. (III, lines 37–40)

John Keats, centuries later in a garden in Hampstead, heard those notes and wrote 'darkling I listen', finding his dark mood lifted as Milton's had been by the redemptive power of poetry. And later still, in bleak December Thomas Hardy heard his 'darkling thrush' and even as he tried to write the bleakest of his poems, conceded to the singing bird, a symbol at once of the soul and poetry, 'some blessed hope whereof he knew and I was unaware'.[14] So Milton 'sings darkling' and something of the power and heroism of his verse is to be found in the contrast and tension between verb and adverb here, between 'sings' and 'darkling'. Even as the word 'darkling' reminds him again of his blindness, even as he lists in beautiful poetry the things he cannot see, those very things are presented afresh to his own inner eyes and to those of his sighted readers.

> Thus with the year
> Seasons return, but not to me returns
> Day, or the sweet approach of even or morn
> Or sight of vernal bloom, or summer's rose
> Or flocks, or herds, or human face divine; … (III, lines 40–44)

This reminder of the power and clarity of inner vision leads to the heart of invocation with which Book III opens:

> So much the rather thou celestial Light
> Shine inward, and the mind through all her powers
> Irradiate, there plant eyes, all mist from thence
> Purge and disperse, that I may see and tell
> Of things invisible to mortal sight. (III, lines 51–55)

By invoking the power of this inner light, Milton is making a particular claim for his own poetry, but perhaps it is also a claim that can be made for all great poetry. It is the claim to 'see and tell of things invisible to mortal sight'. Coleridge claimed that the great folly of his own age (as of ours) was its submission to 'the despotism of the eye', the naive assumption that only the visible is real. The poetic imagination helps us to see the reality of the unseen. For Milton, this was especially important since he knew that the particular task of *Paradise Lost* was to express the apprehensions of heaven in the forms and shapes of the comprehensible earth. He makes this task and its attendant problems clear in Book V in a conversation between Raphael and Adam. When Adam asks Raphael for an account of the war

---

[14]   See below Chapter 7, pp. 182–5, for an analysis of 'The Darkling Thrush'.

in heaven, Raphael has to explain that language about heaven can only ever be the language of analogy, the vocabulary of the imagination:

> for how shall I relate
> To human sense th' invisible exploits
> Of warring Spirits; how without remorse
> The ruin of so many glorious once
> And perfect while they stood; how last unfold
> The secrets of another world, perhaps
> Not lawful to reveal? Yet for thy good
> This is dispensed, and what surmounts the reach
> Of human sense, I shall delineate so,
> By lik'ning spiritual to corporal forms,
> As may express them best, ... (V lines 564–74)

The key to the poet's art is in the lines 'I shall delineate so, / By likening spiritual to corporal forms, / As may express them best, ...' This seems strongly reminiscent of that account of the art and power of the poet in *A Midsummer Night's Dream*:

> And as imagination bodies forth
> The forms of things unknown, the poet's pen
> Turns them to shapes and gives to airy nothing
> A local habitation and a name.[15]

The poet's stories and images always mean more and embody more than their surface visibility, but Raphael's speech does not end there. For Milton, as for Coleridge after him[16], and many others, it is not only humanity that makes poetry but God, and if our poetry is made of words about things, God's poetry is made of the very things themselves. This universe we think so solid and so self-contained, this visible cosmos which we seem content to read literally and only literally, is also the poetry of our maker. It is speech, in the language of form and motion spoken to us from heaven. The business of science is to construe the surface meaning of the text of the universe, but it is the business of poetry to understand the deeper things of which the text is really speaking. So Raphael continues:

> though what if Earth
> Be but the shadow of Heav'n, and things therein
> Each to other like, more then on earth is thought? (V, lines 574–76)

---

[15]   See above Chapter 2, pp. 55–61.

[16]   For a discussion of Coleridge's idea of cosmos as 'eternal language', see Chapter 6.

This idea that the very creation itself is an expression of spiritual things in corporal form is essential to the way we read *Paradise Lost*. For Milton, the account of the outward and visible creation in Genesis, of the separation of darkness and light, of the raising of the firmament, is also an account of what must happen inwardly and invisibly in each person. He is telling the story of the creation of the macrocosm and the microcosm at one and the same time. In the microcosm too there must be a declaration of light, there must be a raising of a solid ground of firmament, and there must be a garden in which we can walk with our maker in the cool of the evening. He makes this clear in the very opening of Book I. Before he ever describes the first actions of the creation in the outward and visible macrocosm, he invokes them for himself in the inward microcosm of humanity: 'what in me is dark / Illumine, what is low raise and support'. It is as though he says 'Whatever had a beginning (Genesis) out there, and in the past, must also have its Genesis in me'. And so he asks the Holy Spirit, who moved in creation on the outward and visible waters of chaos bringing light to the firmament, to move in him, to enlighten him. For Milton, this is not simply the poetic convention of invoking a muse at the start of an epic, but a fundamental reality. It puts him in a unique relation with his subject. For Virgil writing *The Aeneid*, there is an unbridgeable gap between the urbane Roman poet and the events of the heroic age he is describing. But, when Milton comes to describe the Spirit of God moving over the face of the water in the beginning, he does so in the conviction that the very same Spirit is equally present in his mind, and that the Spirit which inspired the writer of Genesis is working through the words of his poem. By making the first moments in the story of creation an event in the inner as well as the outer world, he is showing us how he intends the entire poem to be read. Every subsequent description of a visible event is intended to give us the vocabulary to comprehend and describe the invisible story of our own souls. Raphael likens spiritual to corporeal forms. Milton intends his reader to reverse the process and liken the corporeal forms in the poem's narrative to the spiritual realities of our own souls. So Milton invokes the spirit in Book I:

> And chiefly thou, O Spirit, that dost prefer
> Before all temples th' upright heart and pure,
> Instruct me, for thou know'st; thou from the first
> Wast present, and, with mighty wings outspread,
> Dove-like sat'st brooding on the vast Abyss,
> And mad'st it pregnant: what in me is dark
> Illumine, what is low raise and support;
> That to the height of this great argument,
> I may assert Eternal Providence,
> And justify the ways of God to men. (I, lines 17–26)

For the rest of the poem, passage after passage turns out to be the story, not just of the great outer *mythos* of Christendom, but also the story of what happens inside each one of us. From the first great images of Satan fallen and miserable, but still with the remnants of his lost glory, through to the moving evocation of the hidden garden of Paradise, glimpsed first in a kind of agony of loss through Satan's jealous eyes; in image after image, Milton gives us a vocabulary of icons, a series of luminous and visible pictures of truths about ourselves, which we could not otherwise articulate.

To read *Paradise Lost* is to be reminded again of how to read the two great works that God has left us – his word and his world. Through the lens of Milton's poetry, we see both the familiar passages of scripture and the familiar objects of the world around us with double, not with single vision. He invites us to pass through the glassy surface of experience, on which we might have 'stayed our eye', to glimpse truths which are both beyond and within us.

For the poet of *The Dream of the Rood*, transfigured and transfiguring vision came naturally and was supported by both his pagan culture and his Christian faith. The vision of the cross as *both* bloodstained wood *and* cosmic glory was part of his spiritual inheritance. He had neither to break taboos nor to push against the spirit of his age to give it expression. There was in his age no 'quarrel', as it were, between Theseus and Hippolyta, between Reason and Imagination. In Shakespeare's age the poet was aware of the distinctions between reason and imagination, between comprehension and apprehension, which were beginning to develop in Western culture; but he was still at liberty to arrange for and celebrate the 'marriage', of these distinct powers. And so the marriage of Theseus and Hippolyta at the end of *A Midsummer Night's Dream*, is blessed both by the 'reason' of Athens and by the 'imagination' of Titania's glimmering wood. Likewise, Sir John Davies was confident that a poem on the soul written as a discursive appeal to reason, could be written alongside an imaginative celebration of the cosmos as a love-led dance, because for Davies the Light of Reason is also the Love who dances at the heart of all things. Cosmology and 'spirituality' were in harmony because they were understood to spring from the same source. But at the turn of the seventeenth century the 'Great Divorce' of reason and imagination, of science and faith, was already beginning to tear apart these ancient unities. Donne and Herbert had to stretch language, to create almost violent conjunctions of opposites in their 'metaphysical conceits' in order to bridge that widening gap. Their poetry sounds a note of warning about the disastrous hollowness of cold and single reasoning. The great edifice of Milton's epic stands in some ways like a last bastion of the old way of seeing and reading ourselves in the world; it therefore became increasingly isolated as a poem when the secular tides of scientific literalism rolled in. Nevertheless, at the height of that time, in his profound invocations of light, Milton had perhaps discovered or rediscovered the truth which would turn the tide. As he hesitated on the brink of the mystery of the Holy Trinity in Book III of *Paradise Lost*, he had sensed that there was 'a stream whose fountain who shall tell', which might be the source both of the scientist's cosmos and of the poet's vision. But for the rest of that century, and through nearly all the eighteenth century, poetry lost its status as luminous and illuminated writing set down in the midst of the pages of life, and became instead a kind of marginal decoration, a nostalgic diversion from the prosaic business of the day:

> Know then Thyself, presume not God to scan
> The proper study of Mankind is Man.[17]

These famous lines seem to rebuke the breadth, the height, the depth, of Milton's visions of 'God' and 'Man'. Pope's sense of what it means to say Nosce Te Ipsum, 'Know Thyself', is shrivelled and cramped in comparison with the range of Sir John Davies' thought on the same subject, for Davies' whole point (and Milton's) is that you cannot presume to 'know yourself' unless you are prepared to 'scan' God. But Pope's trite couplet was a sign of the age to come. It is scarcely surprising, after lines like that, that so much of what passes either for theology or poetry in the Enlightenment age, turns out to be mere anthropology.

In the midst of this ruinous divorce between reason and imagination, poets and scientists were asked, as our own children so often are, to take sides. The scientists were expected to live with their father, 'reason', and to hate and deny their mother, 'imagination'. The poets were expected to cling to the skirts of 'imagination' and never dare to walk in the objective world described by 'reason'. In the next chapter, we shall look at the poet who most successfully survived that Divorce, who worked hardest to reunite reason and imagination. His struggle to understand and overcome the dualism and mental blindness of his own age may give us the key to a deeper harmonisation and a recovery of transfigured vision in ours. And we shall see that for Coleridge, as for Milton before him, the way out of these dark dualities was through the mystery of Trinity.

---

[17] Alexander Pope, *An Essay on Man*, Epistle II, lines 1–2, in *Poetical Works*, ed. H. Davis (Oxford, 1966), p. 250.

Chapter 6

A Secret Ministry: Journeying with Coleridge to the Source of the Imagination

Introduction

Throughout this book, we have been making the case that the imagination, far from being a merely subjective realm of fantasy, is, in fact, an essential instrument with which we grasp the truth. In Chapter 1, we looked at the way in which the philosophers of the Enlightenment had sought to make a divorce between reason and imagination, and exclude imagination from any right to truth. Samuel Taylor Coleridge was living and working in the midst of this process. He saw from within, as it developed, the deadening effect of a falsely rationalistic and materialist philosophy. As a leading figure in the Romantic Movement he was already part of the reaction against a purely mechanical and materialist view of the world, but unlike some of the other Romantic poets he was concerned with more than creating beautiful fantasies as an alternative to grim reality. He wanted to challenge the philosophers on their own ground and show that the insights of imagination are insights into reality itself. Although Coleridge is best known for a handful of brilliant poems written in the course of a few miraculous years when he was a young man at the end of the eighteenth century; it is less well known that he spent the rest of his life, the first thirty-four years of the nineteenth century, reflecting on the meaning of that intense experience – the experience of having been the mind through which great works of imagination had been revealed. In this reflection Coleridge found himself compelled to reject the mechanistic, clockwork cosmos of Newton, to reject the distant and detached clock-maker that passed for God with many of his contemporaries. Instead he rediscovered for himself the mysterious and suddenly present God who spoke to Moses from the burning bush, the mysterious and all-sustaining Word made flesh at Bethlehem, and the life-giving Holy Spirit through whom the imaginations of poets are kindled. After all his peregrinations, Coleridge, like his ancient mariner, found haven and firm footing at last in the land of the Trinity. As we come to the end of the Enlightenment project, whose shortcomings Coleridge so strongly attacked whilst he was in the midst of it, we may find in his writings very useful guides for the seas we have to navigate in the new 'post-modern' era.

In the course of this chapter we shall explore some of the key ideas and images in Coleridge's work which might be of most help to us, in the vital task of reintegrating the insights of the imagination with those of the reason. At the heart of Coleridge's poetry and prose is a profound reflection on the nature and meaning of symbols.

Beginning with the experience of language as a set of symbols, Coleridge came to apprehend nature as a complex network of symbols. He asks the question: 'Who makes the symbols in nature?' Is it humanity, with our own imagination? Is it God alone in a single act of creation long since past? Or are these symbols created by a continuous meeting between His imagination and ours? In seeking an answer to these questions, Coleridge came to develop what might be called a 'theology of the imagination'. We will move in this chapter from the roots of this theology in his early poetry to its flowering in his later prose works.

'Frost at Midnight'

We begin this journey with Coleridge with a beautiful conversational poem which he had written in 1798. In 'Frost at Midnight'[1] he explores the the relation between the inner world of our consciousness and the outer world we inhabit, between the imagined images with which we clothe and express our inner thoughts and the images of the world around us, which in their own way also seem to express our minds. The poem has a deceptive simplicity; Coleridge opens it in the beautiful setting of his little cottage in Somerset, sitting up late at night in front of the dying embers of the fire, in quiet and solitude, with his infant son Hartley, slumbering beside him. And a stream of association, partly mediated through the image of the fire dying in the grate, leads him back first to memories of his own childhood, then forward and out to an imagined future for his own child, and, finally, back again to the cottage.

The images in this poem are beautifully realised with great fidelity to nature as Coleridge has observed it. There is no straining to introduce symbolism, or to reduce the things he observes in nature to the status of mere ciphers or allegories. He is not trying to seize upon an image in order to make a point, and indeed he would regard it as an infidelity to nature to do so. In discussing the work of William Bowles, a contemporary whom he otherwise admired, he wrote:

> There reigns thro' all the blank-verse poems such a perpetual trick of *moralizing* every thing – which is very well, occasionally – but never to see or describe any interesting appearance in nature, without connecting it by dim analogies with the moral world, proves faintness of Impression. Nature has her proper interest; & he will know what it is, who believes & feels, that every Thing has a Life of it's own, & that we are all *one Life*.[2]

---

[1]   Samuel Taylor Coleridge, *Poetical Works I, Poems (Reading Text)*, ed. J.C.C. Mays (Princeton, 2001), pp. 453–56 (Volume 16 in CC).

[2]   A letter of 1802 to William Sotheby, cited in John Beer, *Coleridge the Visionary* (London, 1970), p. 139.

Nevertheless, we have the sense throughout this poem that, as well as giving us these beautiful descriptions, Coleridge's mind is communing *through* the appearances of nature he describes – through the seas and hills, the fire, frost and moonlight – with the mind behind nature. Nature herself, celebrated for her own beauties, becomes in the course of this poem both the medium, and indeed the language of that communion.

So the poem opens:

> The Frost performs its secret ministry,
> Unhelped by any wind. The owlet's cry
> Came loud – and hark, again! loud as before. (lines 1–3)

Coleridge is opening his heart and speaking, directly to us in the present continuous, and the detail of the owl's cry, gives us an immediacy and a presence with him, which is part of the poem's many paradoxes; it is a poem in some senses about solitude, and yet we are invited vividly and presently into the intimacy of that solitude:

> The inmates of my cottage, all at rest,
> Have left me to that solitude, which suits
> Abstruser musings: save that at my side
> My cradled infant slumbers peacefully.
> 'Tis calm indeed! so calm, that it disturbs
> And vexes meditation with its strange
> And extreme silentness. (lines 5–10)

Before we get the reflections and echoes between the inner and the outer, which form the poem's main theme, we start with a contrast between the hush of nature and the disquieting sense of movement and restlessness in Coleridge's own mind, which is of course, what kept him awake:

> Sea, hill, and wood,
> This populous village! Sea, and hill, and wood,
> With all the numberless goings-on of life,
> Inaudible as dreams! (lines 10–13)

This is simply a beautiful evocation of the sleeping village of Nether Stowey in its setting among the hills by the sea. But also it introduces subtly to our minds the notion of the potential for speech hidden in silence. The 'Sea, and, hill and, wood, / With all the numberless goings on of life,' are all for the present inaudible, but there is a distinct suggestion that they could speak had we but ears to hear them, that they have about them the intimations of a deeper meaning that adheres to the imagery of dreams.

So Coleridge continues:

> the thin blue flame
> Lies on my low-burnt fire, and quivers not;
> Only that film, which fluttered on the grate,
> Still flutters there, the sole unquiet thing.
> Methinks, its motion in this hush of nature
> Gives it dim sympathies with me who live,
> Making it a companionable form,
> Whose puny flaps and freaks the idling Spirit
> By its own moods interprets, every where
> Echo or mirror seeking of itself,
> And makes a toy of Thought. (lines 13–23)

Now he introduces for the first time the notion of a direct reflection between the inner and the outer. He begins with the first, perhaps the easiest; one might say the lowest level of that sympathy or connection, which is the one that we make in fancy for ourselves. We see something exterior and seize upon it, and our imagination shapes it and turns it to a symbol for that which is within. Coleridge frankly admits that symbol he makes out of the film fluttering in the grate is entirely his own:

> Only that film, which fluttered on the grate,
> Still flutters there, the sole unquiet thing.
> Methinks, its motion in this hush of nature
> Gives it dim sympathies with me who live,
> Making it a companionable form.

And yet he introduces the idea that there is something within us which is not content to look at the mere surface of nature, something which looks out and beyond, and seeks in nature the echo or mirror of the stirrings it feels within itself. Then comes that experience we all have when an outward and visible object becomes, as it were, the gateway or the vehicle through which the mind is drawn, either out into the imaginary world or back through memory to other times. In this case, the object which becomes the gateway to Coleridge's past is the fire in the grate. The poem begins in the present, with Coleridge, a young father, gazing at the last embers of the fire through the grate, and shifts back to Coleridge the schoolboy, staring at the schoolroom fire, remembering the stories he had been told as a still younger boy, at home in the rural vicarage, of how the fluttering back and forth of the final last little film of ash on the fire, knocking at the grate, presaged the arrival of a stranger knocking at the cottage door, which was why the country people called that last flapping film of ash the 'stranger'. So Coleridge writes:

> But O! how oft,
> How oft, at school, with most believing mind,
> Presageful, have I gazed upon the bars,
> To watch that fluttering *stranger*! and as oft
> With unclosed lids, already had I dreamt
> Of my sweet birth-place, and the old church-tower,
> Whose bells, the poor man's only music, rang
> From morn to evening, all the hot Fair-day,
> So sweetly, that they stirred and haunted me
> With a wild pleasure, falling on mine ear
> Most like articulate sounds of things to come! (lines 23–33)

So Coleridge in the cottage at Stowey is reminded, as he looks at the fire, of Coleridge the schoolboy. But in turn, he is reminded of Coleridge the schoolboy at that very time also being reminded by the fire to look further back. It is as though we have not so much a double vision as a triple vision here; he is remembering himself remembering.

For the boy, unhappy at school, looks at the fire and thinks of visitors, home and holidays, and of his early childhood growing up in the little vicarage of Ottery St Mary in Devon: 'I dreamt / Of my sweet birth-place, and the old church-tower'. And when he remembers that, he remembers the experience as a young child, of hearing the bells ring in the Church, 'Whose bells, the poor man's only music, rang /From morn to evening, all the hot Fair-day, /So sweetly'. And then these remembered bells themselves seem to be stirring in his imagination and speaking of that which is beyond themselves: 'So sweetly, that they stirred and haunted me / With a wild pleasure, falling on mine ear / Most like articulate sounds of things to come!' It is as though we pass through one layer after another; each layer seems to becken us to the one beyond it. The passage thus far has been backwards, taking us closer and closer to the source of things in Coleridge's childhood. For, as Coleridge was to remark thirteen years later in one of his lectures on Shakespeare, 'In the Poet was comprehended the man who carries the feelings of Childhood onto the powers of Manhood, who with a soul unsubdued, unshackled by custom, can contemplate all things with the freshness with the wonder of a child …'[3]

But now these remembered bells of childhood speak not only of the past but of the future, 'like most articulate sounds of things to come'. And we are reminded that this vivid image of the bells ringing on the hot Fair-day is itself in the memory of Coleridge the schoolboy, who wakes guiltily from his reverie but takes comfort from the flapping of the *stranger* in the hope that the superstition might genuinely be true, that there would be a knock upon the door that would really set him free from the schoolroom and take him back in fact, not just in fancy, to his childhood home:

---

[3]   Samuel Taylor Coleridge, *Lectures 1808–1819: On Literature, I*, ed. R.A. Foakes (Princeton, 1987), p. 326 (Volume 5 in CC).

And so I brooded all the following morn,
Awed by the stern preceptor's face, mine eye
Fixed with mock study on my swimming book:
Save if the door half opened, and I snatched
A hasty glance, and still my heart leaped up,
For still I hoped to see the *stranger's* face, ... (lines 36–41)

This is a particular childhood memory, and yet in the gathering symbolism of the poem, it becomes much more. For in one sense, this whole poem is about listening for a knock from behind the door of nature; it is about hoping to find that the world around us is not a blank wall, but a door or a window. It is about hoping that we might glimpse that face which is behind nature. In a sense, Coleridge is saying of the whole cosmos what he says of the schoolroom door: 'A hasty glance, and still my heart leaped up, / For still I hoped to see the *stranger's* face'.

He returns us then to the present, to that continuous, immediate present into which he had invited us at the beginning of the poem. He looks down at his sleeping child, and realises that now, he, Samuel Taylor Coleridge, is no longer the child, but an adult, with the care of a child himself. And so he speaks to Hartley:

Dear Babe, that sleepest cradled by my side,
Whose gentle breathings, heard in this deep calm,
Fill up the interspersed vacancies
And momentary pauses of the thought!
My babe so beautiful! it thrills my heart
With tender gladness, thus to look at thee,
And think that thou shalt learn far other lore,
And in far other scenes! (lines 44–51)

He goes on to contrast the childhood he hopes he can provide for Hartley, with his own devastating experience of having been taken from the bliss of his early days at Ottery St Mary, where he had been free to roam the fields, meadows and streams, and had walked in the evening to see the stars with his father, to be pent up in the grime of London as a schoolboy at Christ's Hospital. And he remembers how the stars were the one thing unsmudged by the dirt of the city, the one living link with the memories of his childhood and the beauties of nature:

For I was reared
In the great city, pent 'mid cloisters dim,
And saw nought lovely but the sky and stars. (lines 51–53)

The stars were certainly a link with his childhood. He wrote much later, in a letter to a friend, about an experience as a young child walking out at night (and we must remember this was in the days before the light-pollution that prevents many of us from seeing the stars in their glory):

> I remember that at eight years old, I walked with [my father] one winter evening from a farmer's house a mile from Ottery, and he told me the names of the stars, and how Jupiter was 1000 times larger than our world, and that the other twinkling stars were suns, that had worlds rolling round them, and when I came home, he showed me how they rolled round. I heard him with a profound delight and admiration, but without least admixture of wonder or incredulity, for from my early reading of fairy-tales, and genii etc, my mind had been habituated to the Vast.[4]

But they were also a link with the long tradition in which human beings, amidst the struggles and sufferings of their life on earth, had looked up to the heavens and found in the stars emblems of hope and glory.

Stars and starlight were of huge symbolic importance to Coleridge, and he consciously participated in that great tradition of understanding and celebrating what the stars might mean, the truths that might be revealed by their order and beauty. This tradition of celebrating starlight, and finding in the heavens signs of hope for earth, finds its *locus classicus*, and one of its chief sources, in the opening verse of Psalm 19: 'The heavens declare the glory of God; and the firmament sheweth his handywork. Day unto day uttereth speech, and night unto night sheweth knowledge. There is no speech nor language where their voice is not heard.' Even in this psalm there is the hint that we might hear the voice of what we thought inarticulate which Coleridge develops in 'Frost at Midnight'. If 'night unto night sheweth knowledge', then it is knowledge of a beauty and order unassailable by the depravities of earth.

Beyond that celebrated declaration in Scripture, Coleridge would have been conscious of the many wonderful moments in the course of European literature in which the stars feature as emblems of hope and renewal. He would have known the great passage which forms the last lines of the *Inferno*, in which Dante and Virgil at last emerge from that lowest pit of Hell, besmeared and begrimed and utterly exhausted, and move once more towards a shining world:

> So now we entered on that hidden path,
> My lord and I, to move once more towards
> A shining world. We did not care to rest.
> We climbed, he going first and I behind,
> Until through some small aperture I saw
> The lovely things the skies above us bear.
> Now we came out and once more saw the stars.[5]

---

[4]   *Collected Letters of Samuel Taylor Coleridge*, ed. E.L. Griggs, 6 vols (Oxford, 1956–71), vol. I, p. 354 .

[5]   Canto 34, lines 133–39, in Dante, *Inferno*, trans. R. Kirkpatrick (London, 2006), pp. 311–12.

Gazing at the stars he would have been conscious, too, of the beautiful passage in *The Merchant of Venice* in which Lorenzo speaks to Jessica of the music of the spheres, the sense that we behold in the stars, but cannot hear, a harmony which resonates with something in our souls, which we strain to catch but cannot:

> Sit, Jessica. Look how the floor of heaven
> Is thick inlaid with patines of bright gold:
> There's not the smallest orb which thou behold'st
> But in his motion like an angel sings,
> Still quiring to the young-eyed cherubins;
> Such harmony is in immortal souls;
> But whilst this muddy vesture of decay
> Doth grossly close in it, we cannot hear it.[6]

Coleridge speaks of himself as being 'in the great city *pent*', and the contrast between the dark confines of our life on earth and the splendour and spaciousness of our glimpses of the heavens would have been articulated for him in the opening lines of *Comus*, when the daemon, a spirit from the realm of the stars, comes down to earth and opens that masque with the words:

> Before the starry threshold of Jove's court
> My mansion is, where those immortal shapes
> Of bright aerial spirits live ensphered
> In regions mild of calm and serene air
> Above the smoke and stir of this dim spot
> Which men call earth, and with low-thoughted care
> Confined and pestered in this pin-fold here
> Strive to keep up a frail and feverish being ... (lines 1–8)[7]

The Bible, Dante, Shakespeare and Milton were all forming and focusing Coleridge's imagination. They were deepening the very way in which he saw the stars. Indeed, in his own poetry – in this very passage and, as we shall see, in *The Rime of the Ancient Mariner* (especially its glosses) – and, perhaps most movingly, in the concluding words of the *Biographia*, Coleridge himself developed and enriched this human celebration of the stars. We see them differently because of what he and others wrote.

So in 'Frost at Midnight', Coleridge moves from the memory of himself as a child on the roof of Christ's Hospital watching the stars, to think of how his own child might be brought up:

---

[6]   Shakespeare, *The Merchant of Venice*, Act V, scene 1, lines 58–65, in *The Complete Works*, ed. P. Alexander (London, 1957)..

[7]   In John Milton, *Complete Shorter Poems*, ed. J. Carey (London, 1968), pp.175–76.

But *thou*, my babe! shalt wander like a breeze
By lakes and sandy shores, beneath the crags
Of ancient mountain, and beneath the clouds,
Which image in their bulk both lakes and shores
And mountain crags: so shalt thou see and hear
The lovely shapes and sounds intelligible
Of that eternal language, which thy God
Utters, who from eternity doth teach
Himself in all, and all things in himself.
Great universal Teacher! he shall mould
Thy spirit, and by giving make it ask. (lines 54–64)

In this passage, Coleridge approaches the heart of what he has to say in his poem. He prepares our mind for the notion that the beauties and particularities of nature might be themselves and yet be more than themselves, by beginning first at the level of analogy. He compares the wanderings of his boy as he grows up to a wandering breeze. Then he introduces the word 'image', which he uses, not its usual sense as a noun but in a new sense, as a verb, and he suggests that one part of nature *images* another part of nature, like 'the clouds / Which image in their bulk both lakes and shores / And mountain crags'. Here, the cloud-mountains correspond to the physical mountains – which in turn, of course, are reflected in the lakes. All these examples of one thing imaging and referring to another prepare the imagination to receive the more explicit teaching that nature herself may be *imaging* that which is beyond nature. That she may be not only a distinct series of opaque objects, but also a language of symbols: 'The lovely shapes and sounds intelligible / Of that eternal language, which thy God / Utters'.

This is one of Coleridge's most important insights. He never ceased to be amazed by the fact that nature is intelligible, by the fact that we not only perceive it in a coherent and ordered way, but that its very coherence and order provides us with a vocabulary of symbols with which to explore a similar coherence and order, both within ourselves and beyond or through the veil of nature. Throughout his life, he tried to build a coherent system of thought on the foundation of this insight. In this system, the analogy of language is crucial. In his later prose he works out the foundations and structure of such a system in a rigorous and rational way. But, in one sense, the heart of it had already been disclosed to him intuitively in this poem. As often happens, imagination was the forerunner of reason. In this poem, he expresses the intuition that the world in which we find ourselves, and all its contents, these lakes, these mountains, these shining stars, are themselves *words*, within an eternal language which God utters. And what is taught in that language is not the accumulation of observations and statistics which passes for science, nor is it the tabulation of dry surfaces evoked, for example, in Wittgenstein's *Tractatus* – 'the world is everything which is the case'.[8] For Coleridge, 'that eternal language'

---

[8]   See above Introduction, pp. 5–6.

does not so much teach facts as disclose a presence, the presence of One 'who from eternity doth teach / Himself in all, and all things in himself. / Great universal Teacher!' We shall return to this theme presently when we examine a notebook entry which forms a bridge between his intuitions here and their outworking in *Biographia Literaria*.

The poem then returns through the speculation about Hartley growing up, back to its point of origin in that hush in the cottage, and we return with it; but we return changed by our journey through these images, and we come back to the first image with which the poem began, but in a sense we understand it for the first time. So Coleridge continues:

> Therefore all seasons shall be sweet to thee,
> Whether the summer clothe the general earth
> With greenness, or the redbreast sit and sing
> Betwixt the tufts of snow on the bare branch
> Of mossy apple-tree, while the night thatch
> Smokes in the sun-thaw; whether the eave-drops fall
> Heard only in the trances of the blast,
> Or if the secret ministry of frost
> Shall hang them up in silent icicles,
> Quietly shining to the quiet Moon. (lines 65–74)

When we began the poem, we might have read the words, 'The frost performs its secret ministry unhelped by any wind', simply as an analogy. We might have thought it a quaint poeticism to suggest that frost had in any sense a ministry or service, let alone any of the aura which surrounds a word like 'ministry', the aura of 'religious service', the suggestion that in some sense the minister is concerned with sacraments, with gateways to God. By the time we have finished the poem and grasped that the frost and the moonlight are part of those 'lovely shapes and sounds intelligible of that eternal language' uttered by God, we can understand at last the full freight of meaning concealed in the poem's opening line: 'The frost performs its secret ministry'. It is as though Coleridge is saying, 'hark! and hark again' – when we hear the word 'ministry' in the opening line, we do not know what to make of it; but when we hark again to the closing lines of the poem, we have a completely new understanding of what it might mean to speak of the 'secret ministry of frost'. This in turn opens our imagination to receive the final image of the 'quiet moon' as the image of one who is also a minister of God.

Moonlight and the Mariner

This final picture of the quiet moon is an apt image with which to end 'Frost at Midnight' just as, later, moonlight 'dim glimmering through the window-pane' would be an apt image for the notebook entry.[9] Apt not only because of the way moonlight transfigures the everyday, removing the 'film of familiarity', and is therefore a natural symbol for the transformative power of the imagination (which was, of course, how Shakespeare used moonlight in *A Midsummer Night's Dream*), but apt also because, in the tradition of Platonic and Neoplatonic thinking in which Coleridge participated, moonlight had come to be understood as the proper symbol for the way in which our grasp of eternal truth is rarely seen directly, but is rather mediated through nature.

The sun, in all its naked glory, symbolises the absolute truth in itself, which cannot be apprehended directly by fallen man any more than the naked eye can endure to look directly at the sun. The whole world is revealed to us in a light at the source of which we may not gaze. It is for this reason that the eagle is the type and symbol of St John the Evangelist, for it was believed that the eagle could see directly into the sun and the preface to John's Gospel seems to imply such a direct insight into God in Himself before all creation.

We cannot bear to look at the sun, but when we look to the moon we find 'brilliance made bearable'.[10] When his rays are reflected to us from her, then in her transfiguring light we get an image of what it might be to look at the sun if we could.

Another reason why the moon became so important a symbol is that in the old cosmography she is as it were, a dweller on the threshold between the human and the divine. The circle of the moon is the boundary between our sublunary world of mortality, mutability, change and decay, and the heavens upon whose threshold she treads, the heavens beyond her where the sun and fixed stars are the signs God has set for the eternal and unchanging verities. The moon is the only one of the heavenly bodies who, whilst shining resplendently like the other luminaries, nevertheless changes, and waxes and wanes as we do. For this reason we yearn towards her as a companionable form, and yet also beyond her, as one whose changes, though we share them, we are called to transcend.

This special role of the moon as the one who so reflects the light and beauty of heaven that even fallen and corrupted men who cannot bear to look directly on its light and goodness are reached and moved by her gentler light, is made clear in *The Rime of the Ancient Mariner*.[11] Before the Mariner's 'fall' in shooting the Albatross, the sun is a bright and companionable presence:

> The Sun came up upon the left
> Out of the sea came he!
> And he shone bright, and on the right
> Went down into the sea. (lines 25–28)

---

[9]   See below p. 160.

[10]   The phrase is Geoffrey Hill's from 'The Masque of Blackness' in *Collected Poems* (Harmondsworth, 1985), p. 146.

[11]   Coleridge, *Poetical Works I*, 1834 text, pp 373 –419.

Afterwards, the sun becomes unbearable in both its heat and light. It is the presence of God visited upon the soul which is in the very agony of denying that Presence:

> All in a hot and copper sky,
> The bloody Sun, at noon,
> Right up above the mast did stand
> No bigger than the moon. (lines 111–14)

And more striking still is the image of the sun staring at the Mariner through the bars of the skeleton ship as though through a dungeon:

> And straight the Sun was flecked with bars,
> (Heaven's Mother send us grace!)
> As if through a dungeon-grate he peered
> With broad and burning face. (lines 177–80)

But when the time comes for grace to touch the Mariner's soul and for his vision to be transfigured, then it is by the ministry of the moon that the transformation happens. The Mariner's deed has alienated him from nature, humanity and God. He cannot bear to look upon the seas, to look upon the dead, or to look upon God:

> I looked to heaven and tried to pray;
> But or ever a prayer had gusht,
> A wicked whisper came, and made
> My heart as dry as dust.
>
> I closed my lids and kept them close,
> And the balls like pulses beat;
> For the sky and the sea, and the sea and the sky
> Lay like a load on my weary eye,
> And the dead were at my feet. (lines 244–52)

It is after he has reached his worst agony, seven days and seven nights of longing but being unable to die, that we get the first initmations of change; first in the imagery of the poem itself, and secondly, in the course of what actually happens to the Mariner. The key – almost as it were, musically, the 'signature' – that accompanies these changes, is the image of the 'moving moon':

In his loneliness and fixedness,
he yearneth towards the
journeying moon and the stars
that still sojourn, yet still move
onward; and everywhere the
blue sky belongs to them, and
is their appointed rest and
native country and their own
natural homes, which they enter
unannounced as lords that are
expected, and yet there is a
silent joy at their arrival.

The moving moon went up the sky
And nowhere did abide
Softly she was going up
And a star or two beside (lines 263–66)

Coleridge makes a beautiful and ambiguous play on the word 'moving'. We have to do with a 'moving moon' in every sense. It is in the moon's very nature both that she moves through space and is the cause of movement in others, and also that she moves us in the inner space of our hearts.

Accompanying this verse is the later gloss, which forms a kind of counterpoint to and commentary on the verse: '*In his loneliness and fixedness, he yearneth towards the journeying moon and the stars that still sojourn, yet still move onward* ...' These glosses were added years later when Coleridge republished the poem in 1817, after he had himself lived through much of what the poem describes. They form almost a separate poem and yet one which is in profound conversation with the text it glosses. So, for example, this long and beautiful gloss on the 'journeying moon and the stars that still sojourn yet still move onward', although set there apparently only to explain a single verse, acts as a kind of premonition of the redemption which is to come. At the lowest point in the Mariner's journey, just when he has cried in agony that he wishes to die and yet he cannot, just at the point where his own journey seems endless and hopeless, and home is an unimaginable possibility, just at that point comes a gloss whose imagery moves us from journeying to homecoming. The narrative of the poem will not arrive at a homecoming for many stanzas yet, but the hope of its possibility is mediated to the reader through key words in the gloss. Words like 'belongs', 'rest', 'native country' and 'natural home' gloss the text of the Mariner's exile like the whispers of a good dream. The last phrase of that gloss, 'there is a silent joy at their arrival', anticipates, with its echo of Christ's words about the joy in heaven over the sinner who repents, the final homecoming of the Mariner – even at that point in the story at which such a homecoming seems least likely.

The way in which Coleridge's later gloss on the text of his poem allows us to return to a page we thought we knew and read it in a new way is rather like the experience, for Christians, of repentance, confession and grace. One lives through a page of one's life, and looking back it can seem to have the finality of a printed text, a completed work. How can any of it ever be undone or unsaid, however much one wishes it could? But, in prayer and confession, we offer that page to God

for the commentary of His grace; we invite Him to surround the text of our life
with a gloss that may reveal to us, many years later, glimpses of redeeming love
that were hidden at the time.

The Mariner's redemption can only come from a recognition of the truth he
had denied when he shot the Albatross, the truth that all creatures are God's and
not his. In the following stanzas he looks out again at the water-snakes which he
had previously described as 'a thousand, thousand slimy things', and sees them
utterly transfigured in the moonlight:

By the light of the moon he beholdeth God's *creatures of the great calm*	Beyond the shadow of the ship, I watched the water-snakes; They moved in tracks of shining white And when they reared the elfish light Fell off in hoary flakes … (lines 272–76)
Their beauty and their happiness *He blesseth them in his heart*	O happy living things! no tongue Their beauty might declare: A spring of love gushed from my heart, And I blessed them unaware: Sure my kind Saint took pity on me, And I blessed them unaware.
The spell begins to break	The self-same moment I could pray; And from my neck so free The Albatross fell off, and sank Like lead into the sea. (lines 283–91)

It is as though by seeing these creatures in moonlight he is given, however briefly,
some notion of how God sees them. Certainly Coleridge's own experiences of
moonlight, especially moonlight on water, had something of that quality, as for
example this brief passage from one of the notebooks shows: 'Quiet stream, with
all its eddys & the moon light playing in them; quiet, as if they were Ideas in the
divine Mind anterior to the Creation.'[12]

For Coleridge, the meaning of the moon and moonlight is not a purely
human invention; it is a symbol, but it is not a randomly chosen or arbitrarily
constructed human symbol. It is a symbol which is given, which is moulded by and
participates in the reality it represents. Coleridge distinguished true symbols from
artificial analogies; he summed up his distinction in a late work, *The Statesman's
Manual*: 'The Symbol is characterized by… the translucence of the Eternal through
and in the Temporal. It always partakes of the Reality which it renders intelligible;
and while it enunciates the whole, abides itself as a living part in that Unity, of
which it is representative.' Whereas analogies are 'but empty echoes which the

---

[12]   Cited in Beer, *Coleridge The Visionary*, p. 147.

fancy arbitrarily associates with apparitions of matter, less beautiful but not less shadowy than the sloping orchard or hill-side pasture-field seen in the transparent lake below'.[13]

Coleridge spent most of the second part of his life reflecting in a rigorous and philosophically disciplined way on the very question of what a symbol is, and on the relation between language considered as a set of symbols given and articulated by humanity, and nature considered as a set of symbols given and articulated by God. It is to some of his later prose works that we now turn in order to travel with Coleridge on a journey which traces the full flow of his poetry back to its source in an Imagination which is more than the human.

Symbol and Imagination in Coleridge's Prose

We will begin with a notebook entry which continues, as it were, from where 'Frost at Midnight' left off; it develops the notion that nature might itself be a language. But Coleridge has been thinking more deeply. In 'Frost at Midnight', the phrase 'eternal language' tells us something about God, but doesn't help us to understand his language. In the note, Coleridge is trying to grasp what it might mean to say that the language of God is a 'symbolic' language.

Perhaps the most important of Coleridge's many insights was the profound parallel he discerned between our experience of language and our experience of the world. We could describe language in purely exterior and physical terms. As soon as a word is used it has a quantifiable physical presence – black ink and paper weighing so many grams, an audible sound at so many decibels. Yet, however accurate the measurements and description of language as a purely physical phenomenon were to be, such a description would still say nothing of a speaker's, listener's or reader's actual experience of language. When we use language, we pass through the physicality of the words so swiftly we hardly realise they are there. For, the words we use are, of course, not simply dead physical objects, opaque and referring to nothing but themselves. The words we use are living symbols taking us the instant they are uttered through and beyond themselves, connecting us with an intricate network of reference, reference to other words and reference to the realities in nature and in ourselves of which the words are symbols. For most of us this process of meeting the words only to be ushered through them to that meaning beyond them to which they point is so familiar and unconscious we scarcely notice it is happening. We cease to be conscious of the words, only of the images they summon up. But poets are concerned not only with the meanings of words, but with savouring and celebrating the words themselves, the very sounds. And so it is that, in reading great poetry, our vision is doubled; we become aware simultaneously both of the word as a thing in itself, a chosen

---

[13]   From 'The Statesman's Manual', in *Lay Sermons*, ed. R.J. White (Princeton, 1972), pp. 30–31 (Volume 6 in CC).

sound, a kind of music in the air, and also of that other reality, that mystery of truth of which the word is the gatekeeper. In the language of poetry we meet something which is both itself and a mediator of that which is beyond itself. We can sometimes have the same experience not just with words but with the world. Indeed, as we have seen in earlier chapters, before the Enlightenment most people were free to read the world as being itself symbolic and constantly drawing us to truths beyond itself. For Coleridge, this experience was so constant that it drove him first to doubt and then to demolish the new 'Enlightened' view' that the world was a set of dead objects meaning nothing.

Take, for example, this key passage from a notebook of 1805:

> In looking at objects of Nature, while I am thinking, as at yonder moon dim-glimmering through the dewy window-pane, I seem rather to be seeking, as it were *asking,* a symbolic language for something within me that already and for ever exists, than observing anything new. Even when the latter is the case, yet still I have always an obscure feeling as if that new phenomenon were the dim awaking of a forgotten or hidden Truth of my inner Nature! It is still interesting as a Word, a Symbol! It is *Logos,* the Creator! and the Evolver![14]

This remarkable 'note to self' was itself the fruit of reflection on the kind of writing and the kind of looking and listening at nature that Coleridge had already been engaged in. It turned out also to be the seed for later development in Coleridge's thought, especially the *Biographia* and the lecture on 'Poesy considered as one of the Fine Arts'. It is an enormously dense and rich passage that begins, apparently, in a world clearly divided between subject and object, which Coleridge inherited in the eighteenth century. That phrase 'in looking at objects of nature' could have been written by any materialist or mechanistic philosopher of Coleridge's day. But the sentence continues 'while I am thinking' – and this is one of the first things we observe about Coleridge: he is aware constantly of the fact that we are not merely a passive *tabula rasa*, upon which the outside objects of nature impinge or impress themselves, but constantly active, looking, thinking, shaping beings. And surely this constant awareness of our own conscious activity of the moment, what Coleridge in another place called 'the self-circling energies of the reason',[15] must itself have an influence on not only the way in which we see nature, but perhaps on the very nature itself that we see.

So he continues, 'In looking at objects of nature while I am thinking, as at yonder moon dim-glimmering through the dewy window-pane, I seem rather to be seeking, as it were, asking ...' We move here from the ideas and language about the mind as being passive, to the notion that the mind is actively *asking*, actively *seeking*. And what the mind seeks is not simply the exterior recording of the opaque

---

[14]   *The Notebooks of Samuel Taylor Coleridge*, ed. K. Coburn, 4 vols (New York, 1957–73), vol. II, 2546.

[15]   'Statesman's Manual', in *Lay Sermons*, p. 29.

outsides of dead objects, what it it seeking is *language*, intelligibility, meaning: 'I seem rather to be seeking, as it were, asking for a symbolic language.'

Coleridge has the experience as he sees the moon dim-glimmering through the window pane, that there is, as it were, a meaning behind it, that it is like a word, that he could pass through it and see something beyond it; but he has simultaneously the experience that whatever is beyond it is also resonant with something which is within him, something which 'already and forever exists'. It is as though the experience of perception were a kind of medium or middle-state between a meaning which is beyond and a meaning which is within. It becomes, as it were, a language of communication between the inner and the outer, between the immanent and the transcendent. In some ways, he is rediscovering the correspondence between inner nature and outer nature, which was so beautifully expressed and ordered before the Enlightenment in the images of the microcosm and the macrocosm which we looked at in the poetry of Sir John Davies. It is not surprising that Coleridge was deeply attracted to Davies, and when in the *Biographia Literaria* he wants to talk about the way in which the imagination works, he turns to Davies' poem *Nosce Teipsum*.

So Coleridge continues in this startling little note, and this time he introduces the word 'Word', significantly with a capital W – 'It is still interesting as a Word, a Symbol!' Now, whose word, whose symbol is it? Coleridge in this note is certainly not suggesting that it is simply his own construct. Yes, this moonlight does seem somehow to correspond with something within Coleridge's inner nature, which only that moonlight could express; but Coleridge is not saying that it is he, privately, Coleridge himself, who is, as it were, casting upon the moonlight the spell of its meaning.

'It is still interesting', he says, 'as a Word, a symbol'; but he goes on to say, 'This is Logos, the Creator and the evolver', and here he anticipates by some years the formulation which he gives this idea in the famous thirteenth chapter of the *Biographia Literaria*, where he asks, at last, 'What is the deepest and purest source of creativity, of imagination?' Is there a common source both for the outward and visible forms of nature, and for those inward and invisible imaginative apprehensions of that nature which we find in the human mind? Is there a common source for that beautifully expressed and ordered organic whole, that composition of one in many parts which we call the cosmos, and the beautifully expressed and ordered organic wholes in poetry and art which we call human creation? Might there be a single source for that ordering and imaginative power which is responsible for both? Coleridge anticipates and says, 'this is Logos, the Creator and the Evolver'.

It is not by chance, as Coleridge was later to show, that we find in the world around us so many apt representations and symbols of our own inner states and experiences. For the outward 'objects' of nature are continuously given and made by the divine Mind and Imagination, they are the 'eternal language' of the Divine Poet, whose *poiesis* made us and our minds, and made our minds to be an image and reflection of his own.

If Coleridge is right in thinking that the whole creation including humankind is God's poetry, and that the human being is made in God's image, then we can ask whether the human experience in writing poetry has anything to teach us about God and the world. Not surprisingly, some of the best and most influential of Coleridge's literary critical writing, especially about Shakespeare, has turned out to be reflection on this very question.

Coleridge and Shakespeare

In many ways, Coleridge could be credited with helping the English to rediscover the greatness of Shakespeare; to appreciate Shakespeare for the real virtues of his work, and not, as the eighteenth-century critics have done, to admit him grudgingly to the pantheon of great writers as a kind of honorary rustic, a flawed, natural genius in whom many good things were to be found in spite of his woeful ignorance of the rules of composition. The pre-Coleridgian view of Shakespeare is best summed up in Milton's famously condescending praise 'sweetest Shakespeare, fancy's child, / Warble his native wood-notes wild ...'[16]

This monumental critical failure to understand the power and subtlety of Shakespeare's art arose from the mistake of trying to apply a rigid and literalistic reading of Aristotle's *Poetics*, particularly the so-called 'unities', to Shakespeare's great tragedies. Shakespeare is shown as failing to apply the rules, and the power of his plays is conceded only as a success in spite of this failure.

Following the lead of German romantic philosophers and critics, Coleridge showed how beautifully and subtly wrought the plays are; that far from being 'native wood-notes wild' they are organic wholes, whose inner-structure is perfectly accommodated to bear the weight of every line and animate the whole, whose smallest line or image carries and reiterates the meaning of the whole. However, in the course of rescuing Shakespeare from perverse criticism, he embraced rather than repudiated the notion that Shakespeare is 'natural', as distinct from 'artificial'. Indeed, he took this analogy more seriously than those who had used it as a slight, and it helped him not only to appreciate Shakespeare, but to understand the distinction between the 'mechanic' and the 'organic' in many other spheres as well. This pair of contrasting terms was important to Coleridge in his understanding of 'cosmos' as well as his understanding of literature. Ultimately, the distinction he makes between mechanic and organic form is rooted in his distinction, to which we will come, between Imagination and Fancy. Fancy can manipulate the 'fixities and definites' in order to make a 'mechanic' form which is manufactured according to a prescribed set of rules. But only Imagination, in its Primary and Secondary form, is capable of the primary creative act which gives a living work its organic structure.

---

[16]   'L'Allegro', lines 133–34, in Milton, *Complete Shorter Poems*, p. 138.

In the 1812 lectures, Coleridge praises Shakespeare for rejecting the 'mechanic' manipulation of formal image, so that it conformed to a schema worked up merely by the fancy of man, and praises him for his power, like that of Nature herself, to develop and unfold naturally from the seed and the root, so that the finished work is still in vital touch with its own *fons et origo*:

> The form is mechanic when on any given material we impress a predetermined form, not necessarily arising out of the properties of the material – as when to a mass of wet clay we give whatever shape we wish it to retain when hardened. The organic form, on the other hand, is innate; it shapes as it develops itself from within, and the fullness of its development is one and the same with the perfection of its outward form. Such is the life, such is the form. Nature the prime genial artist, inexhaustible in diverse powers, is equally inexhaustible in forms: each exterior is the physiognomy of the being within, its true image reflected and thrown out from the concave mirror; and even such is the appropriate excellence of her chosen poet, our own Shakespeare – himself a nature humanized, a genial understanding directing self-consciously a power and a[n] implicit wisdom deeper than consciousness.[17]

Here, the parallel between human and divine making is explicit; it is not simply that images from nature provide Coleridge as a critic with metaphors such as 'organic', but rather that there is a genuine continuity and reflection between the 'creativity' of nature, the prime genial artist, and the example of the power of imagination in Shakespeare. The key to understanding the way imagination works in Shakespeare and what it teaches not only about his art, or about art in general, but about nature herself, is that Shakespeare's art is not simply the embroidering by fancy on the grave-clothes of the cold corpse of dead nature, but rather the operation in and through him as an artist of the very same power which itself gives nature life, and that power is the power of Imagination.

What Shakespeare is doing as an artist, as distinct from what we all do in merely perceiving nature at all, is, 'directing self-consciously a power and an implicit wisdom deeper than consciousness'. By the time he came to write the *Biographia Literaria*, Coleridge was prepared to name that power and the Mind behind it more explicitly.

Coleridge on Coleridge

But, perhaps the most important contribution of the literary critical part of *Biographia*, to Coleridge's final insights about God and the human imagination, came in his reflections on his own and Wordsworth's experience as poets writing

---

17   Coleridge *Lectures 1808–1819: On Literature, I*, p. 495.

at the height of their powers. Take, for example, the famous passage in which he describes the occasion of the *Lyrical Ballads*:

> In this idea originated the plan of the *Lyrical Ballads*; in which it was agreed, that my endeavors should be directed to persons and characters supernatural, or at least romantic; yet so as to transfer from our inward nature a human interest and a semblance of truth sufficient to procure for these shadows of imagination that willing suspension of disbelief for the moment, which constitutes poetic faith. Mr. Wordsworth, on the other hand, was to propose to himself as his object, to give the charm of novelty to things of every day, and to excite a feeling analogous to the supernatural, by awakening the mind's attention to the lethargy of custom, and directing it to the loveliness and the wonders of the world before us; an inexhaustible treasure, but for which, in consequence of the film of familiarity and selfish solicitude, we have eyes, yet see not, ears that hear not, and hearts that neither feel nor understand.[18]

This passage is most often cited for the justly famous phrase 'willing suspension of disbelief'; but it also contains two other key ideas for what might be called Coleridge's 'theology of the imagination'. The first is the notion that the poet's business is to discern and establish the links between our inward nature and the matter of his art: so, although he was writing about 'persons or characters supernatural, or at least romantic', persons or characters who, from the point of view of a rationalist, do not properly speaking exist (that is, the Mariner and Cristabel), yet he does so in the full consciousness that these 'shadows of imagination' are the language with which we may speak about 'our inward nature', and may perhaps be the only language in which some parts of that inward nature find expression. In some ways, most of his later writing was an attempt to understand how it was that such a marvellous correspondence between image and truth is possible.

The second key idea here is that poetry is not about lulling the mind, decorating its interior or making a pretended escape from a fixed and dead world, but rather to 'awaken the mind's attention' to a world that is not properly seen at all. Coleridge contends that what we mistake for 'objective' unemotional observation of the natural world is often no more than 'the lethargy of custom', contenting itself with 'the film of familiarity'. The poet, as much as the philosopher or the scientist, is concerned with helping us to look beyond surfaces at what is really there. What he directs us to is not only 'the loveliness and wonders of the world before us', but also something 'inexhaustible'. This last is a vital term. The nature over which our lethargy has cast the film of familiarity is not, in Coleridge's view, fixed and static, but continuously coming to be in the meeting of our minds with the Mind of God.

---

[18]   Samuel Taylor Coleridge, *Biographia Literaria*, ed. J. Engell and W. Jackson Bate (Princeton, 1983), vol. II, pp 6–7 (Volume 7 in CC).

At the core of both of these ideas is Coleridge's sense of a correspondence between 'inner' and 'outer' nature; a correspondence whose meaning he had been seeking since that first jotting in his notebook about seeing the moonlight through the window: 'I have always an obscure feeling as if that new phenomenon were the dim awakening of a forgotten or hidden Truth of my *inner Nature* ...' So, in *Lyrical Ballads*, he felt himself trying 'to transfer from our *inward nature* ... a semblance of Truth'.

His lecture 'On Poesy or Art' brought these obscure feelings or intuitions into crystal clear focus, and made explicit the pivotal role that the arts of the imagination have to play in the mediation between the 'inner' and the 'outer'. In the following quotation, he may have been consciously rewriting the note of 1805, beginning with that same phrase about 'looking at the objects of nature' – but this time, it is not a question of 'dim intuition'; now he is clear both that the 'mirror of nature' presents us with a picture of the inner as well as the outer, and also that it is imaginative poetry which establishes the link between the two:

> In the objects of nature are presented, as in a mirror, all the possible elements, steps and processes of intellect antecedent to consciousness, and therefore to the full development of the intelleigential act; and man's mind is the very focus of all the rays of intellect which are scattered throughout the images of nature. Now so to place these images, totalized, and fitted to the limits of the human mind, as to elicit from, and to superinduce upon, the forms themselves the moral reflexions to which they approximate, to make the external internal, the internal external, to make nature thought, and thought nature – this is the mystery of genius in the Fine Arts ...[19]

The aim of the artist therefore is not simply to describe or imitate the outsides of the objects around him, but so to describe them as to elicit from them what it is that they might mean; so to describe them as to discern in them a hidden correspondence with our inner nature. This is possible without being a merely arbitrary human act, a projection of our psyche on to the inanimate, because of the pivotal role which Coleridge saw for the human mind and imagination made in God's image. It is, as he calls it, 'the very focus of all the rays of intellect which are scattered through the images of nature'.[20]

---

[19]   I am quoting from the slightly expanded version printed by J. Shawcross in the appendix to his edition of the *Biographia Literaria*, 2 vols (Oxford, 1907), vol. II, p. 257. Coleridge's own notes for this lecture are printed in *Lectures 1808–19: On Literature II*, pp. 217–25.

[20]   Shawcross, vol. II, pp. 257–58.

Biographia Literaria: Chapter 13

We turn now to the part of the *Biographia* in which all the ideas we have been tracing in this chapter so far, from the first foray in 'Frost at Midnight' onwards, find their greatest expression and deepest resolution. Throughout the *Biographia* Coleridge speaks of preparing the ground for the more important things he has to say later, and the reader comes at last to the much promised Chapter 13 with a great sense of expectation. That chapter is the most famous and the most perplexing, the most exciting and the most frustrating in all the annals of literary criticism. No sooner has this chapter, titled 'On the Imagination', begun, than it is broken off, and Coleridge interposes a 'letter from a friend' (written by himself!) pleading with him not to try and open the depth and complexity of what he has to say about imagination in so short a space as a single chapter, but to save it for his great proposed work on the constructive philosophy, the *Logosophia*. The letter urges him instead just to give a brief outline of what his conclusions might be and to save the detailed development of his argument for the later work. The letter ends, and Coleridge appends two powerful and provoking paragraphs on Imagination and Fancy – and so ends the chapter.

Richard Holmes, in the second volume of his excellent biography of Coleridge, says of these two paragraphs:

> Coleridge left behind, at the end of Chapter 13, the most famous critical fragment of his career. It became in many ways the prose equivalent of 'Kubla Khan'. Its 199 words – clear, compact, Delphic – were destined to generate as much discussion, as much source-hunting, as much praise and controversy, as the poem. It summed up seven chapters of argument, and defined for the English-speaking world the Romantic concept of creativity.[21]

I shall cite these paragraphs in full, since they are so crucial to our understanding of Coleridge:

> The imagination then, I consider either as primary or secondary. The primary IMAGINATION I hold to be the living Power and prime Agent of all human Perception, as a repetition in the finite mind of the eternal act of creation in the infinite I AM. The secondary Imagination I consider as an echo of the former, co-existing with the conscious will, yet still as identical with the primary in the *kind* of its agency, and differing only in *degree*, and in the *mode* of its operation. It dissolves, diffuses, dissipates, in order to re-create; or where this process is rendered impossible, yet still at all events it struggles to idealize and to unify. It is essentially *vital*, even as all objects [as objects] are essentially fixed and dead.

---

[21] Richard Holmes, *Coleridge: Darker Reflections* (London, 1998), p. 410.

FANCY, on the contrary, has no other counters to play with, but fixities and definites. The Fancy is indeed no other than a mode of Memory emancipated from the order of time and space; while it is blended with, and modified by that empirical phenomenon of the will, which we express by the word CHOICE. But equally with the ordinary memory the Fancy must receive all its materials ready made from the law of association.

Whatever more than this, I shall think it fit to declare concerning the powers and privileges of the imagination is the present work, will be found in the critical essay one the uses of the Supernatural in poetry, and the principles that regulate its introduction; which the reader will find prefixed to the poem of *The Ancient Mariner*.[22]

Here, the intimations which Coleridge had in the notebook of 1805, that the phenomena of nature might form a symbolic language, and that the words of this language might both articulate hidden truths about our inner nature and also point to God the Creator as Logos, all these are made explicit and grounded in a philosophical system: 'The primary Imagination I hold to be the living Power and prime Agent of all human Perception, as a repetition in the finite mind of the eternal act of creation in the infinite I AM.' It is vital that we understand what it means for Coleridge to call the Imagination a 'living power' and an 'agent'. Throughout the first part of the *Biographia*, and indeed throughout the first part of his life, he battled with, and in the end defeated, a system of thought in which not only the imagination and all perception, but mind itself, was understood as a 'passive faculty' rather than a living power, a patient, not an agent. It was a view of the world which saw the mind as, at best, passively recording material phenomena, and at worst as merely a mirage, the accidental by-product of the movement of atoms in a mechanical universe. Coleridge saw the falsehood at the bottom of this view, and these two paragraphs are a kind of cry of triumph in winning that victory. He understood that, from Descartes onwards to Newton, we had simply been beginning from the wrong end of things; as he put it in a letter to Thomas Pool reflecting on his close reading of Newton's *Optics*:

I am exceedingly delighted with the beauty and neatness of his experiments, & with the accuracy of his *immediate* deductions from them – but the opinions founded on these Deductions, and indeed his whole theory is, I am persuaded, so exceedingly superficial as without impropriety to be deemed false. Newton was a mere materialist – Mind in his system is always passive – a lazy Looker-on on an external World. If the mind be not *passive*, if it be indeed made in God's Image, & that too in the sublimest sense – the Image of the *Creator*- there is

---

[22]   Coleridge, *Biographia Literaria, I*, pp. 304–5.

ground for suspicion, that any system built on the passiveness of the mind must
be false, as a system …[23]

The Cartesian-Newtonian system, for all its immediate lucidity, ultimately
made for a universe devoid of mind and intrinsically unintelligible, and made mind
itself almost an absurdity, and something which was to be experienced in isolation,
individually, and only ever on the inside of one's small part of a cosmos which
otherwise consisted of nothing but outsides. Coleridge was now in a position to see
things from an entirely different perspective; he was no longer obliged to confine
his sense of mind, intelligence, joy or wonder, within the circle of the human skull,
but to find it radiating through all the phenomena of the cosmos.

For Coleridge, the physical universe which is the supposed 'object' of our
perception, is not something that merely strikes us from the outside, but something
which is, as it were, being formed continuously, both from our side of it, and
from an apprehended but as yet unknowable other side beyond it. The insight of
the two paragraphs quoted above is that there is a deep connection between that
which is below the level of our consciousness and is continually giving us the gift
of ourselves and our mind, and that which is behind or beyond the phenomena
and is continuously giving them their being, allowing them to well up from its
own *inexhaustible* depths. Even so seemingly simple a thing as perception itself,
let alone composition or art, results from the active powers of our imagination,
meeting and reflecting the active power of that Imagination which has caused all
things to be.

By means of our Primary Imagination, we are constantly participating in a
cosmos whose every part is fraught with the meaning of the Mind of God. For
Coleridge, our Secondary Imagination (what we would now call poetic imagination,
or imagination of the artist) is of the same kind and comes from the same source
as this Primary Imagination and, when we cooperate with it, it too produces and
articulates eternal symbols. By contrast, the Fancy simply manufactures artificial
equivalences which are not, in Coleridge's terms, worthy of the name of 'symbol'.
They have, as he would put it, 'mechanic form' rather than 'organic form', because
they are not rooted in the Mind which is the source of the organic wholeness of the
cosmos, considered as God's act of *poiesis*.

Even as quite a young man, and in his days as a Unitarian preacher, Coleridge
had begun to speculate in this direction, but had drawn a very strict dividing line
between philosophy and religion in general, let alone full-blooded Trinitarian
Christianity in particular. But, by the time he came to write the *Biographia*, he had
indeed experienced 'a more thorough revolution in my philosophic principles and
a deeper revelation into my own heart' and 'my final reconversion to the whole
truth in Christ';[24] and so here, he names the Mind and Imagination behind all

---

[23]   In Samuel Taylor Coleridge, *Selected Letters*, ed. H.J. Jackson (Oxford, 1988), p.
90.

[24]   Coleridge *Biographia Literaria, I*, p. 205.

things, in an allusion to God's self-disclosure to Moses at the burning bush: 'I AM that I AM'.

The second part of this sentence on the Primary Imagination is equally important; Coleridge calls it 'a repetition in the finite mind in the eternal act of creation in the infinite I AM'. In other words, the human mind, far from being an 'epiphenomenon', a ghost in the machine or a kind of mist thrown up by the mere movement of matter, is, in all its imaginative perceiving, correspondent to something else beyond itself, and beyond the cosmos it inhabits. It is scarcely surprising that we find everywhere tantalising repetitions and echoes of ourselves in nature, that the mind is 'everywhere echo or mirror, seeking of itself'; since our mind itself is a repetition, an echo, of the Mind of the Maker in whose image we are created.

Coleridge develops this thought in the later *Philosophical Lectures*, also intended, like the *Biographia*, as a kind of preface to his unwritten *Logosophia*:

> the mind ... then, looking abroad into nature, finds that in its own nature, it has been fathoming nature, and that nature itself is but the greater mirror in which he beholds his own present and his own past being ... while he feels the necessity of that one great Being, whose eternal Reason is the ground and absolute condition of the ideas in the mind, and no less the ground and the absolute cause of all the correspondent realities in nature.[25]

In God, the living power of Primary Imagination actually causes things to exist; indeed, it is the Logos 'through whom all things were made'. In the human being, the Primary Imagination is the living power whereby all things, including humanity itself, are perceived. Because our Primary Imagination is a repetition in our finite mind of God's eternal act of creation, it enables us so to read God's works as to glimpse through them the Mind of their Maker. Unless, of course, we perversely choose to refuse that glimpse, refuse to hear 'that eternal language', which 'God utters', just as we might choose to describe our own language entirely in terms of its physicality and not in terms of its meaning.

If we ask, 'How is it that the Primary Imagination in God, which is the Logos through whom all things are made, the eternal act of creation, can be repeated in our finite mind?' – we will find it in the preface of St John's Gospel. (Coleridge had intended his great unwritten work, the *Logosophia*, to be a commentary on the opening of John's Gospel.) In that preface the Logos is described, first in his being with God, 'In the beginning the Word was with God, and the Word was God' (1:1); and second, in His being with us, 'The Word was made flesh and dwelt among us'. He is also described as *light*, 'In Him was life, and the life was the light of humankind', and again, 'that was the true light with lighteth every one that cometh into the world'. Here, the Logos is understood both as what Davies called 'the

---

[25]   *The Philosophical Lectures of Samuel Taylor Coleridge*, ed. K. Coburn (London and New York, 1949), lecture 11, pp 333–34.

Light that makes the light that makes the day', and as that 'inner light' whereby we perceive truth in the mind. Just as we require the light of day to perceive the objects outside us, so we require another light in which and through which to apprehend 'the inner-landscape':

> That Power which gave me eyes the World to view,
> To see my self infus'd an inward light,
> Whereby my soul, as by a mirror true,
> Of her own form may take a perfect sight,
>
> But as the sharpest eye discerneth nought,
> Except the sun-beams in the air do shine:
> So the best soul with her reflecting thought,
> Sees not her self without some light divine ...
>
> O Light which mak'st the light, which makes the day!
> Which set'st the eye without, and mind within;
> 'Lighten my spirit with one clear heavenly ray,
> Which now to view it self doth first begin.[26]

Davies was himself paraphrasing and versifying a passage from St Augustine's *De Magistro*:

> But when it is a question of things which we behold with the mind, namely, with our intellect and reason, we give verbal expression to realities which we directly perceive as present in that inner light of truth by which the inner man, as he is called, is enlightened and made happy. But here again, if the one who hears my words sees those things himself with that clear and inner eye of the soul, he knows the things whereof I speak by contemplating them himself, and not by my words. Therefore, even when I say what is true, and he sees what is true, it is not I who teach him. For he is being taught not by my words, but by the realities themselves made manifest to him by the enlightening action of God from within.[27]

In *De Magistro*, and more largely, in the Confessions, and the *De Trinitate*, St Augustine was developing what came to be known as the 'doctrine of illumination', the notion of the Logos as the inner-teacher confirming truth in us, as an inner light to which we bring all that is offered to us as truth to see whether it is indeed genuine. Christ is the inner light by which every human being recognises truth as

---

[26]   'Nosce Teipsum', lines 193–204, in *The Poems of Sir John Davies*, ed. R. Krueger (Oxford, 1975), p.12.

[27]   In *The Writings of Saint Augustine*, trans. R. Russel (Washington, DC, 1968), pp.53–54.

truth; the only difference for Christians is that they recognise who that inner light is, they know him by name, and know, in awe, what else he has done for them.

There are many striking similarities between Augustine and Coleridge, and indeed between *De Magistro*/Confession*s* and *Biographia Literaria*. Both Augustine and Coleridge were fascinated by language; Augustine was a professor of rhetoric before ever he was a theologian. It was his pursuit of truth in and through his love of literature and language which in the end compelled him, like Coleridge, to do theology. Like Coleridge, he was living in an age of enormous cultural transition and philosophical scepticism; like Coleridge, he sensed that the beauty and lucidity of God lay beckoning tantalisingly just beyond the veil of phenomena. Like Coleridge, he was led by this apprehension to challenge the philosophers of his day on their own ground. As Coleridge was eventually to do, he came to understand that the mystery and freedom of human consciousness are not opposed to, but rather rooted in, the mystery and freedom of God's life as Holy Trinity.

De Magistro is an early work of St Augustine's written at the point of transition between rhetoric and theology; indeed, its teaching forms the bridge which links the two. The first part of *De Magistro* is concerned with what we now call semiotics: What is the distinction between sign and symbol? What kind of signs are words? How and in what way is it ever possible for one thing to mean another? The second part of the book shows that the revelation of God in Christ is as much concerned with answering these kinds of questions as it is concerned with addressing issues of 'personal salvation'. These are precisely the concerns of the *Biographia*, which is a work that also bridges and connects Coleridge's insights into language, on the one hand, and his apprehensions of God, on the other.

Curiously, both men wrote their respective books in an attempt to communicate their vision of life to their sons. *De Magistro* takes the form of a dialogue with Adeodatus, Augustine's teenage son of whom he was immensely proud. When Adeodatus died the Easter after its composition, Augustine came to think of that dialogue as a memorial to his son's genius and promise. Readers of 'Frost at Midnight' feel they have been brought intimately in touch with Hartley the sleeping infant, and with all Coleridge's hopes and dreams for him as he grew up. So it is moving to know that parts of the *Biographia* may well have been addressed to Hartley the undergraduate, who came to stay with his father while part of the book was being written.[28]

But, if we recognise in Coleridge's use of the doctrine of the Logos a continuation of what St Augustine had begun in *De Magistro*, there is in Coleridge an important new development. Before Coleridge, all the writers who drew on Augustine's doctrine of illumination, including Davies and Milton and others we have seen in this book, associated the Logos as inner light with *Reason*, albeit intuitive reason rather than discursive reason. Coleridge's great breakthrough was to see that it should be understood in terms of the *Imagination*. We do not, in fact,

---

[28]   See Holmes, *Coleridge: Darker Reflections*, p. 386.

come to a perception of the world, or any understanding of it, as a result of a series of logical deductions or calculations of the discursive reason. It is not the case that a certain quantum of manipulable data falls, as it were, ready-made into the mind through the senses, and then we make the necessary calculations to make sense of it. But rather that our minds and hearts go *out* to embrace the world *imaginatively*. There is a kind of 'leap of faith', a sudden shaping and finding of the whole; or rather, there is an alternation between our 'passively receiving' the influx of what seems to be there, and 'actively shaping' its sense and meaning.

Coleridge himself described the imagination as just such an alternation of looking out and taking in, of leaping forward and being borne along; but, given the exclusively passive and deterministic caste of thinking against which he was fighting, his initial image of the 'leap' in the following passage, is essential:

> Let us consider what we do when we leap. We first resist the gravitating power by an act purely voluntary, and then by another act, voluntary in part, we yield to it in order to light on the spot, which we had previously proposed to ourselves. Now let a man watch his mind while he is composing; or, to take a still more common case, while he is trying to recollect a name; and he will find the process completely analogous. Most of my readers will have observed a small water-insect on the surface of rivulets, which throws a cinque-spotted shadow fringed with prismatic colours on the sunny bottom of the brook; and will have noticed, how the little animal *wins* its way up against the stream, by alternate pulses of active and passive motion, now resisting the current, and now yielding to it in order to gather strength and a momentary *fulcrum* for a further propulsion. This is no unapt emblem of the mind's self-experience in the act of thinking. There are evidently two powers at work, which relatively to each other are active and passive; and this is not possible without an intermediate faculty, which is at once both active and passive. (In philosophical language, we must denominate this intermediate faculty in all its degrees and determinations, the IMAGINATION ...)[29]

There is far more about the imagination in this image than even Coleridge purports to get out of it, containing as it does three of the deepest elements of Coleridge's symbolic language about imagination: the river, the light and the shadows. He might have made the point about the way in which our acts of perception are alternately active and passive simply by reference to the water-insect, and no more. But, by placing his insect upon so vividly imagined a stream, with its surface of rivulets, and the sunlight striking through the water to the bottom of it, he is able to suggest far more than he makes explicit. For example, he implies that, however wonderful our imaginative acts of perception might be, we are as yet still only on the surface of things; we move through life on the surface of a stream whose depths we could hardly guess. And yet, we do sometimes glimpse them, for

---

[29]   Coleridge, *Biographia Literaria, I*, pp.124–25.

fringing the shadows we cast are prismatic colours, suggestive of the light we have not yet turned to face.

The image of the stream itself does so much in its life, its movement, its inexhaustibility, its transparency, to cleanse our mind of the alternative images our culture gives us of world and mind, the images of dark, dead matter, of fixed laws, of an inevitably unwinding clockwork mechanism. Along with Heraclitus, Coleridge is reminding us, as in our own age cosmologists and psychologists have reminded us again, that the world flows and the mind, too, is like a stream, both world and mind welling up from hidden depths.

The image of the inexhaustible river, a fountain of life and light, a force to be reckoned with, submerges and surfaces again at different points in Coleridge's life. He was fascinated by the river as something seen, but whose source in unseen. This fascination goes right back to his childhood, to the days when with his friends he tried to find the source of the Otter, a river which was the subject of his first accomplished poem. 'To the River Otter', written when he was still an undergraduate, shows that already the sense of surface and depth, movement and transparency, had entered his imagination.

> What happy and what mournful hours, since last
> I skimmed the smooth, thin stone along thy breast,
> Numbering its light leaps! Yet so deep impresst
> Sink the sweet scenes of childhood that mine eyes
> I never shut amid the sunny ray, but straight
> With all their tints thy waters rise,
> Thy crossing plank, thy marge with willows gray,
> And bedded sand that veined with various dyes
> Gleamed through thy bright transparents! ...[30]

As Coleridge matured both as a man and a writer, he left the cloying sweetness of that early style behind; but the river which was its subject continued to flow through his mind and inform his thought. Letters and Notebook observations of the rivers and waterfalls (or 'forces'), make it clear that he already understood the river as a symbol in his deepest sense of that word:

> The mad water rushes through its sinuous bed, or rather prison of rock, with such rapid curves, as if it turned the corners, not from the mechanic force, but with foreknowledge, but like a fierce and skillful driver, great masses of water, one after the other, that in twilight one might have feelingly compared them to a vast crowd of huge, white bears, rushing one over the other against the wind – their long, white hair shattering abroad in the wind.'[31]

---

[30] Coleridge, *Poetical Works, I,* p. 300.
[31] Coleridge, *Collected Letters*, vol. II, p. 853.

Here, with his rejection of 'mechanic force' and his hint of 'foreknowledge' he is already beginning to associate the river with mind and imagination. This is even clearer in another note, also about a Lakeland waterfall:

> What a sight it is to look down on such a Cateract! – the wheels, that circumvolve in it – the leaping up and plunging forward of that infinity of Pearls and Glass Bulbs – the continual *change* of the *Matter*, the perpetual *sameness* of the *form* – it is an aweful image and shadow of God and the world.[32]

Here, he makes the symbol explicit, and in some respect it has only been in our own century that physicists have come to understand what it might mean to see the apparently static and solid world in terms of the 'leaping and plunging Cataract'. It still remains for theology to recover an understanding of God as 'that Fountain filling, running', from which all things come.[33] In looking out at the world of the early nineteenth century, Coleridge saw a society obsessed only with the surface of the stream, aware only of its lower reaches, and in the *Biographia*, he remembers the projected poem which he and Wordsworth planned while they walked together in the Quantock Hills, but never wrote:

> I sought for a subject that should give equal room and freedom for description, incident, and impassioned reflections on men, nature and society, yet supply in itself a natural connection to the parts and unity to the whole. Such a subject I conceived myself to have found in a stream, traced from its source in the hills among the yellow-red moss and conical glass-shaped tufts of bent, to the first break or fall, where its drops become audible, and it begins to form a channel; thence to the peat and turf barn, itself built of the same dark squares as it sheltered; to the sheepfold; to the first cultivated plot of ground; to the lonely cottage and its bleak garden won from the heath; to the hamlet, the villages, the market-town, the manufactories and the seaport.[34]

Ironically, it was while he was elaborately planning, and signally failing, to write *The Brook*, that Coleridge – accidentally and almost in parenthesis – 'retired to a lonely farmhouse between Porlock and Linton'. And there, 'without any sensation or consciousness of effort', he found 'Kubla Khan'[35] welling up within him, and wrote the great river-poem which was more than any other to embody truths about the imagination which he himself would not make explicit until many years after the poem had been composed.

---

[32]   Ibid., pp.853–54.

[33]   See Heaney's translation of St John of the Cross discussed below in Chapter 8, pp. 219–26.

[34]   Coleridge, *Collected Letters*, vol. I, p. 355.

[35]   Coleridge, *Poetical Works, I*, pp. 509–14.

Were someone at last to master the whole of what Coleridge has said about God the Word as the hidden Source, at once of the world and of the imagination which apprehends that world, were someone to gather all his scattered observations and link them into the living whole which he hoped would have been his *magnum opus*, the unwritten *Logosophia*, they might at the end of their endeavour look back to this little poem written in distraction and fever by the young Coleridge, and find that everything had already been said here, not in technical, theological language, but in what Coleridge called 'the language of living symbols'. The river that rises and runs through this poem is not only a sacred river, but is significantly called 'Alph', a name summoning both Hebrew *Aleph* and Greek *Alpha*, and the title of Christ the Logos, the *Alpha and Omega*. This river with its beauty, its dancing imagery, emerges from invisibility into visibility, and then dives deeply again to depths we cannot measure.

It is this sacred river which makes our ground fertile. Like Kubla, we can measure and fence, cultivate and build, have our art and our life and our imagination make, as it were, our garden on the side of the river, our 'twice five miles of fertile ground', and our 'gardens bright with sinuous rills'. But the river itself we cannot contain; its source is beyond us, and so is the sea to which it flows. All our art and culture, beautiful as it may be, rightly as it may be called 'a miracle of rare device', is, in comparison with the life of the sacred river on whose sides we are camping, no more than the shadow of the dome of pleasure floating mid-way on the waves. And yet the second movement of the poem closes with an intimation that we come from the source of that river flowing out of Paradise, and that we are called to find it again. This intimation is given through the final image of the inspired poet acknowledging the source of his inspiration:

> Weave a circle round him thrice,
> And close your eyes with holy dread,
> For he on honeydew hath fed,
> And drunk the milk of Paradise.

The river is both the river of Imagination and the river of Being, arising from the same source; and Coleridge's own account of writing the poem is just this image of that which wells up and finishes with the image of reflections on the surface of a stream. 'All the images rose up ... as things with a parallel production of the correspondent expressions without any sensation of consciousness or effort ...' and 'All the rest had passed away like images on the surface of a stream onto which a stone has been cast'.[36]

If writing 'Kubla Khan' had been the experience of the twin streams of Being and Imagination, flowing through Coleridge's mind from their unknowable and unimagined Source in 'caverns measureless to man', then the experience of writing the *Biographia Literaria*, the *Lectures on Shakespeare*, the unfinished

---

[36] Ibid., p. 511.

Logosophia, was the experience of trying to follow the twin streams back to their sacred source. As Coleridge himself wrote in a notebook of 1814:

> I have read of two rivers passing through the same lake, yet all the way preserving their streams visibly distinct … In a far finer distinction, yet in a subtler union, such, for the contemplative mind, are the streams of knowing and being. The lake is formed by the two streams in man and nature as it exists in and for man; and up this lake the philosopher sails on the junction-line of the constituent streams, still pushing upward and sounding as he goes, towards the common fountain-head of both, the mysterious source whose being is knowledge, whose knowledge is being – the adorable I AM IN THAT I AM.[37]

Returning, then, to the passage on imagination in the *Biographia*, Coleridge has asserted that the power and prime agent of all human perception is not a material mechanism leaving its mark on the passive mind; but on the contrary, is a living power of imagination, 'the repetition in our finite minds of the eternal act of creation in the infinite I AM'. It is as though the creative word which speaks the cosmos into being echoes back to God from minds made in his image. Where our echo meshes with his Word, we perceive the world.

Many thinkers might have rested content there, in having achieved an epistemology, a theory of knowledge which set the mind free from mere material mechanism and found a central place for imagination as a distinctive and living human power. But Coleridge goes on to try and find a link between this Primary Imagination and what he calls the Secondary Imagination, by which he means what most people would call the poetic imagination. He goes on to say that the reason why a human work of art can have such extraordinary coherence, such inner consistency, and can 'grow to something of great constancy', is because the imagination with which such art is made, is not simply a matter of private inventiveness or so-called self-expression (something Coleridge relegates to the role of Fancy), but is rather itself a living power, a river rising from somewhere deeper than the conscious mind of the artist. It is, as Coleridge calls it, an 'echo of the Primary Imagination', but this time coexisting with the conscious will. It coexists with the conscious will, that is to say the artist consciously cooperates with its agency; but it is not itself simply the product of the conscious will.

This understanding of secondary imagination, the imagination of the artist, as being essentially the same in kind as the Imagination which makes the world, provides the key to Coleridge's greatest literary criticism as well as to the understanding of his own poetry. When he calls Shakespeare a nature humanised, we see that it is not an idle phrase. The heart of his appreciation of Shakespeare which changed forever the way the English read their own poet, was the discovery of organic, as opposed to mechanic, unity in his plays. The discovery that it is

---

[37]   From *Anima Poetae*, reprinted in *The Portable Coleridge*, ed. I.A. Richards (London, 1978), p. 315.

not the fancied rules derived from a reading of Aristotle's *Poetics* which allow us to interpret the life and power of the great tragedies, but rather what Coleridge calls the 'rules of the Imagination'. He says later on, in Chapter 18 of the *Biographia*, that the 'rules of the Imagination are themselves the very powers of growth and production'.[38] This great phrase is often used in the context of his critical appreciation of Shakespeare and Wordsworth, but, if we are really to come to terms with what Coleridge is saying about the link between Primary and Secondary Imagination, we should apply this sentence equally to the worlds of biology, astronomy, cosmology … We should look out, as he did, on the flowing streams around us, on the trees and mountains, on the stars rising in the heavens, and seeing the miraculous growth and production of the world around us, we should say that 'the rules of the Imagination are themselves the very powers of this growth and production'.

Certainly, if we are to understand the vision and power behind those many moments in Coleridge's prose and poetry in which an account of natural beauty becomes a revelation of truth, then we will reach that understanding by tracing *both* world *and* word back to their single source in the holy Logos, the Imagination of God. Coleridge came to comprehend a unity and continuity between his reason and his faith, both welling up from and animated by imagination. In the last words of the *Biographia*, he seems to revisit that evening walk as a little boy, holding his father's hands while the stars came out, but this time the grown man has found himself drawn into the life of another Father, with the Son, and Holy Spirit:

> … Christianity, as taught in the Liturgy and Homilies of our Church, though not discoverable by human Reason, is yet in accordance with it; that link follows link by necessary consequence; that Religion passes out of the ken of Reason only where the eye of Reason has reached its own Horizon; and that Faith is then but its continuation: even as the Day softens away into the sweet Twilight, and Twilight, hushed and breathless, steals into the Darkness. It is Night, sacred Night! The upraised Eye views only the starry Heaven which manifests itself alone: and the outward Beholding is fixed on the sparks twinkling in the aweful depth, though Suns of other Worlds, only to preserve the Soul steady and collected in its pure *Act* of inward Adoration to the great I AM, and to the filial WORD that re-affirmeth it from Eternity to Eternity, whose choral Echo is the Universe.

ΘΕΩι ΜΟΝΩι ΔΟΞΑ.[39]

---

[38]   Coleridge, *Biographia Literaria, II*, p. 84.

[39]   Ibid., pp. 247–48.

Chapter 7

Doubting Faith, Reticent Hope: Transfigured Vision in Thomas Hardy, Phillip Larkin and Geoffrey Hill

If Coleridge is right about the imagination, if it is true that our imagination enables us both to grasp and to shape reality, and that the source and light of imagination springs from the source of the world itself in Christ the Logos, then it should be the case that great poetry written by poets in touch with both their 'Primary' and 'Secondary' Imaginations should witness to this transfiguring light whether or not their poetry is avowedly religious, or the poets adhere in their own lives to any particular religious doctrine. Indeed, it might be the case that a poet consciously holds doctrines which deny the power of his or her own imagination, which deny the possibility of transfiguration, which refuse to make a wager on transcendence. If that were the case, then we might expect to find in certain poets a tension between the surface of their syntax and the depth of their imagery, between the foreclosures of their 'comprehension' and the openings of their 'apprehension'; as though Theseus and Hippolyta were carrying on their argument within the space of a single poem. In this chapter we shall examine the witness of poets who professed *not* to be Christians. But, if their integrity in their own circumstances prevented them from professing faith, the same integrity also prevented their poetry from degenerating into mere atheist propaganda. Instead, like the poets before them, their poetry expresses a doubled, or transfigured vision. Not simply, as we have seen in poets so far, a simultaneous vision of the natural and the supernatural, but also a simultaneous apprehension of doubt *and* faith, despair *and* hope.

Hardy: Transfiguration's Reluctant Witness

Readers of Hardy's novels are only too aware of how vividly he imagined the possibility of a completely bleak world. He shows us again and again what it is like to be in a world where all that is human is crushed by the inhuman; and yet the same novels are haunted by glimpses of beauty and affirmations of courage which are every bit as real as their overarching architecture of despair. This sense of double-witness, of the bringing together of apparently incompatible insights, is equally vivid in the poetry. As a poet, Hardy inherits all the possibilities of lyric beauty explored by the three generations of Romantic poets who had preceded him, whilst remaining grimly aware of all that was hideous, tragic or banal in the new century he was facing. His imagination had at its disposal all the power of poetry to celebrate life; his mind was persuaded that the bleak fact of death is the one thing never to be forgotten. Yet, it is in the very poems in which his mind is most concentrated on making his reader comprehend the bleak fact of death that his imagination opens up windows for a light which transfigures that bleakness. We shall look at this theme of transfiguration in three of Hardy's most beautiful and haunting poems, 'Former Beauties', 'The Darkling Thrush' and 'Afterwards'.

Former Beauties[1]

>These market-dames, mid-aged, with lips thin-drawn,
>   And tissues sere,
>Are they the ones we loved in years agone,
>   And courted here?
>
>Are these the muslined pink young things to whom
>   We vowed and swore
>In nooks on summer Sundays by the Froom,
>   Or Budmouth shore?
>
>Do they remember those gay tunes we trod
>   Clasped on the green;
>Aye; trod till moonlight set on the beaten sod
>   A satin sheen?
>
>They must forget, forget! They cannot know
>   What once they were,
>Or memory would transfigure them, and show
>   Them always fair.

This poem, observing the market dames 'mid-aged with lips thin-drawn and tissues sere' and remembering their former beauty, is ostensibly about a transfiguration that does not happen. On the surface of the poem, were it reduced to prose, Hardy is saying that the market-dames are alienated forever from their youth; that they can neither remember nor be transfigured. The poem opens with the observations of mortality in an unforgiving light, the 'lips thin-drawn and tissues sere', and it nearly closes with the clear negation 'They cannot know what once they were'. But set against these few lines of bleak denial is all the rest of the poem. Hardy the philosopher wants to say that youth is irrecoverable, that transfigurations don't happen; but Hardy the poet knows better. The effect of the whole poem is precisely the transfiguration of these market-dames. The agent of that transfiguration is

---

[1]   In *The Collected Poems of Thomas Hardy* (London, 1952), p. 223.

love; its medium, memory. As soon as he asks the question (intended to be merely rhetorical) 'Are they the ones we loved in years agone and courted here?' – love takes command of the poem, and bleak rhetoric is defeated by renewing poetry. For the next two verses, the heart of the poem, we see with the eyes of imagination the truth which reason cannot see. Of course, we continue to see with the eyes of reason, the outward and visible market-dames, 'mid-aged'; but at one and the same time, we see vividly and undiminished the 'muslined pink young things to whom we vowed and swore'. Of course, we continue to see the 'lips thin-drawn and tissues sere', in the light of a market day; but at one and the same time, we see these women in transfiguring moonlight, dancing 'Clasped on the green ... till moonlight set on the beaten sod a satin sheen'.

For a moment this double vision in Hardy's poem gives us a glimpse of what it might be like to share the experience of St Paul, who writes about seeing, through the outer flesh which perishes, to the person within who is being renewed:

> For though our outward man perish, the inward man is renewed day by day ... while we look not at the things which are seen but at the things which are not seen; for the things which are seen are temporal. The things which are not seen are eternal.[2]

Of course, Hardy the atheist would have nothing to do with any such Scripture, and would 'nobly' repudiate the hope it has to offer; but Hardy the poet knows better. And just as St Paul preaching the Resurrection in the market-place in Athens found a supporting witness in the pagan poets, so, had he preached the Transfiguration in the market-places of Wessex, he might have found a supporting witness in this pagan poet, too.

For two verses at the heart of this poem, Hardy's memory and imagination lead him as Titania once led Theseus through the glimmering wood; a place where, as Hippolyta says, our minds are 'transfigured ... together'.[3] And like Theseus standing in the Athenian sunlight and denying that there is any truth in the experiences we know he has had, so Hardy in the final verse tries to deny the transfiguration to which his poem is witness. Given his bleak philosophy, this is entirely understandable. St Paul delights in the transfigurations he glimpses, yearns for them and celebrates them, because he knows that 'the unseen things are eternal'; he knows that the little glimpses of transfiguring light we have now are an earnest of things to come, of the eternal and exceeding weight of glory which is to be revealed. For Hardy, on the other hand, these glimpses of beauty only serve to underline the pain of mortality, and make it even more unbearable. For

---

[2] 2 Corinthians 4:16,18.

[3] Shakespeare, *A Midsummer Night's Dream*, Act V, Scene 1, line 24, in *The Complete Works*, ed., P. Alexander (London, 1957). See also the discussion of this passage above in Chapter 2, pp. 000–00.

Hardy, these 'Lightenings' (as Heaney later called them[4]) are only Lightenings in the sense that Shelley had used composing a lyric for Hardy before his time, when he wrote 'What is this world's delight? / Lightening that mocks the night, / Brief even as bright'.[5] To remember the youth and beauty of the market-dames is not for Hardy, as it would have been for St Paul to have a foretaste of their glory in the resurrection, but only to underline the tragedy and loss of their inevitable collapse toward the grave. So it is almost in an act of charity that he tries to *unsay* what his poem has said, to unsee what his heart is seeing, and he writes:

> They must forget, forget! They cannot know
>   What once they were,
> Or memory would transfigure them, and show
>   Them always fair

But once again the poet is wiser than the philosopher. He writes in a tense we might call the lost conditional, 'memory *would* transfigure them'; but, in fact, memory *has* transfigured them. The very thing he denies has taken place. Neither he nor we, after reading his poem, can look again at the market-dames, mid-aged, without this transfiguration taking place. It is the poet who triumphs in this poem, and has the last word – the last two words – give away the heart of the poem which is a glimpse not of time, but of eternity, where we are 'always fair'.

The Darkling Thrush[6]

> I leant upon a coppice gate
>   When Frost was spectre-grey,
> And Winter's dregs made desolate
>   The weakening eye of day.
> The tangled bine-stems scored the sky
>   Like strings of broken lyres,
> And all mankind that haunted nigh
>   Had sought their household fires.
>
> The land's sharp features seemed to be
>   The Century's corpse outlent,
> His crypt the cloudy canopy,
>   The wind his death-lament.
> The ancient pulse of germ and birth

---

[4]   Seamus Heaney, 'Lightenings', in *Seeing Things* (London, 1991), pp. 55–66. See also below Chapter 8, pp. 230–31 and 239–40.

[5]   'Mutability', in *Shelley's Poetical Works*, ed. W.M. Rossetti (London, 1878). vol. III, p. 97.

[6]   In Hardy, *The Collected Poems*, p. 137.

Was shrunken hard and dry,
And every spirit upon earth
　　Seemed fervourless as I.

At once a voice arose among
　　The bleak twigs overhead
In a full-hearted evensong
　　Of joy illimited;
An aged thrush, frail, gaunt, and small,
　　In blast-beruffled plume,
Had chosen thus to fling his soul
　　Upon the growing gloom.

So little cause for carolings
　　Of such ecstatic sound
Was written on terrestrial things
　　Afar or nigh around,
That I could think there trembled through
　　His happy good-night air
Some blessed Hope, whereof he knew
　　And I was unaware.

This famous poem reflects the mood of the dying year, the dying century, dying humanity. Hardy fully witnesses the bleakness but sets against it the counter-witness of the thrush's song, holding them together with the tentative syntax of his conditional possibility of some blessed hope. This poem was written on 31 December 1900, and the dying of that winter's day Hardy also took to be the century's death; the end of the nineteenth century with all its hopes of unimpeded progress and universal peace, cheated and defeated. The outward and visible desolation of the day becomes, as it were, the first voice of the poem, and Hardy's choice of language for that voice paints a word-picture of decline and dissolution from which one might think there was no recovery: 'Spectre-grey …dregs … desolate … weakening … tangled … broken … haunted … corpse … crypt… shrunken … fervourless … bleak … frail … gaunt … gloom'. But then Hardy introduces a second voice:

At once a voice arose among
　　The bleak twigs overhead
In a full-hearted evensong
　　Of joy illimited; …

The language chosen for this second voice is drawn not from the realm of death and decay, which was the register of the first voice, but rather from the language of the sacred; it is full of echoes from the Church upon which Hardy thought he had turned his back: 'full-hearted evensong ... joy ... soul ... carolings ... blessed Hope'. The fact that we hear *both* these voices in this poem, that words from two such distinct linguistic registers are woven together in his verse, is a testament to Hardy's integrity and honesty as an artist. It would have been as easy and as tempting to him to have ignored the witness of the thrush, to have gone home and written an unremittingly grim poem, as it is tempting to the authors of religious doggerel to write 'up-beat hymns' which recycle the clichés of hope without ever making contact with the tragedies of life as it is actually lived. Hardy's witness in this honest poem is that he can neither ignore nor believe the thrush. What he sees, as he leans on a gate on that winter day, gives him no hope at all, but he is not prepared to limit reality to 'the things that are seen'; and perhaps the most honest word in the poem is the word 'seemed' which concludes the second stanza. Had he written 'and every spirit upon earth was fervourless as I', he might never have heard the thrush at all; or, hearing it, his mind might have twisted its song into yet another symbol of decay. But, as Heaney would be later, here Hardy is prepared to be 'exposed to every wind that blows'[7] and, even if he expects the finality of a bleak north wind, he does not ignore this faint air from Paradise.

The first two stanzas are concerned with the outward and visible world, with what we can see; Hope comes in the third stanza, when we stop looking at the familiar and listen, suddenly, to the unfamiliar – as when Heaney said, 'what happens next is a music that you never would have known to listen for'.[8]

Perhaps in order to hear Hardy has to stop looking for a moment, and this is where the poem's haunting title comes in, 'The Darkling Thrush'. One might take the word 'darkling' here, simply to refer to the fact that the thrush begins its song just as the day ends and it begins to get dark. But for Hardy, and for any reader of English poetry, the word 'darkling' carries us immediately to Milton and Keats, the two other poets – both in darkness of one kind or another, both listening to birds – who used that word. As we saw in Chapter 5, Milton used it to mark a turning point from despair to hope. After a long passage lamenting his blindness and complaining of the loss of outward sight, he comes to realise that instead he has been gifted with an inward sight to be shared with others through his poetry, and compares himself to 'the wakeful bird' that 'Sings darkling, and in shadiest covert hid / Tunes her nocturnal note'.[9] Keats deliberately echoed Milton when he came to write the 'Ode to a Nightingale'; but this time he applied the adverb 'darkling' not to the quality of the bird's singing, as Milton had done, but to the quality of his listening: 'darkling I listen'[10]. And what Keats hears is not simply the

---

[7]   Heaney, 'North', line 36, in *North* (London, 1975), p.68.

[8]   Heaney, 'The Rain Stick', in *The Spirit Level* (London, 1996), p.1; see also above Introduction, pp. 16–20.

[9]   *Paradise Lost*, Book III, lines 37–39, in *John Milton: Paradise Lost*, ed. A. Fowler (London, 1971), p. 145.

[10]   'Ode to a Nightingale', line 51, in *The Poetical Works of John Keats*, ed. H.W. Garrod (Oxford, 1939), p. 259.

outward sound but the expression of a soul and the intonation of ecstasy: 'Thou art pouring forth thy soul abroad / In such an ecstasy'.[11]

Keats' active imaginative apprehension of one of the 'lovely shapes and sounds intelligible of that eternal language which God utters',[12] embodied beautifully by his art in the 'Ode to a Nightingale', enters into and nurtures Hardy's imagination. Keats' poetry enabled Hardy to make and express the same imaginative apprehension of what the bird's song might mean, and his choice of language, with its echoes of the 'Ode to a Nightingale' – 'had chosen thus to fling his soul' and 'carolings of such ecstatic sound' – acknowledge a debt he had already hinted in the choice of 'darkling 'for the title of his poem.

The two voices come together in the final stanza, where, hearing the 'carolings of such ecstatic sound', the bleak voice of Hardy the philosophical pessimist finds itself shifted from indicative verbs which allow for one thing and one thing only to happen, to modal verb forms which allow for more than one possibility. In the first form, he says 'so little cause for carolings … was written'; but after hearing these carolings, the verb form changes, something new is possible: 'I could think … some blessed Hope'. The suggestion, even conditionally, of the possibility of something more than the merely visible, is beautifully expressed in the choice of the verb 'trembled' and the preposition 'through'. The 'happy good-night air' sung by the bird is one thing; but the poetry at last allows for the possibility that something else, from somewhere else, some 'blessed Hope', might 'tremble through' it. We havee been prepared for all of this by the choice of the word 'seemed' before we heard the bird. Once we know that the things we see might seem rather than be what we think they are, it becomes possible that, if only for a moment, something else might 'tremble through' them. And this redeeming preposition 'through', is the same that opened the world's windows onto heaven for Herbert when he wrote:

> A man that looks on glass
> On it may stay his eye,
> Or if he pleaseth through it pass
> And then the heavens espy.[13]

But, even as Hardy the poet allows the thrush to help him apprehend the possibility of some blessed hope, Hardy the philosopher tries to have the last word, and to close the poem with the claim to be 'unaware' of that hope. 'Unaware' is an extraordinary word with which to close a poem which is supremely a poem of awareness; awareness both of all the signs of mortality, and of all the intimations

---

[11]   Ibid., lines 57–58.

[12]   'Frost at Midnight', lines 58–62, in Samuel Taylor Coleridge, *Poetical Works, I*, ed. J.C.C. Mays (Princeton, 2001), pp. 453–456 (Volume 16 in CC).

[13]   'The Elixir', in George Herbert, *The Complete English Works*, ed. A. Pasternak Slater (London, 1995), p. 180.

of immortality. In some ways, this beautiful poem is a testimony against itself. Its tentative syntax is subverted by its ecstatic imagery.

Afterwards[14]

> When the Present has latched its postern behind my tremulous stay,
>> And the May month flaps its glad green leaves like wings,
> Delicate-filmed as new-spun silk, will the neighbours say,
>> 'He was a man who used to notice such things'?
>
> If it be in the dusk when, like an eyelid's soundless blink,
>> The dewfall-hawk comes crossing the shades to alight
> Upon the wind-warped upland thorn, a gazer might think,
>> 'To him this must have been a familiar sight.'
>
> If I pass during some nocturnal blackness, mothy and warm,
>> When the hedgehog travels furtively over the lawn,
> One may say, 'He strove that such innocent creatures should come to no harm,
>> But he could do little for them; and now he is gone.'
>
> If, when hearing that I have been stilled at last, they stand at the door,
>> Watching the full-starred heavens that winter sees,
> Will this thought rise on those who will meet my face no more,
>> 'He was one who had an eye for such mysteries'?
>
> And will any say when my bell of quittance is heard in the gloom,
>> And a crossing breeze cuts a pause in its outrollings,
> Till they rise again, as they were a new bell's boom,
>> 'He hears it not now, but used to notice such things'?

Ostensibly, this is a poem about the poet's imminent absence from the world; but never has the world been more vividly and magically present. Like 'The Darkling Thrush', it is a poem with two voices alternating between the ordinary and the extraordinary, between a world still covered with the film of familiarity, and a world from which that film has been removed. As Heaney says of this poem, Hardy's 'ultimate achievement is forever to transform that familiar world into something rich and strange'. Heaney gives this poem a pre-eminent place in the introduction to his volume *The Redress of Poetry*, from which we quoted in our introductory chapter; and what he says about the poem there is central not only to Heaney's key notion of the 'frontier of writing', but also to the central theme of this book, the theme of transfiguration. Here is what Heaney says:

---

[14]   Hardy, The Collected Poems, p. 521.

In one way, this is an expression of solidarity with the ordinary world where people stand around after the news of a death, wistful rather than desolate, and repeat the conventional decencies. But in the end, the poem is more given over to the extraordinary than to the ordinary, more dedicated to the world-renewing potential of the imagined response than to the adequacy of the social one. For part of the time, the reader is confined to the company of the neighbours where all that is on offer is conventional wisdom in untransfigured phrases. But then consciousness is given access to a dimension beyond the frontier where an overbrimming, totally resourceful expressiveness becomes suddenly available; and this entry into a condition of illuminated rightness becomes an entry into poetry itself.

'He was a man who used to notice such things,' say the neighbours, on this side of the frontier. 'Which things?' asks the reader, and from the other side the poem answers, 'The May month flaps its glad green leaves like wings, / Delicate-filmed as new-spun silk.' 'To him this must have been a familiar sight,' say the neighbours. 'What must have been a familiar sight?' asks the reader. 'The dusk, when, like an eyelid's soundless blink, / The dewfall-hawk comes crossing the shades to alight / Upon the wind-warped upland thorn', says the poem. 'Anything else?' says the reader. 'Blackness, mothy and warm', says the poem. 'The full-starred heavens that winter sees', things like that. 'My God!' says the reader.[15]

Nobody could call this poem 'escapist'; it seeks to confront rather than to evade the finality of death. And yet the finality of death is counterbalanced by the almost numinous realisation of beauty in each verse. We cannot help feeling that the intensity of the poetry, from beyond what Heaney calls 'the frontier of writing',[16] hints at a vision of beauty which has been granted to the poet after his death and not before, and gives a strange power, or at least an ambiguity, to the poem's title – 'Afterwards'.

Larkin and the 'Almost True'

Philip Larkin was very much a disciple of Hardy's, and learned a great deal from him, both in the technical matter of versification and in exploiting the power of the laconic understatement, as well as the way in which a powerful image can be at once subverted and supported by the tentative syntax in which it is caught. Like Hardy, he modifies the big verbs like 'love' and 'think' with tentative or conditional qualifiers like 'would' and 'could'. The surface teaching of Larkin's verse is in some ways even bleaker than Hardy's; but, as in the case of his master, the surface teaching of the philosopher is shaken by depth-charges dropped by the poet.

---

[15]   Seamus Heaney, *The Redress of Poetry: Oxford Lectures* (London, 1995), p. xvii.

[16]   Ibid., p. xvi.

Larkin is very much the poet of the near miss, the eulogised might-have-been, the glimpse of meaning at once rejected and regretted. The ambiguous witness of his immaculately crafted poetry is brought to focus in the two poems that follow, 'Church-going' and 'For Sidney Bechet'.

Church-going[17]

> Once I am sure there's nothing going on
> I step inside, letting the door thud shut.
> Another church: matting, seats, and stone
> And little books; sprawlings of flowers, cut
> For Sunday, brownish now; some brass and stuff
> Up at the holy end; the small neat organ;
> And a tense, musty, unignorable silence,
> Brewed God knows how long. Hatless, I take off
> My cycle-clips in awkward reverence,
>
> Move forward, run my hand around the font.
> From where I stand, the roof looks almost new –
> Cleaned, or restored? Someone would know: I don't.
> Mounting the lectern, I peruse a few
> Hectoring large-scale verses, and pronounce
> 'Here endeth' much more loudly than I'd meant.
> The echoes snigger briefly. Back at the door
> I sign the book, donate an Irish sixpence,
> Reflect the place was not worth stopping for.
>
> Yet stop I did: in fact I often do,
> And always end much at a loss like this,
> Wondering what to look for; wondering, too,
> When churches fall completely out of use
> What we shall turn them into, if we shall keep
> A few cathedrals chronically on show,
> Their parchment, plate and pyx in locked cases,
> And let the rest rent-free to rain and sheep.
> Shall we avoid them as unlucky places?
>
> Or, after dark, will dubious women come
> To make their children touch a particular stone;
> Pick simples for a cancer; or on some
> Advised night see walking a dead one?
> Power of some sort or other will go on

---

[17]   In Phillip Larkin, *Collected Poems*, ed. A. Thwaite (London, 1988), p. 97.

In games, in riddles, seemingly at random;
But superstition, like belief, must die,
And what remains when disbelief has gone?
Grass, weedy pavement, brambles, buttress, sky,

A shape less recognisable each week,
A purpose more obscure. I wonder who
Will be the last, the very last, to seek
This place for what it was; one of the crew
That tap and jot and know what rood-lofts were?
Some ruin-bibber, randy for antique,
Or Christmas-addict, counting on a whiff
Of gowns-and-bands and organ-pipes and myrrh?
Or will he be my representative,

Bored, uninformed, knowing the ghostly silt
Dispersed, yet tending to this cross of ground
Through suburb scrub because it held unsplit
So long and equably what since is found
Only in separation – marriage, and birth,
And death, and thoughts of these – for which was built
This special shell? For, though I've no idea
What this accoutred frowsy barn is worth,
It pleases me to stand in silence here;

A serious house on serious earth it is,
In whose blent air all our compulsions meet,
Are recognised, and robed as destinies.
And that much never can be obsolete,
Since someone will forever be surprising
A hunger in himself to be more serious,
And gravitating with it to this ground,
Which, he once heard, was proper to grow wise in,
If only that so many dead lie round.

'Church-going', famously opens with perhaps the most unpromising line in English literature: 'Once I'm sure there is nothing going on ...' Had this been the last line of the poem, it would be devastating. As a first line, it is curiously inviting. If there is really 'nothing going on', how is it we are going to find ourselves invited into the heart of a rich poem of some sixty-three lines? There is a parallel between Larkin's entry into the church and our entry into the poem, both at once hesitant and drawn. Larkin cautiously opens a church door, hesitant in case something should be going on, a service for example. And then he steps inside; likewise, after the apparent assurance that 'nothing's going on', *we* step inside the poem, and our experience in reading the poem will continue to parallel Larkin's experience in the church. On the surface, there is nothing going on; for Larkin, the church is empty, and echoes only his own sniggering. For us, the poem is full of surface declarations that whatever has happened here is redundant, over and done with and finished. And yet …

Larkin in the church discovers a presence in absence, a tense, musty, unignorable silence. And we, in the course of moving through the poem as he moves through the church, find ourselves transported from the surface blankness of the first line's 'nothing going on' to the numinous, rich 'blent air' where 'all our compulsions meet, are recognised, and robed as destinies'. Larkin, the twentieth-century atheist, wants to snigger, wants to reduce his tribute to this church to no more than a donated Irish sixpence; wants to mock the church and himself with the mean and the mundane. Despite images of 'cycle-clips' and sneering phrases such as 'up at the holy end', the poet buried in the atheist, the imagination interned by reason, surprises him with 'awkward reverence', with the discovery of something that 'never can be obsolete'. The mocker who enters the church in the first stanza, who sniggers in the second, and reflects that the place was 'not worth stopping for', is arrested in every sense by the word 'yet' which opens the third stanza and is the poem's turning point: 'Yet stop I did'.

On the surface he is still sneering and berating the place; on the surface he is still comically sure that religion is superstition, and that superstition itself 'must die'. But something has happened to undermine his assumptions. The 'tense, musty, unignorable silence, / Brewed God knows how long' alluded to in the first stanza, has begun to work on him, and the deliberately irreverent throwaway phrase, 'God knows' has begun, in the 'unignorable silence', to take on a life of its own. In a desperate attempt to avoid the pressure of the holy upon the present, Larkin finds himself imagining a future in which, ironically, in the midst of its ruins, a sense of the numinous still clings to this 'cross of ground'. But this fantasy of the future when 'dubious women come / To make their children touch a particular stone' and to 'Pick simples for a cancer', will not do; and Larkin knows it. His imagination is drawn back to the life which the community lives in and through that church now: to marriage, birth and death, to the meeting and recognition of our compulsions.

The surface atheist is still protesting desperately, trying to be 'bored' and 'uninformed', calling the place 'an accoutred, frowsty barn', making cheap jibes at 'ruin-bibbers, randy for antique' and Christmas-addicts 'counting on a whiff of gowns-and-bands'. But, in the end, the atheist in him is surprised and silenced by the poet who emerges from the depths and takes charge of things. There is a line of transition, the final line in the penultimate stanza, during the course of which the voice changes its tone from the surface of mockery trying to put a price on the 'frowsty barn', to a depth of insight to which only the repeated word 'serious' is adequate:

> For, though I've no idea
> What this accoutred frowsty barn is worth,
> It pleases me to stand in silence here;
>
> A serious house on serious earth it is,
> In whose blent air all our compulsions meet,
> Are recognised, and robed as destinies.
> And that much never can be obsolete,
> Since someone will forever be surprising
> A hunger in himself to be more serious,
> And gravitating with it to this ground,
> Which, he once heard, was proper to grow wise in,
> If only that so many dead lie round.

Larkin the poet is compelled to say far more than Larkin the sniggering atheist would like to concede; both figures appear in the poem with harrowing honesty. One is taken aback by Larkin's courage in drawing such an unflattering picture of himself as he does in the second stanza, mocking the place he visits, standing at the lectern pronouncing 'Here endeth', and donating his 'Irish sixpence'. Larkin the atheist wants his sniggering echoes to be the last word; for him, the poem should end here, 'Here endeth': Here endeth the lesson, here endeth the church, here endeth religion, here endeth superstition, here endeth the poem. The place was 'not worth stopping for' and, neither, by the way, is life. But it, too, will have its 'here endeth', and there will be no echoes, sniggering or otherwise, and that is just as well, as Larkin was later to say:

> Man hands on misery to man,
> it deepens like a coastal shelf;
> get out as quickly as you can,
> and don't have any kids yourself.[18]

That's what he wants to say, but spiritual honesty compels the poet as much as harrowing honesty compels the pessimist; and so the poem continues, very much as the dark psalms do, with its counterbalancing 'Yet'. Larkin the poet is compelled to witness to something more than the decay and dissolution he had thought was his subject. And when in the end he gives the church its due, and coins for it words of greater worth than his 'Irish sixpence', the word he uses and redeems is 'compulsion'. All the human compulsions, including the compulsive honesty of the poet, are recognised, and robed in the church, and in the final stanza of the poem which reluctantly celebrates the numinous.

This double-voicing of things, this clash of conflicting honesties, continues throughout most of Larkin's work, though some might argue that he loses this at

---

[18]   'This Be The Verse', in Larkin, *Collected Poems*, p. 180.

the end, and that Larkin the prosaic pessimist betrays Larkin the poet and ends up writing untruthful propaganda. Certainly Heaney, in 'Joy or Night',[19] his powerful comparison between Larkin and Yeats in their attitudes toward death, seems to suggest such a betrayal. However, in the great poems of Larkin's middle period we can hear both voices held in astonishing and creative tension.

Whichever voice begins a poem, the other has to be found a place; in 'Church-going', he starts out wanting to sneer but finds that he cannot help celebrating; in the next poem, 'For Sidney Bechet', the voice of celebration sets the tone and seems to triumph, and yet the crescendo to which it seems to be moving, in the meeting of the words 'love' and 'yes', is at the last minute undercut by a grammatical change of person, and the interposition of conditionals and qualifiers.

For Sidney Bechet[20]

> That note you hold, narrowing and rising, shakes
> Like New Orleans reflected on the water,
> And in all ears appropriate falsehood wakes,
>
> Building for some a legendary Quarter
> Of balconies, flower-baskets and quadrilles,
> Everyone making love and going shares –
>
> Oh, play that thing! Mute glorious Storyvilles
> Others may license, grouping round their chairs
> Sporting-house girls like circus tigers (priced
>
> Far above rubies) to pretend their fads,
> While scholars *manqués* nod around unnoticed
> Wrapped up in personnels like old plaids.
>
> On me your voice falls as they say love should,
> Like an enormous yes. My Crescent City
> Is where your speech alone is understood,
>
> And greeted as the natural noise of good,
> Scattering long-haired grief and scored pity.

Ostensibly, this is a poem about a single note played on Sidney Bechet's clarinet, how that note is heard by different people, and what images it awakens in their imaginations: first in the imagination of two groups of unknown fantasists, and finally in Larkin's own imagination. All three ways of hearing the music are

---

[19]   Heaney, *The Redress of Poetry*, p.146.
[20]   In Larkin, *Collected Poems*, p. 83.

prefaced by Larkin's assertion that they are false, that the beautifully imagined French Quarter of New Orleans that rises in the minds of one group, the smoky night-club with its clientele of 'sporting-house girls' and 'scholars *manqués*' evoked in the minds of a second group of listeners, and the ringing clarity of an 'enormous yes' that love speaks directly to Larkin's heart, are all no more than 'appropriate falsehood'.

This is what Larkin says; but the power of his poetry says otherwise. It is as though the voice that speaks through the note is so live and dangerous that Larkin has to spend four stanzas trying to undercut it, and mute it, before it is even allowed to speak. But speak it does; and for the reader, that blown note, love, making the 'natural noise of good' blows away all the wrappings of doubt with which Larkin the cynic has tried to mute it.

The clarity and power with which the poem ends is so great, that the reader is forced to return to Larkin's deprecatory opening in which he dismisses what he is about to say as, 'appropriate falsehood' (just as he did in 'Church-going', saying there was 'nothing going on'), and to question it. We find ourselves remembering Touchstone's wisdom about truth and falsehood in poetry:

> *Audrey*:   What is this poetry? Is it a true thing?
> *Touchstone*:   Our truest poetry is our most feigning.[21]

Of course the 'legendary Quarter', the 'mute glorious Storyvilles', Larkin's 'Crescent City', are all 'feigned', imaginary; but it does not mean they are false. They are fragments of a paradisal city from which comes both music and love. This poem, strangely haunted by 'Kubla Khan', shares with that poem the haunting image of a magic building reflected on the water. Coleridge's 'damsel with a dulcimer' is a muse whose music kindles his imagination to build an imaginary place from which, nevertheless, real truth flows:

> Could I revive within me
> Her symphony and song
> To such a deep delight 'twould win me
> That with music loud and long
> I would build that dome in air,
> That sunny dome![22]

Larkin uses the same substantial verb, 'build', to describe what the music does in the imagination; it builds a 'legendary Quarter', a 'Crescent City'. His 'Crescent City' may be as imaginary as Coleridge's 'sunny dome'; but it does not mean that the voice we hear speaking in either place is speaking falsehood. Rather it

---

21   Shakespeare, *As You Like It*, Act III, Scene 3, line 20; see above Introduction p. 3.

22   'Kubla Khan', lines 42–46,, in Coleridge, *Poetical Works, I*, p. 514.

is almost as though Larkin in his desperate self-censoring has to claim that it is a falsehood before he will permit himself to confess what it is that he has in fact heard this voice saying: 'On me your voice falls as they say love should, / Like an enormous yes.' Not even Larkin's Hardy-esque qualifications, 'they say' and 'should', can rob these words of their power or obliterate from them the echo they still carry from their true source: 'For the Son of God, Jesus Christ ... was not yes and no, but in Him it is always *Yes*; for all the promises of God find their *Yes* in Him.'[23]

Jazz was perhaps the one really positive thing in Larkin's life, but even that had to be hedged around with conditional clauses. This poem gloriously celebrates Bechet's music and for all the way Larkin's surface meaning purports to undermine the 'enormous yes' he hears in that music, his poem still demonstrates the power of art to transfigure our vision and affirm the truth of what our mind still dares not believe.

Lachrymae Amantis: Geoffrey Hill and the Power of Translation

Geoffrey Hill is one of the greatest living craftsmen in the English language and pre-eminently a master of the sonnet. He has a richly ambiguous relationship with the Christian faith, at once fascinated, moved and appalled – especially when that faith is vividly focused in the suffering of Christ and of subsequent martyrs. The act of translation is itself a parable of transfiguration and it is in a translation of a sonnet of Lopes de Vega with which he concludes his own sonnet sequence *Lachrymae* that Hill gives perhaps the finest account of doubting faith and reticent hope.

We will look at some poems from his volume, *Tenebrae* (1978). The very title of this volume conveys Hill's rich ambiguity. *Tenebrae*, of course, means 'darknesses'; but it is also the name given to a liturgical sequence in the Church, making the transition from Crucifixion to Resurrection. Liturgically it is a movement into darkness in order to find light. Throughout the volume, Hill turns again and again to sacred imagery, searching it with all the knowingness of a twentieth-century sceptic; but at the same time, allowing it utterly to search him with all the power of sacred mystery. He finds himself compelled to confront contradictions which he can neither gainsay nor resolve. The sonnet sequence *Lachrymae*, for example, which begins and ends with sonnets addressed directly to Christ, opens with the image of Christ fixed to the Cross; and the poet, equally fixed in a gaze at Christ – neither is able to turn away from the other, and yet for Hill the sonnet is a declaration not of belief but of unbelief.

In some ways, the whole drama of *Lachrymae* is to be seen in its transition from the absolute fixity of the opening sonnet in which no movement is possible, everything is foreclosed and written off, to the extraordinary opening-up of

---

23   2 Corinthians 1:18–20.

possibilities in the final sonnet in which Christ, no longer on the Cross, comes to seek the poet out. The transition is also reflected in the naming of these poems: the first, 'Lachymae Verae', concerns itself strictly with the question, 'What is truth?', what can I honestly say I perceive to be true? But the final sonnet, 'Lachrymae Amantis', allows Love a say, and Love opens up possibilities for truth that Reason and reflection have not seen. 'The Heart has its reasons whereof the Reason knows nothing.'[24]

Lachrymae Verae[25]

> Crucified Lord, you swim upon your cross
> and never move. Sometimes in dreams of hell
> the body moves but moves to no avail
> and is at one with that eternal loss.
>
> You are the castaway of drowned remorse,
> you are the world's atonement on the hill.
> This is your body twisted by our skill
> into a patience proper for redress.
>
> I cannot turn aside from what I do;
> you cannot turn away from what I am.
> You do not dwell in me nor I in you
>
> however much I pander to your name
> or answer to your lords of revenue,
> surrendering the joys that they condemn.

The opening sentence of this sonnet, with its direct address to Christ as Lord, gives a reader the initial impression that this is going to be a sonnet of unambiguous faith. 'Lord' is, after all, given a capital. 'Crucified Lord' might have stood as the opening of any sixteenth-century devotional sonnet, and that is certainly the tradition against which these poems are set. However, woven in with such affirmations of faith, are a series of counter-statements. On the one hand, Hill affirms the heart of faith in calling Christ 'the world's atonement on the hill' – on the other, he denies, in language as bleak and simple as possible, that he is in any way involved in, or reached by, this atonement: 'You do not dwell in me nor I in you'.

---

[24] 'La coeur a ses raisons que la raison ne connait point': Pascal, *Pensees*, Sect. 4, no. 277.

[25] In Geoffrey Hill, *Collected Poems* (Harmondsworth, 1985), p. 145.

The dominant image of the poem is of drowning: the possibility of salvation is therefore figured as solid ground. The ambiguities of the poem are focused in the two lines addressed to Christ:

> You are the castaway of drowned remorse,
> you are the world's atonement on the hill.

The image of Christ as the castaway is ambivalent to say the least. On the one hand, it reflects the notion that he has been literally 'cast away'; cast out by the world. And this reflects both the circumstances of his original crucifixion, as an outcast, thrown out to die on the rubbish dump of Golgotha, and also the present situation, in which a modern culture, which once had Christ as its centre, has cast him out to the fringes. A culture which once saw Christ as central for dealing with its remorse now casts him away and then, too late, finds itself drowning in a remorse that once might have saved and cleansed it.

However, when the two lines are taken together, and we find that, whereas 'remorse' is drowned, the 'castaway' is on the hill, we have another sense: paradoxically, the One who was cast out of Jerusalem, and crucified on Golgotha, stands now on a hill, on solid ground, whilst all the world around him drowns in its sea of troubles. One has the sense of the poet finding no firm footing, drowning in a dream of hell, looking longingly to this figure who is the 'world's atonement on the hill', but convinced that neither of them can move from where they are, that no connection can possibly be established between them. And yet, neither of them can ever ignore the other; they are eternally connected and yet eternally missing one another:

> I cannot turn aside from what I do;
> you cannot turn away from what I am.
> You do not dwell in me nor I in you

It is not sufficient for the (Christian) reader to reply to the poet, 'Of course, you *can* be connected to Christ; of course you can dwell in him and he in you – go to Church, receive Communion.' Because it is precisely this question of the relationship between Christ and the Church of history which is the centre of the poet's doubts. The end of this sonnet, and many passages elsewhere in the sequence, make it clear that the Church, its culture and its history, are a stumbling-block at the very least, and more often an occasion for dread and loathing. Throughout this sonnet sequence Hill makes us intensely aware tht it is precisely those rituals and devotions which were intended to bring us into communion with Christ that have become the rites of betrayal that separate us. Priests have become 'lords of revenue' and 'slavish masters of self-love',[26] while Christ is 'bowed beneath the

---

26   Ibid., p. 150.

gold', 'consigned by proxy to the Judas-kiss / of our devotion'.[27]. The last lines of that sixth sonnet, 'Lachrymae Antiquae Novae', sum up this fear and alienation, especially with the telling final line alluding to the forced conversions – and indeed, forced Communions – perpetrated by the Conquistadors on the indigenous people in their new dominions:

> Triumphalism feasts on empty dread,
>
> fulfilling triumphs of the festal year.
> We find you wounded by the token spear.
> Dominion is swallowed with your blood.[28]

And yet, as the sequence develops, the confrontation between Christ and the poet becomes ever more vivid and intimate. Three of the sonnets begin with the words 'Crucified Lord'. In the fifth sonnet, 'Pavana Dolorosa', a meditation on the religious violence of the sixteenth century and the martyrdoms on both sides, the poet, having tried to explain martyrdom as a kind of 'self-wounding', suddenly sees through and behind it all, to Calvary, and realises that what happens there is something that no amount of intervening history can eradicate or explain away, that in the paradoxes of God's death there, something is offered which cannot be ignored even if it remains, 'unfound':

> None can revoke your cry.
> Your silence is an ecstasy of sound
>
> and your nocturnals blaze upon the day.
> I founder in desire for things unfound.
> I stay amid the things that will not stay.[29]

These tensions and polarities between the necessity and the impossibility of an encounter with Christ intensify throughout the sequence, until by the end of the sixth sonnet, 'Lachrymae Antiquae Novae', they have become almost unbearable. The effect of the seventh and final sonnet, Hill's beautiful reworking of Lopes De Vega,[30] is all the more dramatic for the context in which it comes.

---

[27]   Ibid., p. 150.

[28]   Ibid., p. 150.

[29]   Ibid., p. 149.

[30]   See J.M. Cohen (ed.), *The Penguin Book of Spanish Verse* (Harmondsworth, 1956), p. 247.

Lachrymae Amantis[31]

> What is there in my heart that you should sue
> so fiercely for its love? What kind of care
> brings you as though a stranger to my door
> through the long night and in the icy dew
>
> seeking the heart that will not harbour you,
> that keeps itself religiously secure?
> At this dark solstice filled with frost and fire
> your passion's ancient wounds must bleed anew.
>
> So many nights the angel of my house
> has fed such urgent comfort through a dream,
> whispered, 'your lord is coming, he is close'
>
> that I have drowsed half-faithful for a time
> bathed in pure tones of promise and remorse:
> 'tomorrow I shall wake to welcome him.'[32]

We should say at the outset that the narrative voice of this poem is complex and multi-layered: it is Lopez de Vega whose sonnet Hill is versioning; it is the narrative voice, the poetic persona to whose first-person voice we have become attuned through the whole sonnet sequence; and it is Geoffrey Hill 'the maker' letting whatever part of his own person he wishes to rest in, or be withdrawn from, his work. When I speak of 'the poet' in the following analysis I am referring to this rich mix, this meeting in translation of seventeenth-century Spanish sensibilities with twentieth-century English ones, mediated through a mind that is especially alert to nuance and ambiguity. I am concerned with what is true of the narrative voice in the poem, not speculating about the 'state of faith' of its author, then or now.

This sonnet picks up – but transfigures – the key images with which the sequence opened: dreaming and drowning. The sense of the 'eternal loss', which is hell, is so vivid in 'Lachrymae Verae' that we almost forget the saving clause in that poem: that what we experience there is a dream of hell. The power, therefore, of the phrase 'tomorrow I shall wake' in the final line of the sequence is drawn from the opening of the first sonnet with its dream-imagery. In the first sonnet, the 'Lachrymae', the tears of remorse, are tears cried to no avail; remorse, in that sonnet, is something destructive in which we drown. The word 'drowned' from the first sonnet has been transfigured in the final sonnet to become the redemptive word 'bathed', with its suggestion of baptism. Indeed, one might say that the

---

31   Hill, *Collected Poems*, p. 151.
32   Hill, *Collected Poems*, p. 151.

dramatic structure of the sequence is precisely a movement from the apparently dead finality of 'drowned remorse' to the new possibilities opened up in being 'bathed in pure tones of promise and remorse'.

What makes this redemption of the imagery of despair possible? How have we moved from the fixed certainties of the first sonnet, ('I cannot turn ... You cannot turn ...') to the open possibilities of this final sonnet? The answer is that there has been a complete reversal of roles between Christ and the poet. Whereas, throughout the first six sonnets, Christ is fixed eternally to the Cross, and the poet, at once present to and distanced from that crucifixion, rehearses his gestures and attitudes in its presence: he seeks Christ, he rejects Christ, he praises Christ, he harangues Christ – and all the while the figure on the Cross is fixed and silent; yet in the final sonnet it is the poet who waits helplessly while another moves towards him. It is no longer a question of humankind's search for God, but of God's search for us. Suddenly, the tables are turned; the poet realises that he has been using his doubt not to seek for the truth, but to fend it off – that his very tirades against religion have been part of a strategy to keep himself 'religiously secure'. And now he confronts the possibility that, far from being fixed safely at a distance on a cross in the past, Christ might be walking towards him through this present night of darkness; that the Passion's ancient wounds can neither be consigned nor reduced to history, that they must bleed anew. Moreover, should the impossible encounter with the Crucified and Risen God actually take place, should that 'tomorrow' come in which the poet wakes to welcome him, then it will not be simply a matter of intellectual speculation or the satisfaction of intellectual doubts and dilemmas, but an encounter with Love which fiercely demands nothing less than love in return. The tables are turned completely; in the light of this final sonnet, we realise that so much of the questioning of God and faith which passes in the first six sonnets for sincere scepticism, turns out to be no more than self-evasion. The question that should have been asked first is not 'What is there in God's heart?', but 'What is there in my heart?' – and it is with this question that 'Lachrymae Amantis' opens:

> What is there in my heart that you should sue
> so fiercely for its love?[33]

For all the redemption of imagery and the 'pure tones of promise' with which Hill concludes *Lachrymae*, the two great questions with which the final sonnet opens, the questioning of himself and of God – 'What is there in my heart?' and 'What kind of care brings you ... to my door?' – remain unanswered. The possibility of a waking encounter with the living God is offered in this sonnet, but by the end of the sonnet it has not actually happened; the poet has moved from the 'dream of hell' in which he 'drowned', to a kind of half-waking state in which he has 'drowsed half-faithful for a time.' But the final line of the sequence, 'tomorrow I shall wake to welcome him', remains intentionally ambiguous. We can read it

---

hopefully, as the promise that there will be a real encounter; or we can read it as the perpetual evasion of half-faith, things will be allowed for as possibilities 'tomorrow', but always evaded today.

Apart from the wonderful verbal music and sheer technical brilliance of this sonnet sequence, its most striking achievement is absolute honesty. The poet refuses to become an exclusive propagandist for either of the apparently incompatible truths he apprehends. He has to do them both justice. And, even though he cannot bring himself to credit in the here-and-now the longed for resolution of these opposites, which he puts off to some waking day 'tomorrow', nevertheless the very endeavour to make coherent and beautiful poems of his experience of paradox, the very shaping of the sonnet itself, with its answering rhymes, perhaps suggests the final ordering of a coherent truth which he may not yet express.

Chapter 8

The Replenishing Fountain: Hope and Renewal in the Poetry of Seamus Heaney

The History of a Raindrop

We began with a reading of Heaney's poem 'The Rain Stick'. Its celebration of sudden refreshment in the midst of the dry and desolate, its release of unexpected music from the unpromising; and its final image of the single drop of water, through which we enter heaven, have been paradigms throughout this book for the power of poetry to transfigure vision, for the particular insights into truth to which the imagination gives access. In this final chapter, we shall return to Heaney and look at some more of his poetry in greater detail, focusing particularly on this theme of renewed or transfigured vision.

Behind the achievement of 'The Rain Stick' is a long history, the training of a poet's eye, opening and exposing his heart. We can see something of that story even in the traces that a single image leaves. We first encounter the raindrop, which, in 'Rain Stick', is to become the gate of heaven, in the poem 'Exposure', which concludes Heaney's 1975 collection *North* and is also the final poem in the sequence *Singing School*.

Exposure[1]

It is December in Wicklow:
Alders dripping, birches
Inheriting the last light,
The ash tree cold to look at.

A comet that was lost
Should be visible at sunset,
Those million tons of light
Like a glimmer of haws and rose-hips,

And I sometimes see a falling star.
 If I could come on meteorite!
Instead I walk through damp leaves,
Husks, the spent flukes of autumn,

---

[1]   In Seamus Heaney, *North* (London, 1975), p. 72.

Imagining a hero
On some muddy compound,
His gift like a slingstone
Whirled for the desperate.

How did I end up like this?
I often think of my friends'
Beautiful prismatic counselling
And the anvil brains of some who hate me

As I sit weighing and weighing
My responsible *tristia*.
For what? For the ear? For the people?
For what is said behind-backs?

Rain comes down through the alders,
Its low conducive voices
Mutter about let-downs and erosions
And yet each drop recalls

The diamond absolutes.
I am neither internee nor informer;
An inner émigré, grown long-haired
And thoughtful; a wood-kerne

Escaped from the massacre,
Taking protective colouring
From bole and bark, feeling
Every wind that blows;

Who, blowing up these sparks
For their meagre heat, have missed
The once-in-a-lifetime portent,
The comet's pulsing rose.

'Exposure' is at one level an intensely personal poem about self-doubt in which Heaney exposes to the light of his own judgement – and ours – his fear of failing either his vocation as a poet who must be open to all truth and feel 'every wind that blows', or his vocation to be one of his own people, to articulate the losses and longings of the tribe to which he belongs. He quotes almost the whole of this important poem in his acceptance speech for the Nobel Prize, and sets out some of its background. He had moved south out of Belfast into County Wicklow, a move which had provoked both triumphant crowing from Protestant forces who wished good-riddance to a famous 'papist' and vituperation from Republicans who wanted to hold Heaney captive as a kind of propaganda icon of struggle in the North. Heaney writes:

> Feeling puny in my predicaments as I read about the tragic logic of Osip Mandelstam's fate in the 1930's, feeling challenged yet steadfast in my non-combatant status when I heard, for example, that one particularly sweet-natured school friend had been interned without trial because he was suspected of having been involved in a political killing. What I was longing for was not quite stability but an active escape from the quicksand of relativism, a way of crediting poetry without anxiety or apology.[2]

At another level, it is a poem about vision, using the word 'exposure' almost in the sense of a camera's exposure of a film to light. Ostensibly it is a poem about a vision or epiphany which has been missed: the poet is literally *exposed* to the dripping December weather of Wicklow, because he has gone out to see a comet, to expose the film of his soul to 'those million tons of light'. And the poem appears to end with an admission of failure; the poet has 'missed / The once in a lifetime portent, / The comet's pulsing rose'. But this missed epiphany is only on the surface; the poet missed what he intended to see but was exposed instead to something far more important which turns out to confirm his vocation. Consciously, he is longing for his doubts to be dealt with by some dazzling finality, a 'million tons of light'. He indulges the fantasy of himself being able to blaze away, free from ambiguities and second thoughts: 'If I could come on meteorite!' Yet his honesty will not allow such escapism; we have not arrived at the eschaton, we have still to contend with our darkness and shifting perspectives. But does this mean that we have nothing to go by, no light for the interim, and no standard by which to be judged, and so liberated? The real achievement of this poem is not only in its honest confession of the loss of that wished-for fantasy light, but in the transfiguration of the image with which the poem opens, the cold rain dripping through the branches in Wicklow. At first, this rain seems to be no more than the mood-music of failure:

> It is December in Wicklow:
> Alders dripping, birches
> Inheriting the last light,
> The ash tree cold to look at.
>
> ... Damp leaves
> Husks, the spent flukes of autumn, ...
>
> Rain comes down through the alders,

---

[2] From 'Crediting Poetry', Heaney's 1995 Nobel speech, published in *Opened Ground: Poems 1966–1996* (London, 1998), p. 452.

Its low conducive voices
Mutter about let-downs and erosions …

But the key word, the hinge of the whole poem, as in so many of the great psalms, is the word 'yet'. The healing light to which Heaney needs to expose his self-doubts is not the 'far off, most secret and inviolate rose'[3] of the comet's light, but the last light of the day in which he stands, the light which, for all his doubts, is still there, is inherited by the dripping alders, and is gathered, concentrated, in each glistening drop that falls from the trees around him. The diamond clarity which he seeks has been around him all the time, and is to be found in the very act of poetic faithfulness to his real situation, in the act, as he puts it, of 'blowing up these sparks / for their meagre heat'.

Rain comes down through the alders,
Its low conducive voices
Mutter about let-downs and erosions
And yet each drop recalls

The diamond absolutes.
I am neither internee nor informer;
An inner émigré, grown long-haired
And thoughtful; a wood-kerne

Escaped from the massacre,
Taking protective colouring
From bole and bark, feeling
Every wind that blows; …

In the act of confessing what he thinks is a failure of vision, Heaney's vision is renewed and he is recalled to the 'diamond absolute' of his vocation as a truth-teller. The symbol, in the deepest sense in which Coleridge might have used that word, of this renewed vision and confirmed vocation, the 'outward and visible sign' for Heaney and for us, the 'word' in 'that eternal language which thy God utters', is the light collected in a falling raindrop.

This drop of water seeded with the last light of a December evening, recalling for Heaney the 'diamond absolutes', has itself both a history and a future. In Heaney's poetic consciousness, and in the wider literary tradition in which he participates, the rounded drop of water containing, as it does, a whole world reflected in the surface, concentrates experience as well as light. The experience, for example, of Heaney as a small child, seeing 'the shiny pouches of raindrops

---

[3]   W.B. Yeats, 'The Secret Rose', line 1, in *The Poems*, ed. D. Albright (London, 1992), p. 87.

on the telegraph wires' along the railway crossing near his home, an experience he celebrates in another poem:

The Railway Children[4]

When we climbed the slopes of the cutting
We were eye-level with the white cups
Of the telegraph poles and the sizzling wires.

Like lovely freehand they curved for miles
East and miles west beyond us, sagging
Under their burden of swallows.

We were small and thought we knew nothing
Worth knowing. We thought words travelled the wires
In the shiny pouches of raindrops,

Each one seeded full with the light
Of the sky, the gleam of the lines, and ourselves
So infinitesimally scaled

We could stream through the eye of a needle.

Here, the raindrops are imagined as not only seeded with light, but as bearers of meaning. They carry the words which the children have been told travel the wires of the telegraph. Heaney intimates that what an adult might mistake for ignorance in the children, is really a kind of wisdom: 'We were small and thought we knew nothing / Worth knowing'. The implication is that they did in fact know something worth knowing, something which adults in the grip of dry reductivism ceased to know. For a moment, the imaginative vision of these children, the vision of raindrops full of light and meaning, raindrops that somehow recapitulate the whole world, 'the sky, the gleam of the lines, and ouselves, so infinitesimally scaled', is the vision vouchsafed once to Blake in the 'Auguries of Innocence':

To see a world in a grain of sand
And heaven in a wild flower,
Hold infinity in the palm of your hand,
And eternity in an hour.[5]

It is the same vision which led Coleridge even in his last years, writing a prose work like 'The Statesman's Manual', to go back to the single vivid experience

---

[4]   In Heaney, *Station Island* (London, 1984), p. 45.
[5]   In *The Poetical Works of William Blake*, ed. J. Sampson (Oxford, 1952), p. 171.

– perhaps as a child – of being 'struck with admiration at beholding the cope of heaven as imaged in a dew-drop', and to say that, if only we could think seriously about that, we would think our way to God. It is the vision which gave Dylan Thomas his beautiful glimpse of 'the round Zion of the water bead'.[6]

Heaney makes it clear that this imaginative vision of everything including themselves, 'infinitesimally scaled' in a raindrop, had about it a sacramental quality by concluding the poem in a single line, given space to itself, with an allusion to the saying of Jesus in which the eye of a needle becomes the impossible point of entry into heaven made possible by God: 'We could stream through the eye of a needle.' Small wonder then, that the falling drop glimpsed in the last light of December by the weary and self-doubting adult, is nevertheless able to recall the 'diamond absolutes'. Small wonder too, that the vision in both these poems is revived and given even deeper clarity and resolution in 'The Rain Stick', a poem in which Heaney, having come through the crises and self-doubts chronicled in his earlier volumes, is able 'gladly and freely to credit marvels'. In that poem, alluding again to the same saying of Christ, he names the heaven into which the little boy in 'The Railway Children' had imagined himself streaming; and he has no doubts about setting aside the dismissive rationalism that had made him think he 'knew nothing worth knowing':

> Who cares if all the music that transpires
>
> Is the fall of grit or dry seeds through a cactus?
> You are like a rich man entering heaven
> Through the ear of a rain drop. Listen now again.[7]

Coleridge called on poets to remove the 'film of the familiar', to 'awaken the mind's attention', to make us realise that we have eyes yet see not. The curved reflective surface of the drop, its dizzying changes of scale and perspective, have this effect of making it, as great poetry should be, at once a mirror and a window. And, very much as we saw in the Introduction, not only Shakespeare's 'mirror held up to nature', but also George Herbert's suddenly translucent window; as Heaney makes clear, not only in this poem but especially throughout the volume entitled *Seeing Things*, which preceded it, he is absolutely concerned with the nature and clarity of our vision.

---

[6]   Dylan Thomas, 'A Refusal to Mourn the Death, by Fire, of a Child in London', lines 7–8, in *Collected Poems, 1934–1952* (London, 1952), p. 101.

[7]   In Heaney, *The Spirit Level* (London, 1996), p. 1.

From the Murderous to the Marvellous

The clarity and assurance of a poem like 'The Rain Stick' might give one the impression that Heaney was naturally or easily a celebrant of light and hope, or even suggest that his poems of hope and renewal were achieved by an aversion of the eyes from the themes of darkness, doubt and despair which have been so central to the literature of the twentieth century. Nothing could be further from the truth. The celebrations of light, of music and of renewed vision in Heaney's later poetry, have such great authority precisely because they arise from a lifetime of exposure to 'every wind that blows'. To use a favourite word of his, we may 'credit' Heaney's glimpses of heaven because, like his master Dante, he has also looked closely into darkness and been the cartographer of hell.

Invoking the muse in Book III of *Paradise Lost*, Milton contrasted the ease with which he could 'venture down the dark descent' with the real difficulty of trying to 'reascend'. In the end, the return to light cannot be a matter of human effort, but has to be heard as a calling and received as a gift, particularly in our own dark times when it seems such a paramount duty to bear witness to suffering. We almost need to be given permission, both as writers and readers, to bear witness to the light. So in his Nobel acceptance speech, *Crediting Poetry*, Heaney speaks first of the almost obligatory attention to darkness and suspicion of light which comes with our culture:

> As writers and readers, and sinners and citizens, our realism and our aesthetic sense make us wary of crediting the positive note. The very gunfire braces us and the atrocious confers a worth upon the effort which it calls forth to confront it ...[8]

Heaney's own effort to confront the Troubles into which he was born and to speak humane truth in the midst of atrocity have been justly celebrated and have in their own sphere, contributed to the present hopes for long-term peace. But Heaney has not remained imprisoned in the role of the poet as a diarist of darkness, or as an elevated war-correspondent; rather he has chosen in the midst of that darkness as he puts it, 'to make space ... for the marvellous' as well as for the 'murderous' in his vision of truth. As he goes on to say:

> for years I was bowed to the desk like some monk bowed over his prie-dieu, some dutiful contemplative pivoting his understanding in an attempt to bear his portion of the weight of the world, knowing himself incapable of heroic virtue or redemptive effect, but constrained by his obedience to his rule to repeat the effort and the posture. Blowing up sparks for a meagre heat. Forgetting faith, straining towards good works. Attending insufficiently to the diamond absolutes, among which must be counted the sufficiency of that which is absolutely imagined.

---

8   Heaney, *Opened Ground*, p. 457.

Then finally and happily, and not in obedience to the dolorous circumstances of my native place but in spite of them, I straightened up. I began a few years ago to make space in my reckoning and imagining for the marvellous as well as the murderous.[9]

We will conclude this chapter with a reading of 'Seeing Things', the beautiful triptych which is the fruit of Heaney's mature 'imagining the marvellous'; but before that, it is worth tracing in his earlier poetry something of the journey, the Dantean pilgrimage, which brought him to the glimpses of heaven which hallow his later work.

From the outset Heaney has been concerned with what might be termed a 'double vision', with seeing things both in terms of their detailed particularities and as doorways or windows to something beyond themselves. The poems of his first volume, *Death of a Naturalist*, are full of detailed, particular observations. Even those things in nature from which the eyes would like to withdraw are seen and rendered in careful detail:

> Bubbles gargled delicately, bluebottles
> Wove strong gauze of sound around the smell.
> There were dragon-flies, spotted butterflies,
> But best of all was the warm thick slobber
> Of frogspawn that grew like clotted water
> In the shade of the banks.[10]

But, however minutely observed, he is never content to 'stay his eye' on the surface of the image; rather he is continuously seeking to see through and beyond it, even if that unknown beyond can be apprehended only as darkness. So, in the final poem of that first volume, 'Personal Helicon', he moves from the natural observation of particular wells around his childhood home, to something more, something which amounts to a 'hearing' of his vocation, and the beginning of his lifetime's effort as a poet. After describing wells in which he could see his own reflection, wells in which through darkness you nevertheless saw the sky, wells with echoes which 'gave back your own call / With a clean new music in it', he concludes the poem and his first book with this quatrain:

> Now to pry into roots, to finger slime,
> To stare big-eyed Narcissus, into some spring
> Is beneath all adult dignity. I rhyme
> To see myself, to set the darkness echoing.[11]

---

[9]   Ibid., p. 458.

[10]   Heaney, *Death of a Naturalist* (London, 1966), p. 15.

[11]   Ibid., p.57.

It is scarcely surprising that the title of his next volume is *Door into the Dark*. It begins a lifetime's attention to the too easily dismissible dark, a lifetime's effort to 'set it echoing' and to discern what unexpected glimmers it might contain. The title of the book comes from the first line of his sonnet 'The Forge', one of many poems in which by celebrating a craftsman he also celebrates the craft of poetry. That poem begins with a line expressive of the wise humility which is at the core of Heaney's work: 'All I know is a door into the dark'. But, looking into that darkness, Heaney discerns in the shape and music of the blacksmith a kind of numinous and creative centre to things, imaged in this poem as the anvil:

> The anvil must be somewhere in the centre,
> Horned as a unicorn, at one end square,
> Set there immoveable: an altar
> Where he expends himself in shape and music.[12]

Heaney's choice of words like 'altar' and 'unicorn' (a symbol of Christ), carrying with them a sense of the sacred and numinous, allow the anvil 'somewhere in the centre' of his poem to be both the particular anvil in the dark workshop of an Irish blacksmith, and also an emblem for that unknowable centre in the darkness beyond our perceptions, where our Creator expends himself in shape and music.

Also in that second volume, is a poem about the paradox of going into the dark in order to have vision restored, which turns out to be prophetic of Heaney's entire *oeuvre*:

In Gallarus Oratory[13]

> You can still feel the community pack
> This place: it's like going into a turf stack,
> A core of old dark walled up with stone
> A yard thick. When you're in it alone
> You might have dropped, a reduced creature
> To the heart of the globe. No worshipper
> Would leap up to his God off this floor.
>
> Founded there like heroes in a barrow
> They sought themselves in the eye of their King
> Under the black weight of their own breathing.
> And how he smiled on them as out they came,
> The sea a censer and the grass a flame.

---

12   Heaney, *A Door into the Dark* (London, 1969), p. 19.
13   Ibid., p. 22.

This poem is full of Heaney's sense of what Eliot called, 'the present moment of the past'.[14] He enters the oratory alone, and is yet immediately aware of the community somehow still 'packing the place'. In a sense, this poem develops the hints of *Door into the Dark*: that in order to enhance our vision we need to absent ourselves from the familiar lit surfaces of things, to walk through a door into the dark, to find what is there 'somewhere in the centre'. Heaney journeys in his imagination with the Celtic saints he has remembered into the 'core of old dark', which becomes also the 'heart of the globe'; he describes these early Christians also in terms of their pagan past, as being 'founded there like heroes in a barrow', and dares with them to enter a darkness where there is nothing but the 'black weight' of our own breathing. However, the end of this daring is vision, not blindness: the Saints sought to see no longer with their own eyes, but with the 'eye of their King'. And the real vision is bestowed only on their return, from the darkness of the oratory to the once-familiar world, where they find that the veil of the ordinary has been removed, and they see the familiar transfigured with the flame of praise:

> And how he smiled on them as out they came,
> The sea a censer and the grass a flame.

The tone and structure of this poem anticipate much of what Heaney was to write later. One might argue that his subsequent poetry, from this volume until the moment in the penitential journey of 'Station Island' when he says, 'my feet touched bottom', is prefigured in the journey in this poem. He speaks of entering the oratory as being like going 'into a turf stack', a 'core of old dark walled up with stone' which would be a good description of what he achieves in *Wintering Out* and *North*; and that likewise, the re-emergence in the final couplet, with its sudden discovery that the very creation itself is a numinous sacrament, anticipates the vision Heaney has in *Seeing Things* and *The Spirit Level*. In *North*, he would be going not simply into the turf stack, but beneath the turf into the bog itself, to explore in the core of its 'old dark' themes at the heart of Irish history and sensibility as well as at the depth of his own poetic vision. The allusion to the heroic age and its links with the early Church, to those monks entering their dark oratory as being 'founded there like heroes in a barrow', are also picked up in *North* where Heaney confirms his vocation as a poet in language which echoes both the monastic and the heroic age, as he hears his muse speak in the poem 'North':[15]

> It said, 'Lie down
> In the word-hoard, burrow
> The coil and gleam
> Of your furrowed brain.

---

14   T.S. Eliot, *Selected Prose*, ed. F. Kermode (London, 1975), p. 44.
15   In Heaney, *North*, p. 20.

Compose in darkness.
Expect aurora borealis
In the long foray
But no cascade of light.

Keep your eye clear
As the bleb of the icicle,
Trust the feel of what nubbed treasure
Your hands have known.'

Heaney's fidelity to this difficult vocation, this command to 'compose in darkness', to work without the comfort even of hope for a 'cascade of light'; and yet to be a faithful witness to whatever gleams are there, is absolute and awe-inspiring, both in this poem and those that follow. Even in the poems whose dominant imagery is darkness, cold and exposure, Heaney never loses this calling to clarity. The poet's eye, and – through the exercise of the imagination – the reader's eye, is kept 'clear as the bleb of the icicle'; faithful through the darkness, and therefore clear enough to see when the icicle melts, the 'diamond absolutes' caught in a falling raindrop.

In 'North', the vocation to compose in darkness had been understood both in terms of the monastic vision of 'Gallarus Oratory', and of the heroic age when the *fili*, the early Irish poets, were expected to go into darkness and retreat to compose.

Heaney and Dante

From *Field Work* onwards though, Heaney begins to make explicit another model of his vocation which was perhaps always there but needed now to be made more formally a part of his work, and that was his relationship with the poet Dante. He had already and in various respects been in conversation with Dante, but Dante becomes more explicitly his companion in *Field Work*. In 'The Strand at Lough Beg,' the first of many elegies for those killed in the Troubles, he quotes the *Purgatorio*, and imagines himself cleansing his murdered cousin to prepare his soul for the journey through Purgatory to Paradise, just as at the beginning of the *Purgatorio*, Virgil cleanses from Dante's face the grime and tears of Hell. For, as both Dante and Heaney imply, this is one of the roles of poetry: to cleanse our memories and clarify our vision, ready for that journey. But, although he imagines his cousin Colum as emerged already from the *Inferno*, cleansed and on the road through Purgatory to Paradise, he knows that he himself is not there yet, and the other Dantean references in this book are to the *Inferno*, to the ninth circle of Hell. In 'An Afterwards', he imagines himself frozen there and condemned for his own moral failings. And finally, in the devastatingly vivid translation of the Ugolino passages from *Inferno* 32 and 33 with which *Field Work* concludes, he offers a glimpse of Hell as a context for understanding the agony of the hunger strikers.

There are many reasons for the resonance between Dante and Heaney; Dante is very much a poet's poet, and there is of course a long tradition, going back to Chaucer, of relation to Dante by poets writing in English. In the very structure of his poem Dante models the possibility of a poet from the past turning out also to be the contemporary of a present poet and walking with him on his journey; for this is what Virgil does for Dante. Further, in the *Purgatorio*, there is a particular series of encounters between poets living and dead, in which they discuss their craft, its impact on their own time, and its place in the wider scheme of things. This sense that Dante both models conversation between poets of different ages and languages, and invites us to such a conversation with him, was very much understood in our own time by Eliot and the other high-modernists, especially Joyce and Beckett.

Heaney, simply by virtue of his deep reading, indeed his inhabiting of the European tradition, would have been intellectually engaged with Dante,[16] and would have found in Eliot's prose and poetry, as well as in Yeats', direct models for reimagining Dantean episodes in modern contexts though Heaney's own way of making Dante a contemporary is probably mediated as much through Osip Mandelstam.[17] In some ways, he had personally much deeper connections with Dante than his modernist predecessors; unlike Eliot, Heaney was born and nurtured, as Dante was, in Catholic Christendom. Like Dante, he reimagined the tradition and, by giving it his individual voice, discerned a 'clean, new music' in it. But also like Dante, he is able to stand over against the tradition and question it.

More specifically still, he shares with Dante both the curse and blessing of having been made the exile of a savagely divided city. Dante and Heaney were both forced to question their relationship to their own 'tribe's complicity' in violence. Both of them were under enormous pressure to write propaganda for their own side; a pressure which they both resisted. Rather than absolutise the immediate political crisis, they chose instead both to be faithful to the fierce passions of their contemporary political situation and at the same time to try and see these things as they might look in the light of eternity. Dante too, might have written 'I am neither internee nor informer', an 'inner émigré'. Both poets, while dealing fully with the dark realities of 'the murderous' and the matter of the cities that bred them, nevertheless felt called also to raise their eyes to another light and to 'credit marvels'.

If Dante is supremely the poet of Paradise and the one through whose imagination glimpses and echoes of the unimaginable come most clearly into

---

16   For an interesting discussion of Heaney's engagement with Dante, see Maria Christina Fumagalli *The Flight of the Vernacular: Seamus Heaney, Derek Walcott and the Impress of Dante* (Amsterdam and New York, 2001).

17   See Mandelstam's essay 'Conversation about Dante' and Heaney's 'Envies and Identifications: Dante and the Modern Poet', both printed in *The Poet's Dante: Twentieth-Century Responses*, ed P.S. Hawkins and R. Jacoff (New York, 2001), respectively pp. 40–93 and 239–58.

European literature, it is because he was also the pilgrim through Hell and Purgatory. In identifying with Dante, Heaney discovers the hidden hope that lay in that first command to 'compose in darkness'; he is not to remain in the 'core of old dark' forever, but like the monks in 'Gallarus Oratory', having sought himself and found himself, and us under the 'black weight' of our own breathing, he would be called eventually, to 'straighten up', 'unclench' and 'emerge', as the authoritative celebrant of light.

Between the *Inferno* and the *Paradiso* comes the *Purgatorio*; if Hell is the place where suffering is simply itself and unredeemed, then Purgatory is the place where it is open to the possibility of transfiguration; the place where tears can cleanse. Heaney's next volume of original poetry (as opposed to translation), *Station Island*, was to be, in every sense, his *Purgatorio*, and the sequence 'Station Island' itself, is Dante reimagined and revoiced for our own times.

'Station Island'[18] is a sequence of twelve poems in which the figure of the poet[19] makes two journeys simultaneously. The first is an outward and visible journey around the beds, or 'stations', on Station Island in Lough Derg, also known as 'St Patrick's Purgatory', and still a place of pilgrimage. Heaney has made this pilgrimage three times; the name 'Patrick's Purgatory' may have suggested the link with Dante's *Purgatorio*, which animates the poem. The second and inner journey, enabled by the outward and visible one, is a series of confessional and ultimately purgative encounters with significant people – both in the poet's personal past, and in the past of Irish and European literature. And here, the links with Dante's *Purgatorio*, and more widely with the whole *Comedia*, are crucial.

Dante makes his journey as one of the living; but, in a series of harrowing encounters with the dead, he is forced to re-examine all he is and has been. He is purged both of his pride and of his uncertainty. He is rebuked for wasting life and talent, but is also enabled to resume his life and exert his talent with a new confidence and mastery of touch. In Dante's journey through Hell and Purgatory, he is accompanied and guided by the poet Virgil. At the beginning, and for most of the journey through Hell, Dante's dependence on Virgil is childlike, or childish, to the point of being almost pathetic. He lacks confidence and is continually looking to the master for advice and instruction. But throughout, Virgil, as he teaches and guides Dante, is seeking to build his confidence and independence, because he knows the time will come, at the end of the *Purgatorio*, when the disciple must dare to tread a road on which the master has never set foot, and to be the poet of mysteries which the pagan humanism of Virgil had not yet seen.

The significant moment comes at the end of the *Purgatorio* when, after all they have been through together, Virgil says to Dante:

[18]   In Heaney, *Station Island*, pp.61–94.

[19]   There is a distinction, of course, between Heaney the voice of the pilgrim-poet in this sequence, and Heaney the public figure, let alone Heaney the private man. In what follows I am referring to Heaney the voice of the pilgrim-poet in this sequence.

No longer look to me for signs or word
Your will is healthy, upright, free and whole
And not to heed that sense would be a fault.
Lord of yourself I crown and mitre you.[20]

The uncertain, and sometimes cringing Dante, referring always back to Virgil as 'the master', has at the end of the *Purgatorio* been made a *master* himself. And paradoxically, it is Virgil the pagan who gives him the confidence to write in the *Paradiso* the Christian truths that Virgil had never glimpsed.

Heaney's Purgatorio: *The Journey of 'Station Island'*

Dante's journey is both the journey of a whole culture from paganism to Christendom, and the journey of a man from childhood through adolescence, to a mature mastery as well as psychologically and morally; the journey through unredeemed violence and darkness to the possibilities of redemptive suffering and finally of unassailable peace. So in Heaney's own re-reading and reimagining of the Dantean pilgrimage in 'Station Island' there is a journey through his own life from the little boy in the first poem listening in the bedroom dark to wind and rain in the trees, to the mature poet given his mastery and confidence by Joyce the master, walking confidently out into the rain. But there is a journey also through the literature of Ireland, from the early nature poetry of Sweeney, through the medieval monks and scribes, the sectarian prose of men like Carlton, to Joyce, and finally to Heaney himself. And likewise, and perhaps most profoundly, there is a journey down into the worst of the darkness and the discovery with Dante, with St John of the Cross, and with Eliot, who quoted them both, that 'the way down is the way up'. For in this poem, we are brought lower and lower through layers of history, but also through layers of self-accusation, self-doubt and uncertainty, of loathing and disgust at the self-perpetuating chains of violence and complicity, until that point in his nightmare imagination of the dying hunger striker when Heaney says, 'my feet touched bottom and my heart revived'.

And then we are brought up, again, into the possibilities of redemption; we are enabled to 'credit marvels', to see the 'need and chance to salvage everything'. Finally, at the end of the poem, Heaney, like Dante before him, is sent out from his *Purgatorio*, genuinely purged and changed, given both the permission and the mastery he needs to be as faithful to the vision of light as he was in the past to the vision of darkness.

It would take a whole book to spell this process out in all its mastery, poem by poem; for the purposes of this chapter which is concerned with what makes Heaney's *Paradiso* credible, we need only look at that point in the *Purgatorio*

---

[20]   Dante, *Purgatorio*, trans. R, Kirkpatrick (London, 2007), Canto 27, lines 139–42, p. 259.

where his 'feet touched bottom', and then from there, in the remaining three poems of the sequence, the path of recovery.

The low point in 'Station Island' is reached in Poem ix.[21] The poem begins with the spirit of an IRA soldier and hunger striker who describes his own death in a way that invokes our empathy, and yet at the same time evokes his willingness to kill and his memory of the bomb he has set in a way that horrifies us. His last words combine his own tragic suffering with that of a victim he has shot:

> When the police yielded my coffin, I was light
> As my head when I took aim.

Heaney remembers his funeral and recognises equally in him both the evil and the sacrifice.

> Unquiet soul, they should have buried you
> In the bog where you threw your first grenade,
> Where only helicopters and curlews
> Make their maimed music

In the history of Ireland, the poet feels he has been equally a part of both the music and the maiming. His dream becomes a nightmare:

> I dreamt and drifted. All seemed to run to waste
> As down a swirl of mucky, glittering flood
> Strange polyp floated like a huge corrupt
> Magnolia bloom, surreal as a shed breast,
> My softly awash and blanching self-disgust.

Here, even the images which have throughout been symbols of good in Heaney's work – light and flowing water – seem corrupt and destroyed; the water is not cleansing but 'mucky', running 'to waste', carrying hideous debris. The light neither cleanses nor illumines, but merely glitters on the surface of the flood and reveals only the horror around it. Disgust and self-disgust, left to themselves, redeem nothing, until they can be transfigured by repentance. Are these dark waters to be 'night waters' in the sense that they are like the rivers in Dante's Hell, crossed only once and carrying the damned forever down into hopelessness? Or 'night' waters, in which the word night carries the implicit hope of day, and waters still hold their potential to cleanse? Might the word 'awash', which seems to carry nothing but drifting helplessness, be redeemed to mean washed, purged, cleansed – are these to be the waters of Hell, or of Purgatory?

The change comes in the next line where, amidst the blanching waters of self-disgust, come the redeeming waters of human tears:

---

[21]   *Station Island*, pp.84–86.

> And I cried among night waters, 'I repent
> My unweaned life that kept me competent
> To sleepwalk with connivance and mistrust.'

'Connivance and mistrust', or even just the fear of these, have been one of Heaney's consistent poetic themes; his poetry up to this point is full of self-questioning and mistrust of himself, as though he had never quite lost that first tag he gave himself when he published his poetry under the name 'Incertus'. Whatever truth there might or might not be in the charges he so publicly made against himself of 'tribal complicity', they needed to be dealt with and purged if he was to be free to express, and not to mistrust, such light as might be given to him. So the narrator of these poems 'repents'. This is the moment to which the whole pilgrimage has been moving. And what comes next in the dream-sequence of the poem is the redemption of nightmare imagery; the strange polyp, with its corrupt magnolia bloom drifting in mucky water forever down to nowhere, becomes, instead, first a lighted candle, and then a bright-masted ship which retrieves its course and is 'no more adrift':

> Then, like a pistil growing from the polyp,
> A lighted candle rose and steadied up
> Until the whole bright-masted thing retrieved
> A course and the currents it had gone with
> Were what it rode and showed. No more adrift,
> My feet touched bottom and my heart revived.

The dream imagery changes again; he sees the 'moon through rippled Lough waters', itself an image of the 'molten inside sheen of an instrument' as yet undisclosed. And he wakes to the three images which are to inform his *Paradiso*: light, music and flowing water; and to the one word which is to characterise his poetic vision of these things – 'clarity':

> And then it was the clarity of waking
> To sunlight and a bell and gushing taps
>   In the next cubicle.

It is in this morning light that the narrator, and through him the reader, suddenly realises what the something 'round and clear', the 'shining instrument', was at the end of his dream; and not only what it was, but what it means, and how it might be taken up. How it was miraculously 'still there for the taking':

> Still there for the taking!
> The old brass trumpet with its valves and stops
> I found once in loft thatch, a mystery
> I shied from then for I thought such trove beyond me.

The hidden trumpet glimpsed by the child in loft thatch, which he both longed to play and also shied away from, becomes a symbol of the mystery of redemptive love which Heaney has hesitated to credit, has mistrusted himself to be able to express, from which, he has felt it to be almost his duty to abstain; it is the 'cascade of light' he had thought his muse had taught him not to expect. And now, at last, when he sees from the darkness of this nightmare how desperately it is needed, he discovers that it is still there: it is 'there for the taking'. And that, purged of his own darkness and uncertainties, he might have the temerity to take it up and to blow upon it no uncertain note.

But there are three 'stations' still to travel in the completion of Patrick's Purgatory; and in these, now that his 'feet have touched bottom', the pilgrim-poet must learn to see and to trust the light, to become open to 'the need and chance to salvage everything'. Station X acts almost as an overture to the explicit account of redemption in Station XI. It gives a prophetic image of redeeming transformation by telling two parables whose significance will only be understood in the light of the next poem.[22] The first is the story of an ordinary mug which Heaney lent to a group of actors, and how, when he saw it lifted up into the imaginative space of the play, it was transfigured before him. The key words, almost imitating the whole movement of descent and ascent which is the structure of the *Comedia*, of the salvation story and, of course, baptism, are 'dipped', 'glamoured' and 'restored':

> Dipped and glamoured from this translation,
> It was restored

The second is the story of St Ronan and the Otter.

> As the otter surfaced once with Ronan's Psalter
> Miraculously unharmed, that had been lost
> A day and a night under Lough water
>
> And so the saint praised God on the Lough shore.
> The dazzle of the impossible suddenly
> Blazed across the threshold, a sun-glare
> To put out the small hearths of constancy.

In the first published version of this poem, in the edition of *Station Island* itself, Heaney speaks of this miracle as the 'dazzle of the impossible' suddenly blazing; but lest he should be misunderstood as suggesting that he was still the unpurged 'Incertus', too reticent to 'credit' such a sudden blaze, he rewords this verse when it is reprinted in *Opened Ground*, and consciously echoes the poetic credo he had set out in *Crediting Poetry*, where 'credit' has become a key verb, as poetry enables us to credit, and so to see, realities we would otherwise miss. The

---

22   Ibid., pp. 87–88.

revised verse finishes not with the saint on the lough shore in the past, but with the poet standing, blinking in the present light at the door of the hostel, his vision as purged and renewed as the vision of the monks in 'Gallarus Oratory' had been, 'as out they came, / The sea a censer, and the grass a flame':

> And so the saint praised God on the Lough shore
> For that dazzle of impossibility
> I credited again in the sun-filled door,
> So absolutely light it could put out fire.[23]

But if the poet-pilgrim in 'Station Island', purged by his long, dark journey, has been enabled to credit again the dazzle of impossibility in the sun-filled door, he must still make, with the rest of us in the land of the living, a journey in the dark. These poems are glimpses given in the context of this present darkness, and he must return to the great task of clarifying vision and witnessing honestly in the here-and-now. In the last two poems of 'Station Island', he resumes his calling. In Poem IX, he had 'cried out in repentance' in the midst of a nightmare; in X, he wakes in sunlight and is encouraged by the memory of two stories of redemption and restoration. And so, in XI, he makes confession, and in XII, is restored to mastery of himself and sent out freshly into the world.

The whole sequence 'Station Island' is a masterpiece; but Poem XI is the jewel in its crown, containing as it does not only a fine emblem of sin and redemption, but also a powerful new translation of perhaps the greatest of the poems of St John of the Cross. The poem opens with the poet's memory of having ruined a kaleidoscope he had been given as a child, by plunging it 'in a butt of muddied water', in his desire, even then, to see into the dark. This gift, 'mistakenly abased', becomes an emblem for all that is ruined and 'run to waste' in us. It harks back to the mucky, glittering flood of the nightmare station IX, and supremely it represents the problem of our failed vision with which this entire book has been concerned. The kaleidoscope becomes an emblem of the gift of imagination itself, an instrument in which we may see, refracted through the creation, the glories of God's light. Our fall, collectively and individually, has plunged this kaleidoscope into muddied water. The world we see habitually is not the true world at all, because it is seen through the sludge with which the kaleidoscope is encrusted, a sludge which Coleridge so charitably called 'the film of familiarity and selfish solicitude'. The question is, has the gift been ruined forever? Can the kaleidoscope surface again? Can it ever again become the 'marvellous lightship', the window into heaven? In this poem, Heaney suggests that it can: 'What came to nothing could always be replenished', and the replenishment, the restoration of vision, like the resurfacing of the kaleidoscope, is precisely the business of poetry:

---

[23]   *Opened Ground*, p. 264.

XI[24]

As if the prisms of the kaleidoscope
I plunged once in a butt of muddied water
Surfaced like a marvellous lightship

And out of its silted crystals a monk's face
That had spoken years ago from behind a grille
Spoke again about the need and chance

To salvage everything, to re-envisage
The zenith and glimpsed jewels of any gift
Mistakenly abased …

What came to nothing could always be replenished.

The monk to whom Heaney has made confession understands this absolutely; he understands that Heaney's vocation as a poet comes from the same source as his own vocation to be a monk, and is therefore able to say, 'Read poems as prayers'. It is not that Heaney is asked to, or would be prepared to sloganise for the Catholic Church, but rather that his cleansing of the instruments of our vision, by the power of his imagination as a poet, is part of that whole restoration, even in our darkness, of the vision of Truth which is the work of the whole Trinity, but especially in us of the Logos, the Word who is also the Light. This becomes abundantly clear in the poem Heaney goes on to translate, in which at last, after all his journeying, he arrives at and names the Source of that river which Milton named, 'Siloam's brook', and Coleridge called, 'Alph, the sacred river'.

'Read poems as prayers,' he said, 'and for your penance
Translate me something by Juan de la Cruz.'

Returned from Spain to our chapped wilderness,
His consonants aspirate, his forehead shining,
He had made me feel there was nothing to confess.

Now his sandalled passage stirred me on to this:
How well I know that fountain, filling, running,
   Although it is the night.

But not its source because it does not have one,
Which is all sources' source and origin
   Although it is the night.

---

[24]   *Station Island*, p. 89.

No other thing can be so beautiful.
Here the earth and heaven drink their fill
    Although it is the night.

So pellucid it never can be muddied,
And I know that all light radiates from it
    Although it is the night.

I know no sounding-line can find its bottom,
Nobody ford or plumb its deepest fathom
    Although it is the night.

And its current so in flood it overspills
To water hell and heaven and all peoples
    Although it is the night.

And the current that is generated there,
As far as it wills to, it can flow that far
    Although it is the night.

And from these two a third current proceeds
Which neither of these two, I know, precedes
    Although it is the night.

This eternal fountain hides and splashes
Within this living bread that is life to us
    Although it is the night.

Hear it calling out to every creature.
And they drink these waters, although it is dark here
    Because it is the night.

I am repining for this living fountain.
Within this bread of life I see it plain
    Although it is the night.[25]

Clearly there are many poems by Juan de la Cruz that Heaney could have translated here; but this one has a special resonance, not only with the structure and imagery of the 'Station Island' sequence in which it is placed, but with the whole body of Heaney's work – poems in earlier volumes aw well as those in more recent works which continue to echo the themes of this poem. St John titled this poem *Cantar Del Alma que se huelga de conoscer a Dios por Fe*, 'The Song of

---

[25]   Ibid., pp. 89–91.

the Soul which Delights to Know God by Faith'; the significance is in the phrase about 'knowing God *by Faith*'. St Paul contrasts faith and sight, 'we walk by faith and not by sight'; to know God 'by faith' is to acknowledge the present darkness and yet to see beyond it, to see paradoxically what cannot be seen, for 'faith is the evidence of things not seen'.[26] To know God by faith is both to acknowledge his palpable absence from the world of the visible and yet at the same time to dare to see him 'through a glass, darkly'.[27] This paradox of finding that the visible may also be alive with 'what's invisible'[28] is at the heart of Heaney's vocation as a poet.

Secondly, the two key images of this poem – the fountain whose deepest fathom nobody can plumb, and the light which is both beautiful and invisible – have been key images in Heaney's work since his first volume, and continue to inform his most recent work. So, when he translates that first line, 'How well I know that fountain, filling, running', we hear at this point both Heaney's own voice, for we are still in the midst of one of *his* poems, and, at the same time, the voice of St John of the Cross, for we have begun one of his. They are both saying 'how well I know that fountain, filling, running …' St John's voice carries with it his knowledge of that fountain and all the sources in his soul and in his world from which it flows; it carries *his* knowledge and love of the Song of Songs, and its archetypal image of the fountain sealed, the garden enclosed, his deep meditation on the story, in John 4, of the woman at the well and Christ's promise to her of a fountain welling up in her to eternal life; it carries his participation in the Spanish mystical tradition in which the fountain plays a key role, and his reading of the chivalric romances in which the knights on their mystic quests are granted a vision of the hidden, magical fountain. All these 'sources' flow together as St John, in the midst of the dark night of his own soul, still affirms that he 'knows that fountain'.

Had this translation been published on its own, in a collection of Spanish mystical verse, it would be John's voice alone that we hear; but because the translation is set in the midst of Heaney's poems, and at a crucial point in this sequence, we hear Heaney's voice also and *his* particular knowledge of 'that fountain'. When Heaney says 'how well I know that fountain', he is speaking not just as John does of Scripture and of mystical or literary fountains, but of his own 'Personal Helicon', the 'Wellhead' in the farmyard of his childhood, the 'untoppled *omphalos*' which was at once the outward and visible source of the 'water of life' to Heaney and his kith and kin, and also, in the eternal language of symbol, the inward and spiritual source of his imagination and his entire inspiration.

---

[26] Hebrews 11:1.

[27] 1 Corinthians 13:12.

[28] *Seeing Things* p. 17.

As he writes in 'Personal Helicon':[29]

> As a child, they could not keep me from wells
> And old pumps with buckets and windlasses.
> I loved the dark drop, the trapped sky, the smells
> Of waterweed, fungus and dank moss.

And in his autobiographical prose of the late 1970s, he makes it even more abundantly clear how deeply linked to the heart of his work were these almost numinous childhood encounters with wells and water:

> To this day, green, wet corners, flooded wastes, soft rushy bottoms, any place with the invitation of watery ground and tundra vegetation, even glimpsed from a car or a train, possess an immediate and deeply peaceful attraction. It is as if I am betrothed to them, and I believe my betrothal happened one summer evening, thirty years ago, when another boy and myself stripped to the white country skin and bathed in a moss-hole, treading the liver-thick mud, unsettling a smoky muck off the bottom and coming out smeared and weedy and darkened. We dressed again and went home in our wet clothes, smelling of the ground and the standing pool, somehow initiated.[30]

He describes vividly how the 'shaft was sunk for the pump at the wellhead', which came to symbolise so much for him:

> I remember, too, men coming to sink the shaft of the pump and digging through that seam of sand down into the bronze riches of the gravel, that soon began to puddle with the spring water. That pump marked an original descent into earth, sand, gravel, water. It centred and staked the imagination, made its foundation of the *omphalos* itself.[31]

This wellhead, while remaining mostly a hidden source for so much of Heaney's poetry, is made visible in occasional glimpses, always bringing a deep sense of rootedness and reassurance at various key points in his verse. In the first of the dedicatory poems of *North*, significantly entitled 'Sunlight', it is almost as though he needs to look at this well again and associate its water with light and love, before he dares to go down into the dark of that volume:

> There was a sunlit absence.
> The helmeted pump in the yard,

---

[29]   Death of a Naturalist, p. 57.

[30]   From 'Mossbawn', broadcast on Radio 4 in 1978; published in *Preoccupations* (London, 1980), p. 19.

[31]   *Preoccupations*, p. 20.

Heated its iron,
Water honeyed

In the slung bucket ...[32]

It is there again in *Field Work*, the hidden source which the 'armoured cars' of
the invaders can never touch. In 'The Toome Road':

O charioteers, above your dormant guns,
It stands here still, stands vibrant as you pass,
The invisible, untoppled omphalos.[33]

It is there in the beautiful poem 'A Drink of Water', where a cup of water from
that well is transfigured in Coleridgian moonlight, and Heaney confesses his need
to 'dip, to drink again', and hints at the hidden source of all this refreshment:

Nights when a full moon lifted past her gable
It fell back through her window and would lie
Into the water set out on the table.
Where I have dipped to drink again, to be
Faithful to the admonishment on her cup,
Remember the Giver, fading off the lip.[34]

And, it is there again in *The Spirit Level*, in the wonderful poem 'At the
Wellhead', a poem which consciously recapitulates Juan de la Cruz's themes of
music, water and hidden vision in the midst of darkness. Here he compares the
piano playing of a blind neighbour to the sound of water:

Her notes came out to us like hoisted water
Ravelling off a bucket at the wellhead
Where next thing we'd be listening hushed and awkward[35]

That poem is addressed to a singer, and the wellhead becomes a symbol for the
source of music itself; so Heaney says, 'Sing yourself to where the singing comes
from.'

It was water from this well, in a bucket in the scullery, remembered from
Heaney's childhood, which became a symbol in his Nobel acceptance speech,
both of the poetic imagination and of the soul of humankind:

---

[32]   *North*, p. 8.
[33]   Seamus Heaney, *Field Work* (London, 1979), p. 15.
[34]   Ibid., p. 16.
[35]   *The Spirit Level*, p. 65.

> Ahistorical, presexual, in suspension between the archaic and the modern,
> we were as susceptible and impressionable as the drinking water that stood
> in a bucket in our scullery: every time a passing train made the earth shake,
> the surface of that water used to ripple delicately, concentrically, and in utter
> silence.[36]

He returns to the image of this water in the great three-part *credo* in that
speech, each part beginning 'I *credit* poetry', about the heart of what poetry, as a
redemptive reordering of the human imagination, can do:

> I credit it ultimately because poetry can make an order as true to the impact
> of external reality and as sensitive to the inner laws of the poet's being as the
> ripples that rippled in and rippled out across the water in that scullery bucket
> fifty years ago. An order where we can at last grow up to that which we stored up
> as we grew. An order which satisfies all that is appetitive in the intelligence and
> prehensile in the affections. I credit poetry, in other words, both for being itself
> and for being a help, for making possible a fluid and restorative relationship
> between the mind's centre and its circumference …[37]

Here, the water from that well has become a symbol for his own mind.

All these fountains literal, literary and symbolic, are part of his knowledge,
part of the word 'know', as Juan de la Cruz and Heaney blend their voices to say
'how well I know that fountain, filling, running, although it is the night'.

Yet the fountain of which they speak, although it has to be imagined through
the memory of all these other fountains, is not itself any of these deep sources,
but is a source beyond them. So comes that astonishing second phrase: 'But not
its source because it does not have one, / Which is all sources' source and origin'.
By choosing to translate this poem in this way and in this context, Heaney is
saying that, even this deepest source of his, this 'personal Helicon', has a source
beyond itself: and that source is the 'Eternal Fountain', deep in the heart of the
Godhead, which this poem celebrates. This fountain is the source of the world we
apprehend by imagination and also the source of the source of imagination itself,
the 'Light which makes the light which makes the day',[38] the pellucid light which,
unlike the damaged kaleidoscope of our fallen minds, 'never can be muddied'. All
light radiates from it, even the light gathered in that falling December raindrop,
which reminded Heaney of his 'diamond absolutes'. This source of light can be
found even in darkness. In all of Heaney's poetry there has been a digging down,
a stripping away of layers, an attraction to unfathomable depth. In the first of the
bog poems, he says, in awe, 'the wet centre is bottomless'; and yet in those depths

---

[36]   'Crediting Poetry', in *Opened Ground*, p. 447.

[37]   Ibid., pp. 449–50.

[38]   See above Chapter 4, pp. 000–00.

he is looking also for a centre that can hold, and here he finds it, and finds in it a perpetual source of radiant and refreshing energy:

> I know no sounding-line can find its bottom,
> Nobody ford or plumb its deepest fathom
>   Although it is the night.

> And its current so in flood it overspills
> To water hell and heaven and all peoples
>   Although it is the night.

> And the current that is generated there,
> As far as it wills to, it can flow that far
>   Although it is the night.

Heaney's translation avails itself of a secondary meaning in 'current' as it stands in relation to 'generate', one unavailable to the original poet and yet, in its hint of energy and light, entirely in keeping with its purpose. St John of the Cross goes on, and Heaney in his translation follows him, to locate this 'source of all sources' and 'origin of all origins' in the life of God the Holy Trinity:

> And from these two a third current proceeds
> Which neither of these two, I know, precedes
>   Although it is the night.

Here we have a beautiful resolution in the symbol of mingling currents, which can be 'distinguished but not divided', as Coleridge would say, of that perplexity which reason encounters at the brink of mystery, and with which Milton was so evidently struggling in his own invocation of the fountain of holy light.[39]

Milton hesitates before the technicalities of his own theology, unsure whether this first and original Light is an 'essence' or an 'overflowing', a first-born of creation or an intrinsic part of the Godhead. John's more fluent theology, informed by the poet's mystical experience, finds in the image of the mingled streams in the river, as Coleridge was later to do, an expression of the plurality *and* oneness which is the mystery both of the Godhead and of human consciousness.

Although John of the Cross gives us this verse sounding the heart of a Trinitarian understanding of God, he returns us, at the end of his poem, to our actual experience of the world now, and to the central paradox that in this present darkness we are called to see the invisible, and to hear in its music the call of our Creator. The poem brings us at last to a place in which the mystery, the source of time and space, of light and of imagination, is made manifest in the midst of time

---

39   See above Chapter 6, pp. 000–00.

and space, but apprehended only by imagination – that is, to the mystery of the sacrament:

> This eternal fountain hides and splashes
> Within this living bread that is life to us
>   Although it is the night.

> Hear it calling out to every creature.
> And they drink these waters, although it is dark here
>   Because it is the night.

> I am repining for this living fountain.
> Within this bread of life I see it plain
>   Although it is the night.

As we hear Juan de la Cruz's voice speaking these verses, we know that he understood them in terms of the defined and covenanted Sacraments of the Church, especially the Sacrament of the Eucharist. When Heaney takes up the same words, the context is broadened. Heaney, writing in a secular and post-modernist world, calls us to 'see it plain' in a new way. He takes up the task of helping us in the midst of 'utter visibility' to be alive to what is 'invisible',[40] helping us, in the midst of meaningless or murderous noise, to hear a 'music we would never have known to listen for', and to 'enter heaven through the ear of a raindrop'. The real source and theological root, not only of the title but of the whole achievement of his volume *Seeing Things*,[41] is here in this poem.

There is, of course, one remaining poem to conclude the sequence of 'Station Island'. It is all very well for Heaney the pilgrim-narrator of the sequence to have come in his own soul to a point of personal repentance and renewal, and to have had his 'catholic' vision clarified by the genius of St John of the Cross, but he also remains Heaney the modern poet and the inheritor of the great achievements of Joyce, Yeats and Beckett. If his vision is to have validity both for himself and for the fractured and sceptical world out of which his poems arise and to which they are addressed, then it must be consonant with all he has learnt from those masters of scepticism and anomie. Dante's *Divine Comedy* is a distinctively Christian vision but it has an extra conviction and authority because it carries with it Virgil's *imprimatur*; it is the fruit of an encounter with philosophical reason and with 'pagan' imagination, both of which Virgil represents. So Heaney's later work has an authority which could not simply be achieved by translating or even reinterpreting the great work of Catholic mystics and saints of the past; it has to be achieved by bringing their insights fully into contact with all the fractured tragedy and doubt of our own age, which was the special *metier* of the modernist masters.

---

[40]   See below p. 236.
[41]   Seamus Heaney, *Seeing Things* (London, 1991).

Before Heaney can really 'straighten up' from the 'prie-dieu', credit marvels, and help us, too, to 'see things', he needs the imprimatur of his master, Joyce; and this is what he is given in the final poem of the 'Station Island' sequence.

The first eleven poems of 'Station Island' are all set on St Patrick's Purgatory itself; but the final encounter is back on the mainland. Heaney has finished his pilgrimage and exorcised his demons, and is purged and prepared to take up his vocation as a poet with newly cleansed vision. The hand that reaches down from the jetty to lift him back up into the resumption of his life is that of James Joyce. It is appropriate enough that Joyce disdains to appear on the island itself, to be part of what he dismisses as an 'infantile, peasant pilgrimage'. And yet, although Heaney acknowledges his great debt to Joyce, an acknowledgment which takes the form in the allegory of Joyce helping him up, he also makes it clear that, as with Dante and Virgil, Joyce can no longer be simply his guide; that Heaney himself may not simply guard the Joycean heritage but also direct it towards visions that Joyce himself could not see. All this is very delicately put in this moment of exchanged handgrip and by the allusion to Joyce's blindness, with its reservation in the word 'seemed':

> Like a convalescent, I took the hand
> Stretched down from the jetty, sensed again
> An alien comfort as I stepped on ground
>
> To find the helping hand still gripping mine,
> Fish-cold and bony, but whether to guide
> Or to be guided I could not be certain
>
> For the tall man in step at my side
> Seemed blind ...[42]

Though Heaney is about to step out with Joyce's blessing on roads Joyce never travelled, he nevertheless pays tribute to all the gifts he and the rest of us have received from Joyce's genius. The 'straight walk', the 'eyes fixed straight ahead', the clarity of the singer's voice, 'Cunning, narcotic, mimic, definite / As a steel nib's down stroke, quick and clean.[43]

In the first published version of this poem, there is a middle passage in which Heaney tells Joyce that a passage from Stephen's diary had become for him 'a revelation ... a password in my ears, the collect of a new epiphany'. He omits this passage of tribute in the revision for *Opened Ground*, preferring to go directly to Joyce's final admonition as Heaney takes up again his vocation:

---

[42]   *Station Island*, p. 92.
[43]   Ibid., p. 92.

'Take off from here, and don't be so earnest

> So ready for the sackcloth and the ashes.
> Let go, let fly, forget.
> You've listened long enough. Now strike your note.'[44]

Heaney receives these words as the gift of freedom and possibility, and the revelation is accompanied by the icon of the raindrop:

> It was as if I had stepped free into space
> Alone with nothing that I had not known
> Already. Raindrops blew in my face ...

Joyce sets him free from the burden of rehearsing again and again the Troubles of his own people:

> ... You are raking at dead fires,
> Rehearsing the old whinges at your age.
> That subject people stuff is a cod's game.

Heaney is free to 'strike his own note', to find the light where it is least expected; to find what Joyce called, 'elver-gleams in the dark of the whole sea'
:

> '... it's time to swim

> Out on your own and fill the element
> With signatures on your own frequency,
> Echo-soundings, searches, probes, allurements,
> Elver-gleams in the dark of the whole sea.'

Claritas: *The Beginning of Heaney's* Paradiso

From the end of *Station Island* onward, Heaney is free in a new way to 'strike his own note'. In the next two volumes, he experiments both with translation and with essays in different genres such as allegory and the careful construction of emblems, in an attempt to discern what the signature of his own frequency might be. More and more it becomes clear that he is called so to celebrate the visible as to make it alive with the invisible, to make such music with the audible words of his verse that it catches an echo of Keats' 'unheard melodies'. The great achievements of this new style come in his most recent volumes, from *Seeing Things* onwards. On the way towards them, in *The Haw Lantern*[45] he writes some telling verses that

---

44   Ibid., p. 93.
45   Seamus Heaney, *The Haw Lantern* (London, 1987).

indicate the effects he is trying to achieve, and the means by which he hopes to achieve them.

So, for example, in 'The Spoonbait',[46], he constructs a formal emblem of the invisible soul by means of the known visibility of a spoonbait in a child's pencil case. The poem begins with an almost awkward formality:

> So a new similitude is given us
> And we say: The soul may be compared
>
> Unto a spoonbait that a child discovers
> Beneath the sliding lid of a pencil case

But then the verse takes off with an insight into the power of imagination to help us see and understand more than we could ever catch in the first glimpse of anything. The spoonbait is 'glimpsed once, and imagined for a lifetime'. In some ways, the role of Heaney's poetry since the 1990s has been to give us the insights of a lifetime's imagination which will help us truly to 'see things' we had so far only glimpsed once. The spoonbait itself is then compared to a host of other things; a shooting star, the polished helmet of a hero, but most characteristically and powerfully, in this context, to a single drop of water. And since this poem was published after his translation of the Juan de la Cruz, which locates in the Trinity the 'source' of all these numinous drops of light and water that fall through Heaney's poetry, we can say with certainty that Heaney's characteristic reversal of the story of Dives and Lazarus, his retelling of it so that even for Dives the drop of water *can* fall through the gulf and reach him, is rooted in John of the Cross's powerful line that, the hidden fountain, waters hell and heaven and all peoples'. So, for a moment, the drop that recalled the 'diamond absolutes' for Heaney in the hell of his self-doubt becomes, in this poem, 'Like the single drop that Dives implored / Falling and falling into a great gulf'.

Heaney has come to understand that the deepest music in his poetry is the 'music of what happens', not on the surface of his images, but in and through the echoes of other images that they recall; and so, in the poetic preface to 'Clearances', the sonnet sequence in memory of his mother, he celebrates what she has already taught him about his craft, and implores her directly, through the communion of the Saints, to teach him more:

> She taught me what her uncle once taught her:
> How easily the biggest coal block split
> If you got the grain and hammer angled right.
>
> The sound of that relaxed alluring blow,
> Its co-opted and obliterated echo,

---

[46] Ibid., p. 21.

Taught me to hit, taught me to loosen,

Taught me between the hammer and the block
To face the music. Teach me now to listen,
To strike it rich behind the linear black.[47]

The Art of Seeing Things

In his next volume, *Seeing Things*, Heaney was indeed to 'strike it rich behind
the linear black.' The whole volume is full of those deft strokes that split open the
apparently known and take us straight to the heart of what was invisibly behind
it. It is the book which most clearly celebrates his power to 'straighten up' from
the prie-dieu and 'credit marvels', the beginning of the extended '*Paradiso*' of his
most recent work. This is made explicit in a sonnet like 'Fosterling'.[48] In the octet
he relives his early poems which delved into the heaviness of silted land, and what
he called 'my silting hope, my lowlands of the mind'; and, in an ironic reference
to the film of the opposite name, 'the heaviness of being'. But in the sestet, he
turns all these things around, finishing his poem on the lifting sounds of brighten
and lighten:

>   And poetry
> Sluggish in the doldrums of what happens.
> Me waiting until I was nearly fifty
> To credit marvels. Like the tree-clock of tin cans
> The tinkers made. So long for the air to brighten,
> Time to be dazzled and the heart to lighten.

The first part of the brilliant sequence 'Squarings' which forms the second half
of the book is itself called 'Lightenings', and celebrates a sequence of moments of
vision and encounters with the marvellous. The last of these 'Lightening' poems is
about transfiguration: 'a phenomenal instant when the spirit flares'. This is not the
transfiguration of Christ on the mountain, but rather the transfiguration of the thief
on the cross, in and through the 'transfiguration' of Christ on the cross beside him. It
is about the discovery, in the midst of the dreadful and unpromising, of the promise
of redemption. The pain that 'seems untranslatable into bliss' is nevertheless
translated by Christ the Logos who enters into the thief's pain precisely so as to
transfigure and translate him into Paradise. But this poem celebrates more than the
particular historical moment of the dying thief, hearing the unexpected music of
Christ's promise, 'this day thou shalt be with Me in Paradise' – it also celebrates
what Heaney calls the 'good thief in us', harking to the same promise:

---

[47]   Ibid., p. 24.
[48]   *Seeing Things*, p. 50.

xii[49]

And lightening? One meaning of that
Beyond the usual sense of alleviation,
Illumination, and so on, is this:

A phenomenal instant when the spirit flares
With pure exhilaration before death -
The good thief in us harking to the promise!

So paint him on Christ's right hand, on a promontory
Scanning empty space, so body-racked he seems
Untranslatable into the bliss

Ached for at the moon-rim of his forehead,
By nail-craters on the dark side of his brain:
This day thou shalt be with Me in Paradise.

Unfolding a Triptych

Striking as they are, these and many of the other individual poems in *Seeing Things* in which we see an apparently familiar picture and then see it again in a new light, are only, as it were, lightening sketches for the masterpiece which is at the centre of this volume and the poem from which it takes its title. 'Seeing Things' forms a triptych altarpiece through which the rest of the poems can be understood and appreciated. As with many triptych paintings, the poem consists of a central panel portraying a moment in the life of Christ, which is of universal significance, flanked by two side panels containing so-called 'secular' imagery in which the universal significance of the 'sacred' event is worked out. In the central panel of a typical triptych we might see the crucifixion and be tempted to locate it either only in 'distant Holy-Land' at a distant time, or only in some 'sacred' and isolated theological world; but in the panels beside it we see kneeling alongside the sacred figures of the Saints, perhaps the Holy Virgin or St John, the patron or the artist himself in contemporary clothing. They are present to and participating in the central event of the sacred panel and also present to and sharing with us our own so-called, 'ordinary world'. We can no longer say 'that was then, this is now'. We cannot say as we look at the central panel that we are witnessing a past event. We find ourselves standing at the foot of the Cross – not surrounded by plaster saints and stained-glass images, but in the midst of our contemporaries. The central event may turn up anywhere and compel us to reinterpret all the other events with which it is suddenly juxtaposed.

---

[49]   Ibid., p. 66.

Seeing Things[50]

I

Inishboffin on a Sunday morning.
Sunlight, turf smoke, seagulls, boatslip, diesel.
One by one we were being handed down
Into a boat that dipped and shilly-shallied
Scaresomely every time. We sat tight
On short cross-benches, in nervous twos and threes,
Obedient, newly close, nobody speaking
Except the boatmen, as the gunwales sank
And seemed they might ship water any minute.
The sea was very calm but even so,
When the engine kicked and our ferryman
Swayed for balance, reaching for the tiller,
I panicked at the shiftiness and the heft
Of the craft itself. What guaranteed us –
That quick response and buoyancy and swim –
Kept me in agony. All the time
As we went sailing evenly across
The deep, still, seeable-down-into water,
It was as if I looked from another boat
Sailing through air, far up, and could see
How riskily we fared into the morning,
And loved in vain our bare, bowed, numbered heads.

II

Claritas. The dry-eyed Latin word
Is perfect for the carved stone of the water
Where Jesus stands up to his unwet knees
And John the Baptist pours out more water
Over his head: all this in bright sunlight
On the façade of a cathedral. Lines
Hard and thin and sinuous represent
The flowing river. Down between the lines
Little antic fish are all go. Nothing else.
And yet in that utter visibility
The stone's alive with what's invisible:
Waterweed, stirred sand-grains hurrying off,
The shadowy, unshadowed stream itself.
All afternoon, heat wavered on the steps
And the air we stood up to our eyes in wavered

---

[50]   Ibid., pp. 16–19.

Like the zigzag hieroglyph for life itself.

III

Once upon a time my undrowned father
Walked into our yard. He had gone to spray
Potatoes in a field on the riverbank
And wouldn't bring me with him. The horse-sprayer
Was too big and new-fangled, bluestone might
Burn me in the eyes, the horse was fresh, I
Might scare the horse, and so on. I threw stones
At a bird on the shed roof, as much for
The clatter of the stones as anything,
But when he came back, I was inside the house
And saw him out the window, scatter-eyed
And daunted, strange without his hat,
His step unguided, his ghosthood immanent.
When he was turning on the riverbank,
The horse had rusted and reared up and pitched
Cart and sprayer and everything off balance
So the whole rig went over into a deep
Whirlpool, hoofs, chains, shafts, cartwheels, barrel
And tackle, all tumbling off the world,
And the hat already merrily swept along
The quieter reaches. That afternoon
I saw him face to face, he came to me
With his damp footprints out of the river,
And there was nothing between us there
That might not still be happily ever after.

In the case of Heaney's triptych, the central event is not the crucifixion but the baptism of Christ. And in it his most vital images of water and light find their natural home. But in it, too, his deep concern for the experience of suffering, for the sense of overwhelming and drowning sorrow, also have their place. For baptism is, of course, a mimesis of death by drowning; but also of resurrection and new birth. And so Heaney chooses to flank his central panel portraying the baptism of Christ with two 'secular' panels portraying episodes in his own life strongly connected with the fear of drowning. They are episodes in which there is at once a full understanding of our tragic mortality and yet an intimation of a hope beyond it. That intimation almost invisible in the side panels is made utterly visible in the central panel.

There are many other subtle links between the central and side panels of this poem; in the central panel, Christ 'sees' and 'is seen'; we see him as he sees us. But also we see him seen by his Father in heaven. The side panels are equally concerned with father–son relationships, and with the assurance of being seen. In the first, Heaney, the fearful child in a boat, imagines himself seen from above; and in the third, he is able in the extremity of his father's near death, at last to see him face-to-face. But all these renewals of vision are governed by the central renewal of the way we see things which is given in Heaney's depiction in the central panel: the experience of seeing a work of art, a sculpture representing the baptism of Christ, in such a way as to see not only the event itself, but its true meaning as a source of life and light in his life and ours. The visual paradigm of the triptych is essential for this poem because although the poems which form the sequence are numbered in Latin numerals, and have on the first reading to be read in a linear way; necessarily we read them in that order – I, II, III. It is vital that this order does not dominate our subsequent readings. We must learn 'to strike it rich behind the linear black', and to read the central poem, II, back into I and forward into III. This process is itself a mimesis of the Church's understanding of the Christ-event which occurs at 'the fullness of time'; which is to say that all times, both before and after, find their fulfilment there. So in this reading of the poems we will begin with II, the central panel: *Claritas*. The dry-eyed Latin word'.

Claritas. The opening word of this central poem might stand for the whole of Heaney's achievement in *Seeing Things*, which is to engage our imaginations so that, if only for a moment, we see the once-opaque world with a new and luminous clarity. His choice in *claritas*, of what he calls a 'dry-eyed Latin word', also locates him, as does much of the other poetry in this volume, as a poet who is working right from the heart of both the Classical and the Catholic European traditions. The poem itself is about a work of art in that tradition – the carved façade of a cathedral. And we are given a clarified and penetrating vision in the very medium of the poem itself, for the poem is one work of art, through which we are invited to see another work of art, the façade on the cathedral. This second work of art is (and declares itself to be) a façade. It is by definition only a surface, something which beckons us to that which is behind it. It stands above a door through which we are being invited to enter into the sacred space; within that space will be celebrated the liturgy, which is itself an invitation to 'enter heaven'.

Art of this kind asks both to be *seen* and to be *seen through*; and the element which best represents it is water, at once life-giving and transparent to a light beyond itself. From his opening word *claritas*, Heaney directs our attention to the art of carving which is representing water, and representing water at the very moment when the water itself is made representative of something else. The first paradox of the poem comes in the imaginative transformation of dry, opaque stone, into clear water:

> *Claritas*. The dry-eyed Latin word
> Is perfect for the carved stone of the water
> Where Jesus stands up to his unwet knees

In the syntax and phrasing of the poem, the presence of the water is mediated and suggested by the carving of the stone, and presented to us in the past tense, the 'carved' stone. But Jesus is presented in the present tense. In reading the lines at first we have the sense not of a previously carved representation of Jesus but, for a moment, of Jesus himself, Life itself, standing: 'Jesus stands'. Having *seen* and then *seen through* the water to see Jesus, our view widens to take in the larger scene, and we see St John the Baptist, pouring out more water over his head; and this time we have already moved beyond the second line, past the temporary surface of the artist's work, the carved stone, towards the thing he is representing, the water itself. Half-way through this fifth line, we step further back, and see an even wider picture: now we see the sunlight, falling on the face of the cathedral. We become aware of the great contrast between the dry, bright heat wavering on the steps through the afternoon, and the beautiful refreshing water that is represented to us through the wavering heat-haze. Heaney chooses to describe the sculpting of the water in lines that could equally describe the 'lines' of his own poetry; indeed, he repeats the word *lines* to make the connection clear.

> Lines
> Hard and thin and sinuous represent
> The flowing river. Down between the lines
> Little antic fish are all go. Nothing else.

Heaney's own lines, sometimes hard and sometimes sinuous, have indeed been able to represent 'the flowing river' to his readers. The river that flowed from his 'Personal Helicon', and, as we have seen, continues to flow throughout his work; the river whose 'source' he disclosed by translating John of the Cross. Now he comes in this poem to clarify *our* vision by sharing his own vision of another artist's work, another artist's attempt to represent, through the representation of water, the Source which is 'all sources' source and origin'. As with 'The Rain Stick', where he celebrates the fact that something as sparse and simple as the 'fall of grit and dry seeds through a cactus stalk' can release such cleansing waters, so here he delights that so much can be presented alive to the imagination in just a few hard, thin, sinuous lines. And he invites us to see with him, what he sees 'between the lines', just as surely as his poetry invites us to read between *his* lines. In sharing his imagination of the Jordan in which Christ stands, he changes register to the easy colloquialisms of his childhood, with phrases like 'all go', and here the imagined river, sacralised by the presence of Christ, is not the Jordan, but some clear-flowing little stream in Derry that the child Heaney had paddled in.

Then comes the phrase 'Nothing else.', all by itself and ending a line. How are we to read this? There is something almost teasing, perhaps in a distinctively Irish way, about the placement of these words. Is there the ghost of an ironic question: 'Nothing else? Is that it? Is this carving all there is to see, or are you prepared to look again with me, and find yourself, as they say, seeing things?' 'Nothing else' might be taken as shorthand for the foreclosing finality of glib reductivism. We are 'just a bundle of neurons … nothing else'. The cosmos is a chance concatenation of atoms: nothing else. The music of the rain stick is the fall of grit and dry seeds:

nothing else. In which case, the next line's defiant 'And yet' swings in with the power of all those great reversals in the psalms: 'Nevertheless, I am always with Thee'. It is as though Heaney is saying to the materialists, I can concede you everything about our irreducible materiality … *and yet*, I will always see something more. The phrase 'Nothing else' I think also carries Heaney's admiration for the economy with which the sculptor has transfigured stone. He has used 'just a few lines, hard and thin and sinuous' to represent water – nothing else; and yet those few lines so absolutely engage our imagination that we see between them with utter clarity the 'shadowy, unshadowed streams' of our own childhood.

If there is to be grace in our life, and any vision and crediting of marvels, then such grace and vision has to come, not when we are already on the spiritual heights, but at the point of bleakness, at the point where we feel we have run into the brick wall, the point at which we say 'there is nothing else'. And so it is after that apparent finality, 'nothing else', that he chooses to make the explicit disclosure of what the art of this anonymous sculptor, and his own art, is all about. It is about making the invisible visible:

> And yet in that utter visibility
> The stone's alive with what's invisible:

The juxtaposition there of the words 'visibility' and 'invisible', carefully chosen with their Latin root, carry an echo of the Nicene creed which would be chanted within that cathedral: 'Credo in unum Deum, Patrem omnipotentem, factorem caeli et terrae, visibilium omnium et invisibilium'. These lapidary, dry-eyed Latin words would have sounded and resounded throughout Heaney's childhood. And what do they say? They say first that God is also a 'maker', a poet; he is the 'factorem', the Maker of all things; and like any good artist, only part of what he makes is visible. he is also the Maker of all things invisible. He is the Maker of caeli et terrae, the heavens and the earth. For us now, it is the smaller part of his creation, the terrae, that is visible; but even the 'terrae' is charged and alive with the possibilities of the invisible 'caeli.' As another Catholic poet whom Heaney deeply admired put it, 'The world is charged with the grandeur of God. It will flame out, like shining from shook foil.'[51] When a poet uses his art as Heaney does, to bring us *claritas*, then at any moment and in any place the visible may become alive with what is invisible, and we may glimpse the gateway between earth and heaven through which even a rich man is invited to enter.

And so here, for Heaney, and for us as we read his poetry, the dry, stone façade of the cathedral upon which the hot afternoon sun is beating, is suddenly 'alive with what's invisible'. What are the invisible things that we are now seeing?

---

[51]   'God's Grandeur', in Gerard Manley Hopkins, *Poetry and Prose*, ed. W. Davies (London, 2002), p. 55.

Waterweed, stirred sand-grains hurrying off,
The shadowy, unshadowed stream itself.

None of these things are carved there, and yet we see them clearly; and through them we see something more: for what are we to make of this 'shadowy, unshadowed stream itself'? Of course, it is a visible, remembered stream from his childhood and ours. The outward and visible stream is shadowed, literally, by the trees along its bank, and more profoundly in the way that all things in this world, where we 'see through a glass, darkly', are shadowed; but the stream Heaney sees 'between the lines' on the cathedral façade is both 'shadowy' *and* 'unshadowed'. Through the 'shadowy' stream also runs, invisibly, the 'unshadowed' stream. And what is that? The unshadowed stream is the 'Eternal fountain, hidden away', 'so pellucid it never can be muddied … all light radiates from it.' It is the stream that arises and flows 'down from the Father of lights, with whom is no variableness, neither shadow of turning'.[52] By the end of this poem, we are indeed *seeing things*. We see the most real and yet the most invisible of all things. We see the true Life, the One in whom is Life, and whose 'life is the light of humankind'. By the end of the poem all this making, all this art, and even the water the art represents, and the wavering air through which the represented water is seen, have all become signs that point beyond themselves, towards 'the zigzag hieroglyph for life itself'.

To appreciate the whole sequence fully we must let the light of the invisible, 'unshadowed stream' flow from its place in the centrepiece here, into the scenes depicted in the two side-panels, so that they too may become 'alive with what's invisible'. The first of the two side-panels in this triptych, the 'left-hand panel' as it were, shows us a scene of embarkation. The poet is a small child being 'handed down' into a ferry, and he relives both the vividness of everything he saw and also his vivid fear. But the poem closes with a sudden shift of perspective: in what might almost be an 'out-of-body experience', the poet looks down upon himself and his companions, and sees them, as will become plain, not merely through his own eyes. The poem starts clearly and vividly in the world of the visible; a specific location, a particular time, and all the enumerated things that a small child might see:

Inishboffin on a Sunday morning.
Sunlight, turf smoke, seagulls, boatslip, diesel.

In the second line, Heaney invokes and enumerates all these good things, one by one, 'sunlight, turf smoke …' – almost as a background litany to the way in which the numbered children are handed down one by one into the boat. This careful enumeration both of what the children see and of the children themselves adds to the sense which grows on us in the poem of every precious thing, the whole of life, shipped into the one precarious, riskily faring boat. We enumerate these

---

[52]   James 1:17.

things, partly out of the very fear of losing them, and all this with the movement from phrases like 'one by one' to 'twos and threes' prepares us for the power of the poem's final image, looking down upon our 'numbered heads', with its half-echo of Christ's words that the very hairs on our heads are numbered. On the visible surface of the poem we see only a vignette of children being ferried on a calm day – nothing else?

But 'all the time' we see the surface of this poem, we are being invited to 'see things' in and through it, just as surely as the poet looked over the side of the boat, down through the water and mysteriously from above, down at himself:

> All the time
> As we went sailing evenly across
> The deep, still, seeable-down-into water,
> It was as if I looked from another boat

What do we see when we begin to see through the surfaces of these images? We find that they are not only very specific, a particular ferry on a particular Sunday morning, but also archetypal and universal. When Heaney says, 'our ferryman swayed for balance, reaching for the tiller', we can be sure that this ferryman is also Charon, and through Charon, the archetypal *psychopomp*, the guide of souls, the one who appears on the threshold, when we have to cross it. And lest we should miss this, Heaney includes in this volume, under the title 'The Crossing', his own translation of *Inferno,* Canto 3, lines 18–129, in which Charon ferries the poets. Just as, to make the Dante–Virgil axis quite clear, he opens the book with a translation of *Aeneid* VI, in which Virgil prepares to fare forth from the visible world of the living to the invisible world of the dead, and is counselled by the Sybil to exercise the gift of clarified vision, to 'look up and search deep'.

An entire section of the 'Squarings' sequence of this volume is called 'Crossings', and explores the ways in which outward and visible journeys may also be stations of the soul; the poems in this sequence are full of the numinous qualities of water:

xxxii[53]

> Running water never disappointed.
> Crossing water always furthered something.
> Stepping stones were stations of the soul.

Likewise, the figure of the *psychopomp* is particularly invoked by the notion that in any ordinary and literal situation an ordinary person might turn out to be the soul guide for the soul's journey.

---

[53]   *Seeing Things,* p. 90.

xxvii[54]

Everything flows. Even a solid man,
A pillar to himself and to his trade,
All yellow boots and stick and soft felt hat,

Can sprout wings at the ankle and grow fleet
As the god of fair days, stone posts, roads and cross-roads,
Guardian of traveller and psychopomp.

'Look for a man with an ashplant on the boat',
My father told his sister setting out
For London, 'and stay near him all night

And you'll be safe.' Flow on, flow on
The journey of the soul with its soul guide
And the mysteries of dealing-men with sticks!

And so, as we look at these children 'handed down' into the ferry on a Sunday morning, we find ourselves 'seeing things'. We see the beginning of our own 'faring forth' through life; we remember with Heaney whatever our first glimpses were of life's vulnerability, its precious fragility, as Heaney panics at the shiftiness and heft of the craft itself. But we learn with him, too, to know the paradox expressed in his fear of the very thing that 'guarantees' him, the quick heft and shiftiness of the boat. The very water that he fears will drown him and sink the boat is the same water that buoys him up.

As the journey itself begins, we share with him this growing awareness of being seen as well as seeing, and the boy's imagined vision of himself from above, becomes an emblem both of our consciousness in life and of the intuitive faith that we exist because there is One who beholds us. The source of Heaney's imagined 'other boat, sailing through air' is in an old Irish story which he retells in *viii* of 'Lightenings'[55], a story whose entire purpose is to vindicate the imagination and to rekindle our sense of the marvellous:

The annals say: when the monks of Clonmacnoise
Were all at prayers inside the oratory
A ship appeared above them in the air.

The anchor dragged along behind so deep
It hooked itself into the altar rails
And then, as the big hull rocked to a standstill,

---

[54]   Ibid., p. 85.
[55]   Ibid., p. 62.

> A crewman shinned and grappled down the rope
> And struggled to release it. But in vain.
> 'This man can't bear our life here and will drown,'
>
> The abbot said, 'unless we help him.' So
> They did, the freed ship sailed, and the man climbed back
> Out of the marvellous as he had known it.

So Heaney looks down 'out of the marvellous' *into* the marvellous, and sees both the riskiness of life, and the love it evokes. Both he and we can 'see / How riskily we fared into the morning, And loved in vain our bare, bowed, numbered heads'.

What are we to make of the words, 'in vain'? For all the panic of the little boy in the boat, the sea was very calm. The journey clearly came to a good end, or he would never have grown up to write the poem; and yet somehow, he glimpses even through this little, and (as it turned out) safe journey, the deep tragedy of our mortality. Indeed, this poem really marks the child's first intimation of mortality, his glimpse of the truth with which Milton prefaced *Lycidas*, the lament for a friend who had drowned: 'Si recte calculum ponas, ubique naufragium est' – 'If you reckon rightly, shipwreck is everywhere'.[56] But this intimation of mortality, this looking down on those who seem so certain to be lost, is countered by the other intimation of immortality, carried implicitly, as we have seen, in the penultimate word, 'numbered'. He has his first glimpse of our shared, human tragedy of loving *in vain*, of the shocks and grief of parting and bereavement. But in the sudden shift of perspective, in looking down, there is implied at least the vision of One whose love for us is not in vain, but whose love has the power to bring us at the end of an invisible journey, if we choose it, to fulfilment.

Taken by itself, one might find the weight in the balance of this poem, dipping as the boat itself dips down towards gunwales in the water, down towards the side of mortality, 'risky and in vain'; but of course it is set beside the centrepiece, which is the true point of balance in this triptych. What light does that centrepiece shed on the things we see in this first panel? There, the water, which Heaney fears, and fears will close over his head, is redeemed. For there, 'John the Baptist pours out more water' over the head of Christ; and the water is not the sea of troubles or the sign of mortality, but the 'zigzag hieroglyph of life itself'.

On the right-hand side of the triptych stands another picture: in this, the child Heaney sees his father walking back from the river near their house, having nearly drowned, and having nearly taken Heaney with him. For a moment, father and son meet absolutely in the intimacy of their shared mortality, face to face at last. The nearness of death strips away all the veils, and they really see each other. Heaney tells it quite consciously as a fairy-story, beginning with the formula 'Once upon a time', and finishing with the words 'happily ever after'. He does this both to evoke childhood, and also to celebrate the renewed 'childlike vision' of the adult poet

---

56   See Milton, *The Complete Shorter Poems*, ed. J. Carey (London, 1971), p. 232.

who had waited till he was 'nearly fifty, to credit marvels'. It is the riskiness of our faring, the nearness of our mortality, the immanence of our ghosthood, that brings out in each of us the love we have for one another. After this nearly fatal accident, Heaney's father returned, as it were from the dead: he is no longer simply 'my father', but 'my undrowned father':

> Once upon a time my undrowned father
> Walked into our yard.

As a little boy on that day, Heaney had wanted to go with his father driving the horse-drawn tackle that sprayed the potatoes on the field near a riverbank; but he 'wouldn't bring me with him'. His father comes back from the riverside, and Heaney sees him through a window and suddenly sees the soul in the man:

> I was inside the house
> And saw him out the window, scatter-eyed
> And daunted, strange without his hat,
> His step unguided, his ghosthood immanent.

There are echoes here of what Heaney observes in the poem on the Good Thief we have already quoted, as 'a phenomenal instant when the spirit flares with pure exhilaration before death'; and also of Poem *xxxiv* in 'Crossings'[57] where, seeing the young man on his way to Vietnam, he suddenly sees through the flesh to the soul:

> Yeats said, To those who see spirits, human skin
> For a long time afterwards appears most coarse.
> The face I see that all falls short of since
>
> Passes down an aisle: I share the bus ...
>   Vietnam-bound,
> He could have been one of the newly dead come back ...
> Having to bear his farmboy self again,
> His shaving cuts, his otherworldly brow.

He sees at once the visible and the invisible; the utter visibility of the flesh, but flesh 'alive with what's invisible', alive with soul, precisely because of the nearness of death. His father tells him how the horse had reared up, how the whole rig had been swept over into the deep. And for Heaney, this acknowledgement of their shared vulnerability and of the unexpected gift of life after such a near-miss becomes a station of the soul, a marking point in the relation of father and son. For a moment, they see each other as God sees them both, face to face:

---

[57]   *Seeing Things*, p. 92.

I saw him face to face, he came to me
With his damp footprints out of the river,
And there was nothing between us there
That might not still be happily ever after.

The language here is clearly echoing the passage in St Paul which in some ways underlines the whole effort of *Seeing Things*: 'For now we see through a glass, darkly; but then face to face: now I know in part; but then shall I know even as also I am known.'[58] Like the picture on the first panel, this vignette from Heaney's life is also concerned with the fear of drowning, with the sense that the very water that sustains life also threatens it. But, like that first panel, it is hinged upon and balanced by the centrepiece of the triptych, the baptism of Christ; what light does that central picture cast on this one?

There are a number of deliberate echoes in the language, especially the language of paradox. In the right-hand picture, Heaney meets his 'undrowned father'; in the central picture, Jesus stands up to his 'unwet knees'. But the deepest parallels are the figurative ones. In the right-hand picture, we have a vivid portrayal of the relation between father and son, a relationship of love, which has been clarified and renewed in the face of death. But we view this moment in the light of that central icon of the timeless relationship of God the Father and God the Son, in and through the outpouring of God the Holy Spirit, which is shown forth in the baptism of Christ; for, in the Baptism of Christ, the whole Trinity is present: there indeed, on the very point of contact between earth and heaven. We see the heavens opened and as the Holy Spirit is poured upon him the Son receives and returns the love of the Father. But the river, in which he stands, the river of this flowing relationship of love in the eternal life of the Father and the Son, is not confined to the picture; it flows out from the picture to water 'hell and heaven and all peoples'. It flows in the first instance, out from this central poem into those two moments in Heaney's childhood which stand on either side in this triptych; it flows from this poem into our reading and understanding of Heaney's other verse; and it flows out from 'between the lines' of the poetry into the reader's own imagination. Most of the time it is implicit and invisible, but here, in 'Seeing Things', the 'shadowy unshadowed stream' which is 'Alph the sacred river' rises to the surface from its hidden source and Heaney allows us to see visibly the spring which enriches the opened ground of his poetic imagination.

---

[58]   1 Corinthians 13:12.

Conclusion

This book has been written as both a vindication and a celebration of the poetic imagination; a defence of its status as a truth-bearer and an exploration of the kinds of truth it is capable of bearing. In particular I have been concerned to demonstrate the essential power of imagination to bridge the gap between immanence and transcendence, to mediate meaning between unembodied 'apprehension' and embodied 'comprehension'. I have also been concerned to show that a study of poetic imagination turns out to be a form of theology; that in seeking to understand how multiple meanings come to be' bodied forth' in finite poems which 'grow to something of great constancy' we discover a new understanding of the prime embodiment of all meaning which is the Incarnation. And this new understanding of incarnation in its turn gives us a new confidence in the ultimate significance of our own acts of poetic embodiment. But if poetry as a manifestation of particular embodiment speaks of the immanence of God, then poetry as a means of cleansing and transfiguring vision speaks of God's transcendence. Throughout this book I have sought to celebrate moments of transfigured vision in poetry, and also to help discern the source of that truth which transfigured vision sees, of that unexpected music which the imagination hears. In an age of faith it was possible for poets – from the anonymous poet of *The Dream of the Rood*, who saw the Cross transfigured in light, to Milton invoking 'holy light' – to find the Source of transfigured vision and to name that source as Christ, the logos and the light of the world. From the mid-seventeenth century onward, things could not be so simple again as poets and philosophers alike faced the challenge of a reductive science that pulled down over the windows of vision shutters bearing the bleak inscription 'Nothing else'. We have seen how the poets, to whom the clarification of our vision had been entrusted, fought a rearguard action, and especially how Coleridge did this, both by writing poetry full of clarified, imaginative vision, and also by undertaking the hard, philosophical work necessary to reinstate the imagination as an instrument with which we grasp reality rather than evade it. We have seen that, in order to make sense of the actual experience of writing and reading poetry, he was compelled to rediscover the mystery of God as Holy Trinity. For Coleridge, poetry is not a fanciful compensation for the irreducible bleakness of things; it is part of the evidence that all things are, at least potentially, luminous with the light of God. Coleridge was a prophet sent more for our own age than for his; he foresaw the inadequacy of the whole Cartesian-Newtonian model with its foreclosed rigidities and its too-easy submission to what he called the 'despotism of the eye'. Now we live in an age when that rigid system, against which Coleridge was protesting, is being overthrown. Those blinding shutters inscribed 'Nothing else' are being drawn up; and now it is not only the major poets in our midst, like Heaney, but also the scientists themselves and the philosophers of science, rediscovering the vital role that imagination has to play in their endeavours, who are helping to remove these 'blinds'.

This cleansing and training of vision through a revitalised imagination, is a common task for Science, Poetry and Theology. My purpose has been to highlight the essential role in fulfilling this common task that is played by the poetic imagination.

Bibliography

Works Cited

Ackroyd, Peter, *Albion The Origins of the English Imagination* (London: Chatto & Windus, 2002)

Adey, Lionel, *C.S. Lewis' 'Great War' with Owen Barfield* (Wigton: Ink Books, 2002)

Augustine, *The City of God Against the Pagans,* edited and translated by R.W. Dyson (Cambridge: Cambridge University Press, 1998)

———, *Confessions*, translated by R.S. Pine-Coffin (London: Penguin, 1961)

———, *De Magistro* in *The Writings of Saint Augustine*, translated by Robert Russell, Fathers of the Church 59 (Washington, DC: The Catholic University of America Press, 1968)

Avis, Paul, *God and the Creative Imagination: Metaphor, Symbol and Myth in Religion and Theology* (London: Routledge, 1999)

Bacon Francis, *The Philosophical Works of Francis Bacon*, edited by J.M. Robertson (London: Routledge, 1905)

Barfield, Owen, *History in English Words* (Great Barrington, MA: Lindesfarne Books, 2002)

———, *Poetic Diction* (London : Faber & Gwyer, 1928)

———, *The Rediscovery of Meaning and Other Essays*, 2nd edn (San Rafael, CA: Barfield Press, 2006)

———, *Saving the Appearances: A Study in Idolatry* (London: Faber, 1957)

———, *What Coleridge Thought* (London; Oxford University Press, 1972)

Becket, Samuel, *Waiting for Godot* (London: Faber & Faber, 1956)

Bennett, J.A.W., *Poetry of the Passion: Studies in Twelve Centuries of English Verse* (Oxford: Oxford University Press, 1982)

Beer, John, *Coleridge the Visionary* (London: The Macmillan Press, 1970)

Blake, William, *A Descriptive Catalogue* (1809; reprinted Oxford: Woodstock, 1990)

———, *The Poetical Works of William Blake*, edited by John Sampson (Oxford: Oxford University Press, 1952)

Brown, David, *Tradition and Imagination: Revelation and Change* (Oxford: Oxford University Press, 1999)

Bullet, Gerald (ed.), *Silver Poets of the Sixteenth Century* (London: Everyman, 1960)

Chaucer, Geoffrey, *The Complete Works of Geoffrey Chaucer*, edited by F.N. Robinson (Oxford: Oxford University Press, 1974)

Cicero, *De Republica, De Legibus*, text and translation by C.W. Keyes (London, Heineman: Loeb Library, 1928)

Carpenter, Humphrey, *The Inklings: C.S. Lewis, J.R.R. Tolkien, Charles Williams, and Their Friends* (London : George Allen & Unwin, 1978)

Cohen, J.M., *The Penguin Book of Spanish Verse* (Harmondsworth: Penguin, 1956)

Coleridge S.T., *The Collected Works of Samuel Taylor Coleridge*, General Editor Kathleen Coburn, [16] vols, Bollingen Series LXXV (Princeton: Princeton University Press, 1970–2002); abbreviated as CC. The following individual volumes in this series are cited in my text:

    Aids To Reflection, edited by John Beer (Princeton, 1993), Volume 9 in CC

    Biographia Literaria, edited by James Engell and W. Jackson Bate (Princeton, 1983), Volume 7 in CC

    Lay Sermons, edited by R.J. White (Princeton, 1972), Volume 6 in CC

    Lectures 1808–1819 on Literature, edited by R.A. Foakes (Princeton, 1987), Volume 5 in CC

    Marginalia, Vol. II, edited by George Whalley (Princeton, 1984), Volume 12 in CC

    Poetical Works, edited by J.C.C. Mays (Princeton, 2001), Volume 16 in CC

———, *Biographia Literaria*, edited by J. Shawcross (Oxford: Oxford University Press, 1907)

———, *Collected Letters of Samuel Taylor Coleridge*, edited by E.L. Griggs, 6 vols (Oxford: Oxford University Press, 1956–71)

———, *The Notebooks of Samuel Taylor Coleridge*, edited by Kathleen Coburn, 4 vols, Bollingen Series L (New York Pantheon Books, 1957–90)

———, *The Philosophical Lectures of Samuel Taylor Coleridge*, edited by Kathleen Coburn (London and New York: The Pilot Press, 1949)

———, *The Portable Coleridge*, edited by I.A. Richards (London: Penguin, 1978)

———, *Selected Letters*, edited by H.J. Jackson (Oxford: Oxford University Press, 1988)

Coulson, John, *Religion and Imagination* (Oxford: Oxford University Press, 1981)

Dante, *Dante in English*, edited by Eric Griffiths and Mathew Reynolds (London: Penguin, 2005)

———, *The Divine Comedy*, translated by Robin Kirkpatrick, 3 vols, Penguin Classics (London: Penguin 2006–8)

———, *The Vision of Dante*, translated by H.F. Carey (Oxford: Oxford University Press, 1923)

Davies, Sir John, *The Poems of Sir John Davies*, edited by Robert Krueger (Oxford: Oxford University Press, 1975)

Dearborn, Kerry, *Baptized Imagination: The Theology of George MacDonald* (Aldershot: Ashgate, 2006)

Donne, John, *The Poems of John Donne*, edited by Sir Herbert Grierson (Oxford: Oxford University Press, 1949)

———, *The Sermons of John Donne*, edited by George R. Potter and Evelyn M. Simpson, 10 vols (Los Angeles: University of California Press, 1953–62)

Eliot, T.S., *Collected Poems 1909-1962* (London: Faber, 1974)

———, *Four Quartets* (London: Faber, 1944)

———, *Selected Prose*, edited by Frank Kermode (London: Faber, 1975)

Fiddes, Paul S., *Freedom and Limit: A Dialogue between Literature and Christian Doctrine* (Basingstoke: Macmillan, 1991)

Flieger, Verlyn, *Splintered Light: Logos and Language in Tolkien's World* (Grand Rapids, MI: Eerdmans, 1983)

Ford, David, *The Musics of Belonging; the Poetry of Micheal O'Siadhail* (Dublin: Carysfort Press, 2007)

———, *The Shape of Living* (London: Fount, 1997)

Fumagalli, Maria Christina, *The Flight of the Vernacular: Seamus Heaney, Derek Walcott and the Impress of Dante* (Amsterdam and New York: Rodopi, 2001)

Gardner, Helen (ed.), *The Faber Book of Religious Verse* (London: Faber & Faber, 1979)

Guite, Malcolm, 'Our Truest Poetry is Our Most Feigning ... Poetry, Playfulness and Truth', in Trevor A. Hart and Steven R. Guthrie (eds), *Faithful Performances: Enacting Christian Tradition* (Aldershot: Ashgate, 2007)

———, 'Poet', in Robert MacSwain and Michael Wood (eds), *The Cambridge Companion to C.S. Lewis* (Cambridge: Cambridge University Press, forthcoming 2010)

———, 'Through Literature', in Jeremy Begbie (ed.), *Beholding The Glory: Incarnation Through the Arts* (London: DLT, 2000)

Hamer, Richard, *A Choice of Anglo-Saxon Verse: Selected with an Introduction and Parallel Verse Translation* (London: Faber & Faber, 1970)

Hardy, Thomas, *The Collected Poems of Thomas Hardy* (London: McMillan, 1952)

Hawkins, Peter S. and Rachel Jacoff (eds), *The Poet's Dante: Twentieth-Century Responses* (New York: Farra, Straus & Giroux, 2001)

Heaney, Seamus, *Death of a Naturalist* (London: Faber, 1966)

———, *A Door into the Dark* (London: Faber, 1969)

———, *Electric Light* (London: Faber, 2001)

———, *Field Work* (London: Faber, 1979)

———, *The Haw Lantern* (London: Faber, 1987)

———, *North* (London: Faber, 1975)

———, *Opened Ground: Poems 1966–1996* (London: Faber, 1998)

———, *Preoccupations: Selected Prose 1968–1978* (London: Faber, 1980)

———, *The Redress of Poetry: Oxford Lectures* (London: Faber, 1995)

———, *Seeing Things* (London: Faber, 1991)

————, *The Spirit Level* (London: Faber, 1996)

————, *Station Island* (London: Faber, 1984)

Herbert, George, *The Complete English Works*, edited and introduced by Ann Pasternak Slater (London: Everyman, 1995)

Hill, Geoffrey, *Collected Poems* (Harmondsworth: Penguin, 1985)

Holmes, Richard, *Coleridge: Darker Reflections* (London: Harper Collins, 1998)

Hopkins, G.M., *Poetry and Prose*, edited by Walford Davies (London: Everyman, 1998)

Hulme, T.E., *Selected Writing*, edited by Patrick McGuiness (Manchester: Fyfield, 1988)

Keats, John, *The Letters of John Keats*, edited by M.B. Forman, 3rd edn (Oxford: Oxford University Press, 1947)

————, *The Poetical Works of John Keats*, edited by H.W. Garrod (Oxford: Clarendon Press, 1939)

Langland, William, *The Vision of Piers Plowman: A Complete Edition of the B-Text*, edited by A.V.C. Schmidt (London: Everyman, 1978)

Larkin, Phillip, *Collected Poems*, edited, with an introduction, by Anthony Thwaite (London: Faber, 1988)

LeClercq, Jean, OSB, *The Love of Learning and the Desire for God* (London: SPCK, 1978)

Lewis, C.S., *The Collected Poems of C.S. Lewis*, ed. W. Hooper (London: Fount, 1994)

————, *The Discarded Image: An Introduction to Mediaeval and Renaissance Literature* (Cambridge: Cambridge University Press, 1964)

———— [pseud. Clive Hamilton], *Dymer* (London: J.M. Dent, 1926)

————, *Surprised by Joy* (1955; London: Fount, 1987

Lovelock, James, *Gaia: Medicine for an Ailing Planet* (London: Gaia Books, 2005)

————, *The Revenge of Gaia* (London: Penguin, 2007)

Macrobius, *On the Dream of Scipio*, translated by W.H. Stahl (New York: Columbia University Press, 1952)

Mahon Derek, *Selected Poems* (London: Penguin, 1993)

Midgely, Mary, *Science and Poetry* (London: Routledge, 2001)

Milton, John, *The Complete Shorter Poems*, edited by John Carey (London and Harlow: Longman, 1968)

————, *Paradise Lost*, edited by Alastair Fowler (London and Harlow: Longman, 1971)

Muir, Edwin, *Collected Poems* (London: Faber, 1960)

O'Driscoll, Dennis, *Stepping Stones: Interviews with Seamus Heaney* (London: Faber, 2008)

Pettet, E.C., *Of Paradise and Light: A Study of Vaughan's Silex Scintillans* (Cambridge: Cambridge University Press, 1960)

Pickstock, Catherine, *After Writing: On the Liturgical Consummation of Philosophy* (Oxford: Blackwells, 1998)

Pope, Alexander, *Poetical Works*, edited by Herbert Davis (Oxford: Oxford University Press, 1966)

Prickett, Stephen, *Romanticism and Religion: The Tradition of Coleridge and Wordsworth in the Victorian Church* (Cambridge: Cambridge University Press, 1976)

Reilly, R.J., *Romantic Religion: A Study of Owen Barfield, C.S. Lewis, Charles Williams and J.R.R. Tolkien* (Athens, GA: University of Georgia Press, 1971)

Roszak, Theodore, *The Voice of the Earth* (London: Bantam, 1993)

———, *Where The Wasteland Ends: Politics and Transcendence in Post Industrial Society* (London: Faber, 1973)

Sayers, Dorothy, *The Mind of the Maker*, edited, with an introduction, by Susan Howatch (1941; London: Mowbray, 1994)

Shakespeare, William, *The Complete Works*, edited, with an introduction and glossary, by Peter Alexander (London: Collins, 1957)

Shelley, P.B., *Shelley's Poetical Works*, edited by W.M. Rossetti (London: E. Moxon & Co., 1878), Volume III

Sprat, Thomas *A History of the Royal Society of London for the Improving of Natural Knowledge* first edition 1667. Online edition edited by Jack Lynch available at: andromeda.rutgers.edu/~jlynch/Texts/sprat.html

Swanton, Michael, *The Dream of the Rood* (Manchester: Manchester University Press, 1970)

Steiner, George, *Real Presences* (London: Faber & Faber, 1989)

Thomas, Dylan, *Collected Poems, 1934–1952* (London: J.M. Dent, 1952)

Tillyard, E.M.W., *The Elizabethan World Picture* (London: Chatto & Windus, 1960)

Tolkien, J.R.R., *Tree and Leaf* (London: Harper Collins, 2001)

Vaughan, Henry, *Poetry and Selected Prose of Henry Vaughan*, edited, with an introduction, by L.C. Martin (Oxford: Oxford University Press. 1963)

Wittgenstein, Ludwig, *Philosophical Investigations*, translated by G.E.M. Anscombe (Oxford: Oxford University Press, 1968)

———, *Tractatus Logico-Philosophicus*, translated by David F. Pears and Brian McGuinness (London: Routledge, 2001)

Yeats, W.B., *The Poems*, edited by Daniel Albright (London: Everyman, 1992),

Further Reading

Beer, John, *Coleridge's Poetic Intelligence* (London: The Macmillan Press, 1977)

Boyle, Nicholas, *Sacred and Secular Scriptures: A Catholic Approach to Literature* (London: DLT, 2004)

Brown, David, *Discipleship and Imagination: Christian Tradition and Truth* (Oxford: Oxford University Press, 2000)

Carey, John, *John Donne: Life, Mind, and Art* (London: Faber, 1990)

Frye, Northrop, *The Great Code: The Bible and Literature* (London: ARK Paperbacks, 1982)

Gardner, Helen, *Religion and Literature* (London: Faber & Faber, 1971)

Heaney, Seamus, *District and Circle* (London: Faber, 2006)

Herbert, George, *A Choice of George Herbert's Verse*, edited by R.S. Thomas (London: Faber, 1967)

Holmes, Richard, *Coleridge: Early Visions* (London: Hodder & Stoughton, 1989)

Jasper, David, 'The Study of Literature and Theology', in Andrew Haas, David Jasper and Elisabeth Jay (eds), *The Oxford Handbook of Literature and Theology* (Oxford: Oxford University Press, 2007)

Lewis, C.S., *A Preface to Paradise Lost* (Oxford: Oxford University Press,1942)

Perkins, Mary Anne, *Coleridge's Philosophy: The Logos as Unifying Principle* (Oxford: Oxford University Press, 1994)

Prickett, Stephen, *Word and Words: Language, Poetics and Biblical Interpretation* (Cambridge: Cambridge University Press, 1986)

Raine, Kathleen, *Defending Ancient Springs* (Oxford: Oxford University Press, 1967)

Sayers, Dorothy, *The Poetry of Search and the Poetry of Statement and Other Posthumous Essays on Literature, Religion and Language* (London: Gollancz, 1963)

Soskice, Janet, *Metaphor and Religious Language* (Oxford: Oxford University Press, 1985)

Ward, Keith, *Rational Theology and the Creativity of God* (Oxford: Oxford University Press, 1982)

Williams, Charles, *The English Poetic Mind* (Oxford: Oxford University Press, 1932)

———, *The Figure of Beatrice* (London: Faber, 1943)

Wright T.R., *Theology and Literature* (Oxford: Oxford University Press, 1988)

Index